THE MAJOR PREMIERSHIP

Also by Peter Dorey

BRITISH POLITICS SINCE 1945

THE CONSERVATIVE PARTY AND THE TRADE UNIONS

The Major Premiership

Politics and Policies under John Major, 1990–97

Edited by

Peter Dorey
Lecturer in Politics
Cardiff University

First published in Great Britain 1999 by
MACMILLAN PRESS LTD
Houndmills, Basingstoke, Hampshire RG21 6XS and London
Companies and representatives throughout the world

A catalogue record for this book is available from the British Library.

ISBN 0–333–73681–8

 First published in the United States of America 1999 by
ST. MARTIN'S PRESS, INC.,
Scholarly and Reference Division,
175 Fifth Avenue, New York, N.Y. 10010

ISBN 0–312–21839–7

Library of Congress Cataloging-in-Publication Data
The Major premiership : politics and policies under John Major,
1990–97 / edited by Peter Dorey.
p.   cm.
Includes bibliographical references and index.
ISBN 0–312–21839–7 (cloth)
1. Major, John Roy, 1943–   . 2. Great Britain—Politics and
government—1979–1997.   3. Conservative Party (Great Britain)
I. Dorey, Peter, 1959–   .
DA591.M33M34   1999
941.085'9'092—dc21   98–38458
                                                                        CIP

This book is printed on paper suitable for recycling and made from fully managed and sustained forest sources.

10   9   8   7   6   5   4   3   2   1
08   07   06   05   04   03   02   01   00   99

Printed and bound in Great Britain by
Antony Rowe Ltd, Chippenham, Wiltshire

To Geoff & Audrey
with love

Contents

List of Tables and Figure   ix

Notes on the Contributors   x

Introduction: John Major – 'One of Us'?   xiii

1   Chaos or Cohesion? Major and the Parliamentary
    Conservative Party
    Philip Cowley   1

2   A Permanent Revolution in Whitehall: the Major
    Governments and the Civil Service
    Kevin Theakston   26

3   Centralisation and Fragmentation: John Major and
    the Reform of Local Government
    John Kingdom   45

4   Renewed Consultation or Continued Exclusion?
    Organised Interests and the Major Governments
    Rob Baggott and Victoria McGregor-Riley   68

5   Strategic Errors and/or Structural Binds?
    Major and European Integration
    Daniel Wincott, Jim Buller and Colin Hay   87

6   Renewed Hope for Peace? John Major and
    Northern Ireland
    Christopher Norton   108

7   Devout Defender of the Union: John Major and
    Devolution
    J. Barry Jones   126

8   The 3 Rs – Reform, Reproach and Rancour:
    Education Policies under John Major
    Peter Dorey   146

9   Rolling Back the (Welfare) State: the Major
    Governments and Social Security Reform
    Michael Hill   165

10   No Return to 'Beer and Sandwiches': Industrial
     Relations and Employment Policies under John Major
     Peter Dorey   179

11   The Limits of Likeability: the Major Premiership
     and Public Opinion
     David Broughton   199

12   Despair and Disillusion Abound: the Major
     Premiership in Perspective
     Peter Dorey   218

Chronology of John Major's Premiership   250

Bibliography   255

Index   269

List of Tables and Figure

Tables

1.1	Ideological support in the 1990 leadership election	3
1.2	Conservative cohesion during the Maastricht rebellions	10
1.3	Backbench attitudes to European integration	13
1.4	Elections and defections, 1990–97	15
1.5	Dissent by government backbenchers, 1945–97	19
1.6	Size of rebellions, 1992–97	20
1.7	Number of dissenting votes cast by rebellious government MPs, 1992–97	21
4.1	Green Papers and Consultative Documents under the Major government	76
4.2	Green Papers and Consultative Documents, 1976–96	77
10.1	Average hours worked per week by full-time employees in EU member states, 1996	194
10.2	Employees' views about what ought to be the primary objective of trade unions, 1989 and 1996	196
11.1	John Major's public image	205
11.2	Margaret Thatcher's public image	206
11.3	The best party to handle economic problems (poll)	211
11.4	The best party to handle problems (poll)	212
12.1	Class and voting in the 1997 election (and 1992 figures)	241
12.2	Vote by region in 1997 (and change since 1992)	242
12.3	Voter's expectations in the 1997 election	245
12.4	Issue saliency in the 1997 election	245

Figure

4.1	Consultation periods under Thatcher and Major	78

Notes on the Contributors

Rob Baggott is Reader in Public Policy at De Montfort University, Leicester. He is the author of *Pressure Groups Today* (1998) and *Health and Health Care in Britain* (2nd edition, 1998). He has also published articles in *Public Administration, Parliamentary Affairs, Policy and Politics, Journal of Social Policy*, and *Talking Politics*.

Jim Buller is a Lecturer in Politics in the Department of Political Science and International Studies at the University of Birmingham. He is the author of *National Statecraft and European Integration: the Conservative Governments 1979–97* (1998), and has also written a number of articles and chapters on British foreign policy and on Britain's relations with the European Union.

David Broughton is Lecturer in Politics in the School of European Studies at Cardiff University. He is the author of *Public Opinion Polling and Politics in Britain* (1995), and was co-editor of the annual *British Elections and Parties Yearbook* from 1991 to 1996 inclusive.

Philip Cowley is a Lecturer in the Department of Politics at the University of Hull, and Research Secretary of the Centre for Legislative Studies. He is editor of *Conscience and Parliament* (1998), and co-editor of the annual *British Elections and Parties Review*, as well as the author of articles in a range of journals, including the *British Journal of Political Science, Political Studies, Party Politics*, and the *Journal of Legislative Studies*.

Peter Dorey is Lecturer in Politics in the School of European Studies at Cardiff University. He is the author of *British Politics since 1945* (1995), *The Conservative Party and the Trade Unions* (1995), and various articles and chapters on Conservative politics in Britain. He has recently completed a monograph, *The Politics of Pay: Governments and Wage Determination in Post-War Britain* (forthcoming), and is currently writing *The Labour Party and Constitutional Reform*.

Colin Hay is a Lecturer in the Department of Political Science and International Studies at the University of Birmingham, and currently a Visiting Fellow in the Department of Political Science at MIT. He is also a research affiliate at Harvard University. He is the author of *Re-stating Social and Political Change* (1996), which was awarded the British Sociological Association's Philip Abrams Memorial Prize.

Michael Hill is Visiting Professor in the Department of Social Policy and Politics at Goldsmiths College, University of London. He is Emeritus Professor of Social Policy at the University of Newcastle-upon-Tyne. His recent publications include *Understanding Social Policy* (fifth edition, 1997), *The Policy Process in the Modern State* (1997), and *Social Policy: a Comparative Analysis* (1996).

J. Barry Jones is Senior Lecturer in Politics in the School of European Studies at Cardiff University. He is the co-author (with Michael Keating) of *Labour and the British State* (1985) and co-editor (with Michael Keating) of *The European Union and the Regions* (1995). He has also written numerous articles and chapters on Welsh politics, devolution, and regionalism in Europe.

John Kingdom is Reader in Politics at Sheffield Hallam University. He has written various books and articles on British politics, including the prize-winning *Government and Politics in Britain* (2nd edition, 1999).

Victoria McGregor-Riley is Lecturer in Public Policy in the Department of Health and Continuing Professional Studies at De Montfort University, Leicester. She is currently working on a monograph on medical pressure groups.

Christopher Norton is Senior Lecturer in Politics at the University of Wolverhampton. He is currently working on a study of Nationalist politics in Northern Ireland since 1940.

Kevin Theakston is Reader in Government at the University of Leeds. He is the author of *Junior Ministers in British Government* (1987), *The Labour Party and Whitehall* (1992), *The Civil Service since 1945* (1995) and *Leadership in Whitehall* (1998).

Daniel Wincott is a Lecturer in the Department of Political Science and International Studies at the University of Birmingham.

He is the author of a number of articles on European integration, in journals such as _Public Administration_, _Journal of European Public Policy_, _Journal of Common Market Studies_ and _International Political Science Review_. He is currently writing _Politics, Law and European Integration_ (forthcoming, 1999).

Introduction: John Major – 'One of Us'?

From the very outset of his premiership, John Major appeared an enigmatic character, deemed to be devoid of any coherent philosophy or ideological baggage, yet confidently being claimed as 'one of us' by the left and right 'wings' of the Conservative party on the grounds that he subscribed to their particular variant of Conservatism (Gilmour and Garnett 1997: 351). Other Conservatives viewed Major primarily as a managerialist rather than an ideologue, someone whose prime objective would be to unite the party by healing the divisions which had emerged, or been exacerbated, under Margaret Thatcher's leadership.

There were five main reasons why some Conservatives (and commentators in general) initially considered Major to be a 'one-nation' Conservative, and who would therefore herald a return to a more conciliatory and consensual Conservatism after eleven years of Thatcherite radicalism.

Firstly, Major himself intimated that his beliefs most closely corresponded to the 'one-nation' Conservative tradition in the Party, claiming that he was a 'social liberal' (as opposed to a 'social authoritarian' of the Thatcherite right), and citing Iain Macleod – who had himself been a 'disciple' of Rab Butler in the late 1940s – as his 'mentor' from the pantheon of prominent post-war Conservative politicians and thinkers. Such pronouncements led a number of commentators to accept that the 'one-nation' strand of British Conservatism 'accurately reflected Major's own philosophical position. . . . The emphasis on "one nation" values . . . a reflection of his own values' (Seldon 1997: 126).

Secondly, Major made much in his early speeches of his desire to create 'a country that is at ease with itself', an objective which was widely construed as an acknowledgement that Thatcherism had fostered discord and division in British society. Major's perorations were therefore interpreted as an indication that he wished to recreate 'one nation', and promote a new era of social partnership, unity and inclusion. To this extent, much was made by some commentators of the inclusion of a lengthy section entitled 'Responsibility for Others', in the Conservative party's 1992 manifesto.

Thirdly, there was a clear assumption by many leftish Conservatives that the whole point of the 1990 leadership election was to vote for a candidate who represented a break with, and departure from, Thatcherism. If Conservative MPs were merely going to vote for a leader from the Thatcherite wing of the party, then why had they bothered deposing Thatcher in the first place? On the basis of this reasoning, therefore, Major's election as Conservative leader and Prime Minister was assumed by many on the left of the party to constitute *a priori* a break with Thatcherism, and thus a return to 'one-nation' Conservatism.

Fourthly, Major's personality was viewed by a number of Conservatives and commentators as being emollient and genial, these characteristics apparently confirmed by the immediate return to collegial Cabinet meetings and genuine discussions between Ministers; a 'Cabinet of chums'. John Major's apparently emollient character and style of leadership were viewed by many as further evidence that Major was essentially a 'one-nation' Conservative, for such emollience had also been a feature of previous left-wing Conservatives such as Macmillan, Monckton and Macleod.

Fifthly, some commentators assumed that Major's own apparently humble social background (raised in Brixton, leaving school with few qualifications, and not attending any university) was itself likely to encourage greater sympathy for the less well-off and the 'underdog' in British society, such sympathy being associated with 'one-nation' Conservatism rather than Thatcherism. Yet this particular assumption seemed the least credible, for the experience of the Conservative party during the last twenty years or so has been that those from the least privileged backgrounds have tended to be the most hostile towards 'one-nation' Conservatism.

Indeed, a number of commentators have discerned a clear link between the Conservative party's abandonment of 'one-nation' principles and policies and the replacement of MPs from privileged or socially exclusive backgrounds by somewhat more meritocratic recruits from relatively humble origins, the latter tending to be devoid of the *noblesse oblige* which the previous generation of 'one-nation' Conservatives evinced (Critchley 1992: 58; Critchley 1994: 195; Dorey 1996; Montgomery-Massingberd 1986).

Yet, in spite of these assumptions about John Major's apparent 'one-nation' inclinations, he secured very little support from Conservative MPs on the left of the party in the second ballot of the leadership contest. On the contrary, the vast majority of left-inclined

Conservative MPs voted for one of the other leadership candidates, namely Michael Heseltine and Douglas Hurd. For example, Heseltine's supporters included Lord (Peter) Carrington, Julian Critchley, Sir Ian Gilmour, Keith Hampson, Emma Nicholson, Lord (James) Prior, Lord St John of Fawsley (Norman St John-Stevans), Peter Temple-Morris, and Peter Walker. Douglas Hurd, meanwhile, attracted the support of such leftish Conservatives as Tony Baldry, Kenneth Clarke, Tristan Garel-Jones, Alan Howarth (who several years later defected to the Labour Party), Chris Patten, Nicholas Scott and Lord (William) Whitelaw.

Of those few left-inclined Conservative MPs who supported John Major in November 1990, the most notable were John Gummer, Ian Lang, David Mellor, Gillian Shephard and Peter Thurnham.

By contrast, Major received considerable support from the right of the parliamentary Conservative party, where he was widely viewed as 'one of us', having intimated that while he might be liberal on social issues, he was 'dry' on economic affairs, and thus likely to maintain the economic policies and priorities of the Thatcher governments. In view of the *economism* and *reductionism* of the Thatcherite right, Major's apparent willingness to continue with the economic principles of the 1980s was sufficient to secure him the support of most MPs on this wing of the party. However, also of immense importance was the determination of the Conservative right to 'stop Heseltine', which itself rendered it necessary that they support Major (the third candidate, Douglas Hurd, being despised for his apparently privileged background and patrician politics). Certainly, Thatcher herself made it publicly known that Major was her clear choice for the Party leadership, whereupon she was accompanied by colleagues such as Alan Clark, Michael Forsyth, Michael Howard, Norman Lamont, Peter Lilley, Francis Maude, Gerry Neale, Michael Portillo and Norman Tebbit in voting for Major.

Other Conservatives and sympathetic commentators viewed Major primarily as a managerial leader and political tactician (memories of Harold Wilson occasionally being invoked) for whom holding the Conservative party together was virtually an end in itself. Indeed, Major's official biographer asserts that: 'Major himself was neither a conceptual nor a strategic thinker; rather he was a tactical operator . . . by temperament and choice a conciliator' (Seldon 1997: 133, 738). Another prominent academic described Major as 'a "balancer" . . . more a healer than a warrior, preferring to console rather than confront' (Norton 1996: 65).

Right from the outset, therefore, there was considerable ambiguity about the implications of John Major's elevation to the Conservative leadership. He initially appeared to be all things to all men (and women), with Conservatives on different wings of the party proclaiming him 'one of us'. Indeed, it has been claimed that the 'difficulty in pinning him down was part of John Major's attraction to the parliamentary party, which was in need of unification' (Hogg and Hill, 1995: 7; see also, Junor, 1996: 201). Yet by the end of his premiership six-and-half years later, this apparent ambiguity had been transformed into a fatal weakness, with 'one-nation' Conservatives and Thatcherites alike believing that John Major had betrayed them and their particular brand of Conservatism. Furthermore, the subsequent dislike of John Major which emerged in parts of the Conservative party was to become entirely mutual.

Part of the ambiguity arising from the election of John Major as Conservative party leader derived from differing interpretations of precisely why Margaret Thatcher herself had been rejected – albeit narrowly – by Conservative MPs in November 1990. For some Conservative MPs, it was Margaret Thatcher's style of leadership – increasingly autocratic and imperious – rather than her policies and ideology which had become the problem in 1990. For such MPs, John Major appeared to offer the opportunity to continue with the Thatcher revolution, but with a rather less strident or confrontational style ('Thatcherism with a human face', Kenneth Clarke termed it).

At the same time, some Conservative MPs were highly appreciative of many of Margaret Thatcher's 'achievements', but felt that on particular issues, most notably Europe and the poll tax, she had displayed serious errors of judgement which were damaging to Britain's national interest and/or the Conservative party's electoral prospects. Such Conservatives were thus particularly enamoured with John Major's apparently more pro-European views and his willingness to replace the poll tax.

For others in the parliamentary Conservative party, Thatcherism had gone too far, or outlived its usefulness, and was thus no longer appropriate for the changed economic and social circumstances facing British government in 1990 and beyond. A return to a more constructive and consensual style of Conservatism and governance was deemed desirable, and for some Conservative MPs, John Major appeared to offer precisely such a style. This did not mean support for a return to pre-Thatcher policies as such, but a belief that the

Thatcher revolution had gone far enough (even too far, in some respects), and that 1990 constituted the time to draw a line in the sand, to heal the divisions which Thatcherism had engendered during the 1980s. As Kavanagh expressed it: 'A number of Conservative MPs thought that Thatcherism as a continuing agenda was finished. But beyond repealing the poll tax, there was little support for rolling back its main planks. . . . There was nothing comparable in 1990 to the call for a sharp change of direction in 1945 or 1979' (Kavanagh, 1994: 8–9).

That Major's elevation to the premiership heralded no 'sharp change of direction' is amply borne out in the chapters which follow. Indeed, the most striking feature of the various policies, initiatives and reforms examined by the contributors to this volume is the extent to which they followed a broadly Thatcherite trajectory. His personal style and rhetoric were undoubtedly less combative and confrontational than Margaret Thatcher's, but the substance of most of the policies pursued during John Major's premiership was predominantly Thatcherite.

PETER DOREY

1 Chaos or Cohesion? Major and the Conservative Parliamentary Party

Philip Cowley

INTRODUCTION

For most of John Major's premiership, the term 'Conservative party unity' appeared to be an oxymoron. By 1993, a mere 19 per cent of the electorate considered the Conservatives to be united. This figure fell to 13 per cent in 1994, to 12 per cent in 1995, and was down to single figures for parts of 1996. 'Not since polls asked the question in the early 1970s has the party been so widely regarded as split' (Crewe, 1996: 432). For the party of which it was once said that its secret weapon was loyalty, it was a remarkable state of affairs.

The blame for this has been laid largely – though not exclusively – at the feet of the party's parliamentarians. When the Conservatives gathered for their first party conference following defeat in the general election, 'speaker after speaker was loudly cheered whenever they criticised the parliamentary party, and its divisions' (Riddell, 1997). It was a view with which John Major was in agreement. Just before the 1997 general election he confessed that 'I love my party in the country, but I do not love my parliamentary party' (Seldon, 1997: 3), and he was later to claim that 'divided views – expressed without restraint – in the parliamentary party made our position impossible' (*The Times*, 8 October 1997).

Such a view of the Conservative parliamentary party in this period is understandable. Mass and elite perceptions of the party as disunited were not wrong. Conservative MPs were deeply divided over the issue of European integration, the very issue that came to dominate Major's premiership. Major faced the most sustained Conservative backbench rebellion in post-war history against the Bill to ratify the Treaty of European Union (more commonly known as the Maastricht treaty). During the course of the 1992 parliament, he saw four Conservative MPs defect to other parties, and removed the whip *en bloc* from eight others, the scale of both events unprecedented in post-war Conservative politics. In 1995 he resigned as leader of the party, thereby triggering a leadership contest, in an attempt to reassert his authority.

John Major's premiership could not, therefore, be described as one where there was harmony within the Conservative party. However, as will become clear, although the parliamentary party was rebellious under John Major, its behaviour was not as anarchic as is sometimes claimed.

MARRIAGE

The Conservative parliamentary party elected John Major leader on 27 November 1990. The first round of the contest for the leadership in 1990 had seen the incumbent Prime Minister, Margaret Thatcher, challenged by Michael Heseltine. Thatcher secured more votes than Heseltine – indeed she received the support of a majority of the parliamentary party – but she narrowly failed to fulfil the second condition necessary for a victory on the first round: the need to gain 15 per cent more of the votes of those entitled to vote than her challenger (Cowley, 1996a). Thatcher then withdrew, a decision that allowed two of her Cabinet colleagues, Douglas Hurd and John Major, to contest the second round against Heseltine. John Major received 185 votes, Michael Heseltine 131, and Douglas Hurd 56. Although Major was just short of the requisite majority, his two rivals announced that they would not contest the third ballot. He became prime minister the next day.

The composition of those 185 votes is important. Major's support came from the centre and right of the parliamentary party. He was almost totally rejected by those on the left. Just one of the 27 MPs classified by Norton (1990) as a 'wet' supported Major; and he received the support of fewer than a quarter of those classified as 'damp' (Cowley, 1996b). As Table 1.1 shows, there were statistically significant differences between the views of Major's supporters and those of his rivals. Those differences put Major's supporters to the 'right' (broadly defined) of the rest of the party. Most importantly of all, when multivariate analyses are conducted

Table 1.1 Ideological support in the 1990 leadership election (showing mean values)

	For Major	Not for Major	For Heseltine	Not for Heseltine	For Hurd	Not for Hurd
Tax/spending	2.8	3.5***	3.6	2.9**	3.2	3.1
State ownership	6.1	5.6***	5.5	6.1**	5.8	5.9
European Union	3.0	4.5***	4.7	3.2***	4.1	3.6
Abortion	4.5	3.9*	3.9	4.4	3.8	4.3

* Indicates ANOVA was significant at 0.05 or lower, ** at 0.01 or lower, *** at 0.001 or lower.

Note: table shows mean values of responses of a representative sample of Conservative MPs to four statements: 'There is scope for a further reduction in the level of state involvement in the British public sector'; 'It may be necessary to increase taxes in order to finance necessary improvements in public services such as health and education'; 'The process of European integration must continue, even if this involves some dilution of the sovereignty of the British Parliament'; 'Abortions are too freely available in Britain, and the grounds on which they can be obtained should be made more restrictive'. MPs were given seven options, ranging from disagree very strongly (coded 1) to agree very strongly (coded 7).

Source: Cowley and Garry (1998: 487).

to take into account any interrelationships between MPs' views on the issues, Europe emerges as the *sole* significant ideological variable (Cowley and Garry, 1998: 488–93). In short, most Eurosceptics backed Major and most Europhiles backed Heseltine.

This should not be too surprising. By the time of Major's election, Europe had emerged as the most important issue dividing the Conservative party (Garry, 1995). It was one of the central factors in Margaret Thatcher's downfall, facilitating the contest from which Major emerged victorious (Norton, 1992), for he was (rightly) perceived as being the most Eurosceptic of the three candidates.

Although this helped deliver him the premiership, it left Major with two long-term problems. First, although he was (in relative terms) the most right-wing and Eurosceptic of the three candidates, he was not (in absolute terms) very right-wing or Eurosceptic. Hurd and Heseltine were what Norton (1990) calls 'damps' (in effect, less sodden versions of the party's 'wets'). John Major was a member of the party faithful, a grouping of Conservative MPs who support the party rather than ideological strands of thought. He was not a Thatcherite. Some Thatcherite MPs accepted this, but voted for Major *faute de mieux*. 'There was', said one Eurosceptic MP to this author, 'no one else'. Other Thatcherites convinced themselves – or allowed Major's campaign team to convince them – that Major was 'one of them'. When they later came to realise that he was not, some felt betrayed (see Gorman, 1993).

The second – and related – problem was that Major was not the first choice of most of those who voted for him. Nearly all of Major's supporters in the second round of the contest had voted for Margaret Thatcher in the first. With a few exceptions, Major was, to be blunt, very much a second best for all but his most enthusiastic supporters.

HONEYMOON

The first parliament of John Major's premiership – the two sessions from November 1990 to April 1992 – has elsewhere been described as his honeymoon (Crewe, 1996). Overnight, Major transformed the Conservative party's standing in the opinion polls, while his own poll ratings were also impressive. Major's relationship with his parliamentary party throughout this period was similarly good.

Visible rebellion was both sporadic and limited. Conservatives MPs rebelled – defined here as voting against the instructions of their whips – on 35 separate occasions on the floor of the House. There were a further 24 rebellions in standing committee. These rebellions involved 96 MPs, just over a quarter of the parliamentary party, but were less frequent than under Margaret Thatcher. In the first three sessions of the 1987 parliament, Conservative MPs rebelled in 13 per cent of divisions. In the last two – under Major – they rebelled in 11 per cent. Furthermore, whereas Margaret Thatcher had faced some substantial rebellions, most of the rebellions under Major were small: 13 of the 35 on the floor of the House consisted of a solitary MP. Only eight saw ten or more MPs vote against their party. The largest rebellion – which occurred during the passage of the Dangerous Dogs Bill on 10 June 1991 – consisted of just 19 MPs.

Nor were there any persistent rebels in the first two years of Major's premiership. Over half (48) of the 86 MPs who voted against the government on the floor of the House did so only once. Only nine MPs (that is, 10 per cent of those who rebelled at least once and just 2 per cent of all Conservative MPs) voted against their party on more than five occasions. Even the most persistent rebel, Richard Shepherd, cast just eight dissenting votes against the government in the 332 divisions that took place between 28 November 1990 and the 1992 election.

There were, however, signs of tensions to come. Prophetically, Major's first backbench rebellion occurred over Europe, when seven Conservative MPs voted for a rebel amendment to a 'take note' motion on the EC budget on 4 December 1990, less than a week after Major had become Prime Minister. There were to be a further six rebellions relating to Europe before April 1992. The most serious concerned the Inter-Governmental Conferences, and especially the European Council at Maastricht, due to take place in December 1991 (see Ware, 1996a). There had been a small rebellion in a pre-Maastricht debate on 20 November 1991, when six MPs voted against a motion endorsing the government's 'constructive negotiating approach'. The government won comfortably, with a majority of 101, but reports from Richard Ryder, Major's Chief Whip for most of his premiership, claimed that there were between 40 and 42 Conservative MPs who would vote against any resulting treaty that contained the Social Chapter or other extensions to Qualified Majority Voting (Seldon, 1997: 245). In the event, as a result of Major's negotiations, just seven voted against the government when the House 'warmly endorsed the agreement secured by the government at Maastricht' on 19 December by a majority of 86. Another nine – including a vocal Margaret Thatcher – abstained.[1]

Opposition to the treaty was so limited that Major considered rushing the ratification process through parliament before the general election, but he eventually decided that a hasty ratification would cause more problems with the timetabling of other Bills, especially that abolishing the poll tax, than it was worth. He was later to view his decision as a lost opportunity (Hogg and Hill, 1995: 161–2).

This, therefore, is the first qualification to any picture of Major's backbenchers as especially rebellious. Even if Major's parliamentary Conservative party was particularly rebellious after 1992, there was very little backbench unrest for the first two years of his premiership. Major's most rebellious backbencher was loyal in 98 per cent of divisions; the majority of his rebels rebelled only once; and the majority of the parliamentary Conservative party did not rebel at all.[2] For a government with a majority of around 90, this was small fry.

THE 1992 ELECTION

The general election of April 1992 had three consequences for the Conservative parliamentary party. First, and most obviously, victory meant that the party was denied the 'luxury' of opposition. The splits within the party had to be resolved while governing, a much harder task than in opposition.

Second, the election produced noticeable changes in the composition of the parliamentary party. Of the 368 Conservative MPs at dissolution in 1992, a quarter (94) left the Commons either through retirement (56) or defeat (38). In their place, came 54 new MPs (63 if parliamentary 'retreads' are included), and this intake was more Eurosceptic than previous cohorts (Baker *et al.*, 1995a: 9). Meanwhile, mainly as a result of the large number of retirements at the 1992 election, only 21 Conservative MPs – those 'forged as politicians in the hey-day of the post-war consensus' (Criddle, 1992: 223) – remained from the pre-1970 parliaments.

The effect of this should not be overstated. The left of the party remained, albeit discernibly diminished, and was still too large to be ignored. At the same time, few of those who were to cause trouble in the 1992 parliament had entered the Commons on John

Major's coat-tails; of the most persistent rebels in the 1992 parliament, just three – Iain Duncan Smith, Barry Legg and Walter Sweeney – were 1992 entrants. Most of the Conservative MPs who caused Major problems after 1992 were already in parliament when he was elected leader.

Yet the 1992 election did alter the balance of power in the parliamentary Conservative party, because, probably for the first time, the majority of the party were now either Eurosceptic or had distinctly Eurosceptic leanings (Norton, 1997: 94).

The most important consequence of the election was the third: the peculiarities of the electoral system meant that, despite receiving the largest number of votes cast for a party in British political history, the Conservatives began the 1992 parliament with a majority of just 21 (Curtice and Steed, 1992). By-election losses, coupled with withdrawal of/resignation from the party whip, were subsequently to whittle the majority away even further, and Major was to finish the parliament with a 'majority' of –3, a situation never before faced by a Conservative premier. The three Conservative election victories of 1979, 1983 and 1987, by contrast, had produced majorities of 43, 144 and 101. Under such conditions government defeats in the Commons were rare – Mrs Thatcher suffered just three in eleven years – and potential rebels could be treated with a certain disdain (Nicholas Winterton once being curtly dismissed by a whip with the words: 'I'm too busy to waste my time with a tosser like you' (Seldon, 1997: 286)). From 1992 onwards, it did not take many such 'tossers' to threaten the government's majority. Each potential rebellion had to be taken seriously.

One study of the party in this period describes Major as 'weak' without once acknowledging the difficulties of governing with a majority which was often in single figures, if not lower (Evans and Taylor, 1996: Chapter 9). They were difficulties of which Major was very well aware. In the supposedly off-the-record conversation with ITN's Michael Brunson in April 1993 in which Major appeared to call three members of his Cabinet 'bastards', he described the size of his majority as 'the real problem'. 'Don't overlook that', he argued. 'I could have [*sic*] all these clever decisive things which people wanted me to do – but I would have split the Conservative Party into smithereens.'

MAASTRICHT

Despite its small majority, the Major government did not antici-
pate significant problems with the ratification of the Maastricht treaty
when parliament resumed after the election. The party whips expected some dissent – as they did on two other Bills – but they
hoped to pass the European Communities (Amendment) Bill through
parliament before the summer recess (Seldon, 1997: 291). The Bill
received its second reading on 21 May with a majority of 244 (the
Labour front bench having abstained). Twenty-two Conservative MPs
voted against, and a further number abstained. Despite the increase
in the size of opposition (up from seven before the election), the
whips remained confident that the Bill could easily be passed.

But the result of the Danish referendum on 2 June forced the
government to postpone the Bill's committee stage, 'to consider
further the legal and practical implications of the Danish referendum result' (HC Debates, 3 June 1992: c.827). Sceptic opinion within
the party had been hardening even before the Danish referendum.
'Those on the right of the Conservative Party who had tolerated
but never approved of the Maastricht Treaty had started to make
a fatal elision between the treaty, the ERM and the recession'
(Stephens, 1997: 199). But the Danish referendum result emboldened them. A total of 84 Conservatives – a quarter of the parliamentary party – signed an Early Day Motion (EDM) calling on
the government to use the postponement of the Bill to make a
'fresh start' in its European policy (see Baker *et al.*, 1993). Before
the Bill's progress could resume, Britain was forced out of the ERM,
an event which undermined the government's European policy and
hardened sceptic opinion yet further (Seldon, 1997: 318–20).

Rather than being 'over by summer', the Maastricht Bill did not
receive its third reading until more than a year after its introduction into the House.[3] The committee stage – taken on the floor of
the House – alone took 163 hours spread over 23 days (Ware, 1996b).
The rebellion at second reading was to be just the first of 62 rebellions
by Conservative MPs.[4] These rebellions involved 50 MPs, who between them cast more than 1100 dissenting votes. There were also
a very large – but ultimately unquantifiable – number of abstentions.[5]

Despite intense whipping of its MPs (Baker *et al.*, 1993), the
government suffered two defeats before the treaty was ratified, and
avoided others only by a series of retreats and U-turns (Baker *et al.*,
1994; Riddell, 1994: 52). The government needed support from

the Liberal Democrats to win the vote on the so-called 'paving' motion in November 1992 to enable the committee stage to begin, and only managed to get the treaty ratified after making the vote on the social chapter in July 1993 a vote of confidence. Conservative rebels were then confronted by a stark choice: if they supported the government they got the Maastricht treaty; but if the government fell, any incoming Labour government would both ratify the treaty and opt-in to the social chapter. 'The Prime Minister', said one rebel, 'has got the party by the goolies' (Gorman, 1993: 1). As a result, only one Conservative – Rupert Allason – failed to vote with the government, which won by a majority of 40. The treaty was then ratified on 2 August 1993.

The Conservative rebellions during the 1970s over entry into the EEC were described then as the 'most persistent Conservative intraparty dissent in post-war history' (Norton, 1978: 80). The Maastricht rebellions easily usurped that title (Ludlam, 1996; Sowemimo, 1996). The average rebellion over the European Communities Bill in 1972 involved fewer than ten MPs (Ludlam, 1996: 106). Only once did more than 20 Conservatives rebel, when 22 voted in favour of an amendment calling for a referendum (Norton, 1975: 435). The average rebellion over Maastricht, by contrast, involved over 18 MPs, with 35 rebellions involving 20 or more. The largest rebellion – at the Bill's third reading on 20 May 1993 – saw 41 Conservative MPs vote against the government, just three short of double the largest rebellion in 1972.

Yet the Maastricht rebels were not as one in their beliefs. Some were die-hard opponents of British membership *per se*. Some objected to further integration on constitutional grounds, others on economic grounds (Riddell, 1994; Baker *et al.*, 1993; see also Sowemimo, 1996). But their disparate membership did not prevent them making common cause against the treaty. Table 1.2 shows the 35 largest rebellions – those which consisted of 20 or more dissenting votes – indicating the MPs who voted against their whips on each vote. As is clear, the rebels – especially the most persistent ones – formed an extremely cohesive grouping. That cohesion was reinforced both by their own whipping system, and by the increased extent of factional organisation within the party (Norton, 1997: 94).

What was surprising about the rebellions, however, was not how many MPs rebelled, but – given the depth of hostility to the treaty within the Conservative parliamentary party – how few. Of the 84

Table 1.2 Conservative cohesion during the Maastricht rebellions

Name	19	82	83	110	111	112	113	115	116	117	118	127	128	129	130	136	137	161	163	174	203	219	232	233	234	235	237	238	244	245	246	247	248	277	359	Total
Taylor	*	*	*	*	*	*	*	*	*	*	*	*	*	*	*	*	*	*	*	*	*	*	*	*	*	*	*	*	*	*	*	*	*	*	*	53
Cash	*	*	*	*	*	*	*	*	*	*	*	*	*	*	*	*	*	*	*	*	*	*	*	*	*	*	*	*	*	*	*	*	*	*	*	52
Winterton, N	*	*	*	*	*	*	*	*	*	*	*	*	*	*	*	*	*	*	*	*	*	*	*	*	*	*	*	*	*	*	*	*	*	*	*	50
Winterton, A	*	*	*	*	*	*	*	*	*	*	*	*	*	*	*	*	*	*	*	*	*	*	*	*	*	*	*	*	*	*	*	*	*	.	*	50
Gill	*	*	*	*	*	*	*	*	*	*	*	*	*	*	*	*	*	*	*	*	*	*	*	*	*	*	*	*	*	*	*	*	*	*	*	47
Jessel	*	*	*	*	*	*	*	*	*	*	*	*	*	*	*	*	*	*	*	*	*	*	*	*	*	*	*	*	*	*	*	*	*	*	*	46
Gorman	*	*	*	*	*	*	*	*	*	*	*	*	*	*	*	*	*	*	*	*	*	*	*	*	*	*	*	*	*	*	*	*	*	*	*	45
Skeet	*	*	*	*	*	*	*	*	*	*	*	*	*	*	*	*	*	*	*	*	*	*	*	*	*	*	*	*	*	*	*	*	*	*	*	45
Knapman	.	*	*	*	*	*	*	*	*	*	*	*	*	*	*	*	*	*	*	*	*	*	*	*	*	*	*	*	*	*	*	*	*	*	*	45
Walker	.	*	*	*	*	*	*	*	*	*	*	*	*	*	*	*	*	*	*	*	*	*	*	*	*	*	*	*	*	*	*	*	*	.	*	43
Marlow	*	*	*	*	*	*	*	*	*	*	*	*	*	*	*	*	*	*	*	*	*	*	*	*	*	*	*	*	*	*	*	*	*	*	*	42
Shepherd	*	*	*	*	.	*	*	*	*	*	*	*	*	*	*	*	.	*	*	*	*	*	*	*	*	*	*	*	*	*	*	*	*	*	*	42
Lawrence	.	*	*	.	.	*	*	*	*	.	*	*	*	*	*	*	*	.	*	*	*	*	*	.	*	*	*	*	*	*	*	*	*	*	*	40
Budgen	*	.	*	*	.	*	*	*	*	*	*	*	*	*	*	*	*	*	*	*	*	*	*	*	*	*	*	*	*	*	*	*	*	.	*	40
Spicer, M	*	*	*	*	*	*	*	*	*	*	*	*	*	*	*	*	*	*	.	*	*	*	*	*	*	*	*	*	*	*	*	.	*	*	*	40
Cran	*	*	*	*	*	*	*	*	*	*	*	*	*	*	*	.	*	*	*	*	*	.	.	*	*	*	*	*	*	*	*	*	*	*	*	38
Lord	.	*	*	*	*	*	*	*	*	*	*	*	*	*	*	*	*	*	*	*	*	*	*	*	*	*	*	*	*	*	*	*	*	.	*	37
Wilkinson	.	*	*	.	*	*	*	*	*	*	*	*	*	*	*	*	*	*	*	*	*	*	*	*	*	*	*	*	*	*	*	*	*	*	*	36
Body	*	*	*	*	.	*	*	*	*	*	*	*	*	.	*	*	*	*	*	*	*	*	*	.	*	*	*	*	*	*	*	*	*	*	*	34
Biffen	*	*	*	*	.	*	*	*	*	*	*	.	.	*	*	*	*	.	*	*	*	*	.	*	*	*	*	*	*	*	*	*	*	*	*	30
Tapsell	*	*	*	*	*	*	.	*	*	*	*	.	*	*	*	.	.	*	*	*	*	*	.	*	*	*	.	*	*	*	*	*	*	*	*	29
Gardiner	.	*	.	*	*	*	*	.	*	.	*	.	.	*	*	*	*	*	*	*	*	*	.	*	.	.	.	*	*	*	*	*	*	*	*	26
Butcher	*	.	*	.	*	*	*	*	*	*	*	.	.	*	.	*	*	*	.	*	*	.	.	*	.	*	.	*	*	*	*	.	*	*	*	25
Sweeney	.	*	.	*	.	*	.	*	*	.	.	*	.	*	*	*	.	*	.	*	*	.	.	.	*	.	.	*	*	*	*	.	*	*	*	24
Legg	.	*	.	*	.	*	*	*	*	*	*	.	.	*	*	*	*	*	*	*	*	.	.	.	*	*	*	*	*	*	*	.	*	*	*	20
Carlisle	.	.	.	.	.	.	.	.	.	.	*	.	.	*	*	*	*	*	*	*	*	.	.	*	*	*	*	*	*	*	*	*	*	*	*	22
Cartiss	*	*	.	*	.	.	.	.	.	*	.	.	.	.	.	.	.	*	*	*	*	.	.	.	.	.	.	*	*	*	*	*	*	*	*	22
Hawskley	.	.	*	.	.	.	.	.	*	.	*	.	.	.	.	.	.	.	*	.	.	.	.	.	.	*	.	.	*	*	*	*	*	*	*	19
Porter	*	*	.	.	.	*	*	*	*	.	.	.	.	.	.	.	.	.	.	.	.	.	.	.	.	.	.	*	*	*	*	*	*	*	*	17
Pawsey	*	.	.	.	.	.	.	.	.	.	.	.	.	.	.	.	.	.	.	.	.	.	.	.	.	.	.	.	*	*	*	*	*	*	*	15
Allason	.	*	*	*	*	*	.	.	.	*	.	.	.	.	.	.	.	.	.	.	.	.	.	.	.	.	.	.	.	.	*	.	*	.	*	12
Boyson	.	.	.	.	.	.	.	.	.	.	*	.	.	.	.	.	.	.	.	.	.	.	*	.	.	*	.	.	.	*	*	*	*	*	*	12
Duncan Smith	.	*	*	.	.	.	.	.	.	.	.	*	.	*	.	.	.	.	.	.	.	.	.	.	.	.	.	.	.	.	.	.	*	.	*	12

Name	Total
Townend	8
Fry	6
Hunter	6
Greenway	5
Bendall	4
Moate	4
Bonsor	3
Clark, M	2
Deva	2
Jenkin	2
Leigh	2
Whittingdale	2
Dunn	1
Mans	1
Robathan	1

Note: * indicates a dissenting vote against the government. Only divisions with 20 or more dissenting votes shown. Total is number of dissenting votes cast throughout all 62 Maastricht rebellions.

signatories to the fresh start EDM, for example, 41 did not cast a single vote against any part of the treaty (see also Hague and Berrington, 1995). Similarly, the extensive survey evidence carried out among Conservative MPs during the parliament showed that doubts about European integration extended deeper into the parliamentary party than the size of the rebellions over Maastricht (see Baker *et al.*, 1995a; 1995b; 1996). Table 1.3 shows the responses Conservative MPs gave to a series of questions about European integration. The table reveals three features about the debate over Europe within the Conservative parliamentary party. Firstly, the majority of the parliamentary party recognised the benefits to the UK of membership of the EU. The majority of the party were not opposed to the EU *per se*. Secondly, however, on most issues the majority of the Conservative parliamentary party were sceptical about any further integration. The third feature of the table is crucial in explaining why the issue was so dangerous for the Conservatives: on most issues there were substantial minorities who took a different position from the majority. For example, whilst 61 per cent of backbenchers thought that monetary union was not desirable, 30 per cent, which represented about 80 backbenchers, thought it was desirable. Scepticism, then, was dominant in the parliamentary party – and more dominant than the open rebellion on the floor of the House over the Maastricht treaty revealed – but it was not predominant.

Over two-thirds of the Maastricht rebels had supported John Major in 1990. The Bill's passage – and in particular, the tactics that were used – alienated many of them from his leadership. Most of those who were pleased with the Bill's passage were those who had not voted for him in 1990. From that point on, John Major had little ideological support from any sector of his parliamentary party.

CONTINUING CONFLICT

The government faced a series of other rebellions during the parliament. Plans announced in October 1992 to close 31 coal-mines and make over 30 000 miners redundant had to be postponed when it became clear that enough Conservative MPs would rebel to defeat the government (Negrine, 1995: 52–3). The government's promise to review the policy limited the eventual rebellion to just half-a-dozen Conservative MPs, plus a handful of abstentions. Plans for the privatisation of the Royal Mail were shelved in 1994, again

Table 1.3 Backbench attitudes to European integration (percentages)

Statement	Strongly agree or agree	Neither	Disagree or strongly disagree
The disadvantages of EC membership have been outweighed by the benefits	59	9	32
The globalisation of economic activity makes European Union (EU) membership more, rather than less, necessary for the UK	62	8	30
An Act of Parliament should be passed to establish explicitly the ultimate supremacy of Parliament over EU legislation	56	16	28
Britain should block the use of QMV in the areas of foreign and defence policy	87	6	7
EMU is not desirable	61	9	30
The establishment of a single EU currency would signal the end of the UK as a sovereign nation	51	11	38
Britain should never rejoin the ERM	52	15	33
There should be a national referendum before the UK enters a single currency	55	4	41
Britain should adopt the Social Protocol	5	2	93
Cohesion funds should be phased out	66	18	16
The 1996 IGC should not increase the supranational powers of EU institutions	88	5	7
The Commission should lose the right to initiate legislation	61	4	35

Source: Ludlam (1996: 117) and Baker *et al.* (1995b)

after it became clear that there was sufficient backbench opposition to defeat the scheme (Crick, 1997: 409–10).

In November 1994, the government was forced to make the passage of the European Communities (Finance) Bill an issue of confidence to ensure its passage (Alderman, 1996a). Eight Conservatives still failed to support the government and had the whip withdrawn as a consequence. (A ninth MP, Sir Richard Body, resigned the whip in protest at their treatment, despite having supported the government.) The government then lost a vote on its planned increase in the level of Value Added Tax on domestic fuel on 6 December 1994, when seven

Conservatives (three of whom were without the whip) voted against the government. A further eight – five without the whip – abstained. The government lost by 319 to 311 and cancelled the VAT increase, the Chancellor consequently having to introduce other measures to recoup the £1bn shortfall arising from the defeat.

The government were also defeated on a 'take note' motion, on the government's handling of the Common Fisheries Policy on 19 December 1995. Two Conservatives cross-voted, more than ten abstained, and the government lost by 299 to 297 votes. In late 1995, the government withdrew its Family Homes and Domestic Violence Bill, and in April 1996, it allowed free votes on the key parts of its Family Law Bill, in both cases because it was clear that (again) sufficient MPs would rebel against the Bill to defeat it (Read and Marsh, 1997).

April 1996 also saw 66 Conservative MPs support Iain Duncan Smith's Private Members' Bill to give parliament power to over-turn rulings of the European Court of Justice, while June witnessed 76 Conservatives vote for Bill Cash's Bill requiring a referendum before any change to the relationship between Britain and the EU could take effect. Although Private Members' Bills are tradition-ally unwhipped, the government whips advised MPs to abstain on both bills. Over 90 ignored that advice and voted for one or both of the Bills. The largest rebellions of the parliament against the whips occurred later in 1996, when in a series of rebellions, up to 95 MPs – over a quarter of the parliamentary Conservative party – voted against parts of the Firearms (Amendment) Bill.

Conservative MPs also showed a willingness to pursue an inde-pendent line on several ostensibly free votes, but where there was a clear and known government line, such as Members' Pay and Allowances, in both July 1992 and July 1996, and over the planned implementation of the restrictions on MPs' links with outside or-ganisations in November 1995 (Johnston *et al.*, 1997).[6]

EJECTIONS AND DEFECTIONS

During Major's premiership, 10 MPs were deprived of their mem-bership of the parliamentary party ('lost the whip'), while another resigned the whip.[7] A further four defected to other parties. These 15 MPs are listed in Table 1.4.

In just under two years, therefore, Major's governments removed

Table 1.4 Ejections and defections, 1990–97

Lost whip	Resigned whip	Defected
John Browne (1992)	Sir Richard Body (1994)	Alan Howarth (1995)
Deselected but intended to stand in 1992 election against official Conservative candidate	In protest at treatment of EC (Finance) bill rebels	Joined the Labour Party.
		Emma Nicholson (1995)
		Joined the Liberal Democrats
Rupert Allason (1993)		Peter Thurnham (1996)
Failed to support government in final Maastricht vote		Resigned the whip (Feb), joining the Liberal Democrats (Oct)
Nicholas Budgen Michael Carttiss Christopher Gill Teresa Gorman (1994)		Sir George Gardiner (1997)
Tony Marlow Richard Shepherd Sir Teddy Taylor John Wilkinson		Joined the Referendum Party
Failed to support government in EC (Finance) bill votes		

the whip from more than twice the number of Conservative MPs (4) to have lost it during the rest of the century (Norton, 1995). Defections on the scale seen after 1992 were also unprecedented in post-war Conservative politics. None of this helped the Conservatives portray themselves as a united party. The MPs who lost the whip *en masse* after the EC (Finance) Bill vote, together with Sir Richard Body, attracted extensive media attention, even giving press conferences and staging photo opportunities. Each of the defectors made disparaging comments about their previous party (see, for example, Nicholson, 1996), all of which served to reinforce the perception of disunity.

There are, however, good grounds for not treating the various ejections and defections as evidence of a party falling apart at the seams. Withdrawing the whip *en masse*, as happened after the EC (Finance) Bill vote, was without precedent in the Conservative party, but failing to support the government in a vote of confidence was not. In 1972, 15 Conservative MPs had voted against their own government in a vote of confidence over the European Communities Bill (with another five abstaining), without suffering any disciplinary action. The eight Conservatives deprived of the party whip during Major's premiership had merely abstained. Thus, what was unprecedented was not the dissent itself, but the government's reaction (Norton, 1995). The only MPs to lose the whip in different circumstances was John Browne, and he lost it for reasons that were as much electoral – allowing his local party to argue that he was not a 'proper' Conservative (Pearce, 1992) – than disciplinary.

The defections are harder to dismiss. Baston (1996) argues that 'parties that fray at the edges . . . are usually about to come apart at the seams'. This may be true (although it has yet to happen). However, what is striking about the defections is that only one came from the right of the party, and only after the MP concerned had been deselected by his local party. The others were from the centre or left of the party, and in all but one case involved some personal rather than wholly political motivation (even if, for obvious reasons, the defectors liked to justify their actions in political terms). Perhaps the most significant effect of the defections – other than the effect they had on the public's image of the Conservative party – was that they each reduced Major's majority by two. Had it not been for the defections, the government would have ended the parliament with a small majority (Cowley, 1995).

THE LARGEST REBELLION

For most of Major's premiership (beginning in earnest during the Maastricht saga), there were rumours of challenges to his leadership. Major dismissed these as 'like Billy Bunter's postal order: widely talked about, but it never actually arrived' (Seldon, 1997: 515). In the end, tired of waiting, Major himself initiated the process that was to lead to his second leadership contest. On 22 June 1995, after yet another depressingly bad series of local election results, a bruising (and disrespectful) encounter with the 'Fresh Start' group of Conservative MPs, and amid talk of a challenge to his leadership in November, Major resigned as Conservative Party leader – but not as prime minister – to precipitate a leadership contest (Alderman, 1996b), urging his detractors to 'put up or shut up'.

They put up, with John Redwood resigning from the Cabinet to stand against Major. The results, announced on 4 July, were:

John Major	218
John Redwood	89
Abstained/Spoilt/Did not vote	22

To win on the first ballot a candidate in a Conservative leadership contest needs to clear two hurdles. He or she must gain both (i) an overall majority of the votes of those entitled to vote; and (ii) 15 per cent more than any other candidate of the votes of those entitled to vote. Major cleared both these hurdles comfortably, as well as managing to clear the so-called 'third hurdle', the need to win 'convincingly' (Cowley, 1996a; 1996c).

Conservative Party divisions over Europe explain most, but not all, of the result. At their core, the 111 MPs who did not vote for John Major comprised the Maastricht rebels, with about 80 per cent of those MPs who broke ranks over the Maastricht Bill either abstaining or backing Redwood (more usually the latter). This was particularly true of the Bill's more dedicated opponents: of those who voted against the Maastricht Bill on 11 or more occasions, nearly 90 per cent did not support Major. Yet, together, these rebels account for only around one-third of those who failed to back the Prime Minister. Around them was a wider Eurosceptic element. Some 60 per cent of the signatories to the Fresh Start EDM, for example, either voted for Redwood or abstained. And of the 111 Conservative MPs who did not back John Major, over 60 per cent could be classed as Eurosceptic, whereas of those who voted for

Redwood, the figure was nearer 85 per cent. In addition, as well as a scattering of those who felt they could not win under Major, or who felt personally aggrieved towards him, there was also a small group – no more than 10, most of whom abstained – who wanted to depose Major in order to instal Michael Heseltine (see Crick, 1997: 414; Hogg and Hill, 1995: 280).

When he called the contest, Major had claimed that he was being opposed by a 'small minority'. While winning it secured his position until the general election, it also showed that this was not true: the results revealed that a third of his parliamentary party – or close on half his backbenchers – did not want him to continue.[8] It also showed the weakness of his position. In 1990, as we have seen, he had been supported by those on the centre and right of the party. The intervening five years had seen much of that support fall away, most notably as a result of Maastricht. In 1995, therefore, much of Major's support came from the centre and left of the party by default: it came from people who had rejected him in 1990 but who feared the alternative(s) in 1995.

THE 1992 PARLIAMENT IN CONTEXT

Major, then, faced a series of high-profile rebellions throughout his second parliament as prime minister. It is important to put these rebellions into some context. There were 1294 divisions (votes) in the 1992 Parliament. In total, Conservative MPs cast dissenting votes in 174, or 13 per cent, of those divisions.[9] In absolute terms, this is clearly not a high figure, with only one in every eight votes witnessing any Conservative dissent. The other seven saw complete Conservative cohesion. More importantly, in relative terms, this figure is no higher than the level of dissent seen in other recent parliaments. Table 1.5 shows the levels of dissent by government backbenchers in all post-war parliaments.

For those who believe that the Major governments were ones of anarchic behaviour by backbenchers on a scale never seen before, Table 1.5 might be a surprise. Rather than heading the table, the 1992 parliament ranks fourth, just above Margaret Thatcher's first parliament, the Thatcher/Major parliament of 1987 (with Major's part of the latter being relatively quiet) and the 1959 parliament. The 1992 parliament was less troublesome than Mrs Thatcher's middle (1983) parliament and it was noticeably less troublesome than

Table 1.5   Dissent by government backbenchers, 1945–97

Rank	Date	Party	% of divisions seeing dissenting votes
1	1974–79	Lab	20
2	1970–74	Con	19
3	1983–87	Con	16
4	1992–97	Con	13
jnt5	1987–92	Con	12
jnt5	1979–83	Con	12
jnt5	1959–64	Con	12
8	1966–70	Lab	8
9	1974	Lab	7
10	1945–50	Lab	6
11	1950–51	Lab	2
jnt12	1955–59	Con	1
jnt12	1951–55	Con	1
14	1964–66	Lab	0.25

Source: updated from Cowley and Norton (1996).

two of the parliaments of the 1970s: Edward Heath saw his back-benchers defy their party whips in 19 per cent of divisions; and between October 1974 and 1979, Harold Wilson and James Callaghan saw their MPs revolt in 21 per cent of divisions. Based on this measure, then, the 1992 parliament appears not to have seen particularly high levels of dissent from Conservative MPs. Instead, it was of a piece with most post-1970 parliaments: cohesion remained the norm, dissent the exception.

As important as the frequency of the rebellions was their size. As Table 1.6 shows, these rebellions could occasionally be concentrated: 44 of the rebellions saw 20 or more Conservatives cast dissenting votes. Two rebellions – both over the issue of firearms control – saw more than 90 Conservative MPs defy their whips. In this, the period from 1992 was somewhat more rebellious than the three parliaments that preceded it. Between 1979 and 1992 just 9 per cent of rebellions involved 20 or more Conservative MPs (Cowley and Norton, 1996: 17). From 1992 to 1997, that figure had increased to 25 per cent. Yet the majority of rebellions remained limited: 63 (over a third) saw a solitary MP dissent, while another 52 (30) per cent saw between two and nine MPs break ranks. In other words, two-thirds of the rebellions consisted of fewer than ten MPs.

Table 1.6　Size of rebellions, 1992–97

Dissenting votes	N	As % of rebellions
1	63	36
2 to 9	52	30
10 to 19	15	9
20 to 29	32	18
30 to 39	6	3
40 to 49	2	1
50 to 59	0	0
60 to 69	1	1
70 to 79	0	0
80 to 89	1	1
90 to 99	2	1
Total	174	100

These rebellions involved a total of 175 MPs, or just over half of the parliamentary party. Given that, at any time, just under one-third of the party is in government (the 'payroll vote'), this demonstrates that dissent was fairly widespread. However, as Table 1.7 shows, even those Conservative MPs who were prepared to defy their whips did not do so often. Three-quarters of the dissenters broke ranks on fewer than ten occasions (that is, they were loyal to their whips in 99 per cent or more of divisions). Again, such levels of rebellion were not exceptional when compared to previous parliaments. Heath, for example, had seen 12 of his MPs rebel on 50 or more occasions, compared to eight of Major's (Norton, 1978). Furthermore, when compared to the 1974–79 Labour government, Major's backbenchers were extremely loyal: between 1974 and 1979, 268 MPs broke ranks; almost a quarter of Labour rebels voted against their party on more than 40 occasions, with nine doing so more than 100 times (Norton, 1980). By contrast, just 17 of Major's MPs (or 5 per cent) voted against him on 40 or more occasions, with the most rebellious MP – Sir Teddy Taylor – doing so on 70 occasions. Yet even he voted against his party in only one in every twenty divisions.

The same story is true in standing committees, where 'whipped' Conservative MPs cast a total of just 54 dissenting votes in 36 separate rebellions spread over 12 Bills.[10] The 36 rebellions constituted just 2.6 per cent of the 1360 divisions which took place in committee

Table 1.7 Number of dissenting votes cast by rebellious government MPs, 1992–97

Dissenting votes	N	As % of dissenting MPs	As % of parliamentary party
1	26	15	8
2 to 9	106	61	32
10 to 19	12	7	4
20 to 29	8	5	2
30 to 39	6	3	2
40 to 49	9	5	3
50 to 59	4	2	1
60 to 69	3	2	1
70 to 79	1	1	–
Total	175	101	52

Note: final two columns do not sum to total due to rounding. Percentage figures exclude the two deputy speakers from the base.

during the parliament. The total number of dissenting votes (54) as a percentage of the potential number of dissenting votes (around 18 400) was a vanishingly slight 0.3 per cent. As on the floor of the House, then, cohesion rather than chaos appears to have been the norm. Indeed, compared to previous parliaments, Conservative MPs between 1992 and 1997 were particularly cohesive in committee. In the 1983 Parliament, for example, Conservative MPs cast some 317 dissenting votes, spread over 183 divisions. This represents five times more rebellions (and approximately six times more dissenting votes) than in the 1992 Parliament. In total, between 1979 and 1992 Conservative MPs rebelled in 8 per cent of divisions in standing committee (Melhuish and Cowley, 1995: 60), approximately three times more often than they did from 1992 onwards.[11]

There was, therefore, no collapse in party discipline, either in standing committee or on the floor of the House, during John Major's premiership. In standing committee, Conservative MPs were less rebellious than they were during the Thatcher years, while on the floor of the House they were hardly any more rebellious than they had been during Thatcher's premiership. More than four out of every five divisions on the floor of the House saw all the Conservative MPs present enter the same lobby. When the government's ranks did break, the number of Conservative MPs dissenting was usually fewer than ten. Even the most rebellious MP was loyal in more than 9 out of ten votes. In this, the voting behaviour of the Conservative party in the 1992 parliament was of a type seen since 1979.

Furthermore, these data are dominated by the Maastricht rebellions. Over 60 per cent of the dissenting votes cast during the parliament by Conservative MPs took place during the passage of the Maastricht Bill. The majority of the Maastricht rebellions consisted of 20 or more cross-voting MPs. By contrast, of all the other rebellions, only ten (9 per cent) involved more than ten Conservative MPs. Similarly, with Maastricht excluded, no Conservative MP voted against the whips on more than 18 occasions, and only five MPs rebelled on more than ten occasions. Dissent in the 1992 parliament, then, was heavily front-loaded. The first session – which saw the Maastricht rebellions – saw Conservative MPs rebel in 23 per cent of divisions (93 rebellions, spread over 401 divisions). The remaining four sessions between them saw 81 rebellions, spread over 893 divisions, a rate of 9 per cent. For the majority of the parliament, therefore, Conservative MPs were behaving much as government MPs did in the late 1960s, when MPs were described as voting with 'Prussian discipline' (Beer, 1969: 350–1).

CONCLUSION

The above data should be treated with caution. Dissenting votes have the advantage of being what Truman called 'hard data' (see Ozbudun, 1970: 305), but they also suffer from disadvantages. On some occasions (as with the privatisation of the post office, or the Family Homes and Domestic Violence Bill) the government backed down, in the face of certain rebellion and probable defeat, or (as with pit-closures) offered concessions in order to limit the size of any rebellion. On other issues – as with Sunday trading and divorce – the government offered free votes, thus largely removing the issue from the party-political battle and avoiding any 'dissent'. And, as we have seen, in some cases – as over Maastricht or the EC (Finance) Bill – the government limited rebellion only through extensive use of patronage and threats or by making an issue one of confidence. All these events will have given the public the (accurate) impression of division yet resulted in few dissenting votes. The same applies to the leadership election in 1995, or to the ejections and defections from the parliamentary Conservative party.

Furthermore, removing the Maastricht rebellions in this way is somewhat hypothetical. The rebellions in the first session conditioned the remainder of the parliament: one MP admits to quietly absenting himself from votes rather than dissenting because he had no wish to add to the impression of a rebellious party. Another confessed to voting for plenty of things he did not agree with for the same reason: 'I often held my nose when voting with the government.'[12] Had the Maastricht rebellions not taken place, the behaviour of MPs in the last four sessions of the 1992 parliament might therefore have been different.

Yet the exercise still has considerable substantive value. First, it allows us to dismiss some of the wilder claims about the behaviour of Major's backbenchers. It is, for example, not true that during Major's premiership, MPs were more likely to rebel (Evans and Taylor, 1996: 268), nor is it true that the number of rebellions since 1992 had been unprecedented (Neville, 1997: 32). Similarly, Joe Rogaly's (1994) argument that the Major government resembled the last days of the Callaghan government is wide of the mark, at least as far as the behaviour of the parliamentary party is concerned. As we have seen, the PLP of the 1970s was far more rebellious than Major's parliamentary party. In five years the Labour government suffered 23 defeats because some of its own MPs voted with the Opposition. Even Heath, despite being Prime Minister for a shorter period and enjoying a larger majority than Major, suffered six (see Norton, 1978). In the seven years of his premiership, Major by contrast, suffered just four defeats on the floor of the House (on 'whipped' votes) caused by his own backbenchers rebelling, and he managed to pilot all but one of the 195 government Bills introduced in the 1992 parliament on to the statute book. This is not to argue that Conservative MPs were not behaving rebelliously throughout Major's premiership, and especially after 1992, but it is to argue, however, that many rebellions took the form of conversations with journalists or appearances in the media, rather than in the division lobbies of the House of Commons.

Second, the data show that it is possible to be mesmerised by the legislative battles that occurred over Europe, most noticeably Maastricht, and thus to miss the consensus that exists among the parliamentary party on many other issues (Riddell, 1992). As we have seen, once the Maastricht rebellions finished at the end of the first session of the 1992 parliament, there were remarkably few rebellions. Those rebellions that did occur were either extremely limited (almost half consisted of just one MP) or sporadic (such as firearms). They also tended to reflect policy at the periphery of the political debate in Britain – such as divorce or firearms – rather than core debates about public expenditure or the role of the state. Concentrating on the sizable doctrinal splits over Europe, while important, can therefore obscure the relative harmony that existed on much else.

Note

This chapter draws on research carried out as part of a larger ESRC funded project examining parliamentary behaviour since 1979. In addition, the Nuffield Foundation's Small Grants Scheme funded the research into the 1995 leadership contest. Matthew Bailey and Mark Stuart both helped with the research.

The author is also indebted to Timothy Heppell of Newcastle University, whose own research on the divisions in the parliament helped to identify a number of mistakes in the original data.

NOTES

1. Seldon (1997: 250) claims only three abstentions. Notwithstanding the problems – discussed in note 5 below – of definitively measuring abstentions, this is almost certainly incorrect. Five of the MPs that Seldon claims voted for the government did not in fact vote in the division.
2. Nor were there were any defeats on the floor of the House, and there were just six – par for the course – in standing committee.
3. Good accounts of the Bill's tortuous passage can be found in Baker *et al.* (1994), Rawlings (1994a, 1994b) and Ware (1996b).
4. This includes the vote on the ruling of the Chairman of Ways and Means (division 242) and on the Social Protocol (divisions 358 and 359). All three votes were occasioned by, and inextricably linked to, the Bill's passage.
5. It is difficult definitively to measure abstentions, since there is no way to distinguish between those that 'actively abstain' and those who are merely absent. This often leads to the number of abstentions being a matter for debate. Take, for example, the vote over the Committee of the Regions. Baker *et al.* (1994) claim there were 16 Conservative abstentions; Ludlam (1996: 105) claims 18; *The Financial Times* (9 March 1993) claimed 19, as does Norton (1997: 84). For this reason, while the text of this chapter may include reference to the number of MPs believed to have been abstaining on some votes, the analysis is conducted solely with dissenting votes.

6. Indeed, the very first vote of the 1992 parliament demonstrated the willingness of Conservative MPs to pursue an independent line. Over 70 broke with the rest of their party – and the entire cabinet – to support Betty Boothroyd as the new Speaker (Routledge, 1995: Ch. 8).
7. In addition, Sir John Gorst announced in December 1996 that he was withdrawing cooperation from the government, but he did not in fact resign the whip.
8. According to several accounts, Major came close to resigning, believing the result was not good enough to justify carrying on (see Cowley, 1997; Norton, 1997). Major's biographer disagrees (Seldon, 1997: 587).
9. Votes cast while MPs were without the whip are excluded from this total and from all the tables. Inclusion of such whipless votes would make little difference to the overall figures: between them the whipless MPs cast just 13 votes against the government.
10. In addition, Peter Thurnham, while an Independent Conservative, cast ten votes against the government on two Bills.
11. The government suffered 19 defeats in standing committee caused by its own backbenchers rebelling, again roughly of a piece with previous parliaments.
12. Conservative MPs to author.

2 A Permanent Revolution in Whitehall: the Major Governments and the Civil Service
Kevin Theakston

THATCHER'S LEGACY

The Thatcher decade had been a traumatic one for the civil service. There were significant cuts in its size, with staff numbers falling by 20 per cent, and a determination by Thatcher to 'deprivilege' civil servants. The 1980s also witnessed the deterioration of pay in the civil service *vis-à-vis* the private sector, and a bitter, protracted strike in 1981. There was also the banning of trade-union membership at the government's Communications Headquarters (GCHQ) at Cheltenham. Not surprisingly, morale in the civil service plummeted whilst Thatcher was Prime Minister.

By post-war standards, Thatcher was radical both in her refusal to recognise the career civil service as an interest in its own right, and in her resolve to tackle what she believed to be Whitehall's inefficiencies and political pretensions (Theakston 1995). Not since William Gladstone had a peace-time premier effected such a great impact on the civil service.

The Thatcher Governments' reforms of the civil service were based on a mixture of private sector business practices and 1960s managerialism, with Thatcher herself imbuing them with added impetus and political 'clout'. Yet the various initiatives – efficiency drives, the Rayner scrutiny programme and the Financial Management Initiative – failed to yield a fundamental change in the culture and methods of Whitehall during Thatcher's first two terms of office.

It was the launch of the Next Steps programme in 1988, involving the creation of semi-autonomous executive agencies to run the service-delivery and operational tasks of government, which promised a more radical and far-reaching transformation of the organisation and functioning of the civil service machine, although initially: the programme was subject to considerable scepticism, coupled with hostility inside the Treasury, and slow progress during the first two years.

Meanwhile, the 1980s had also seen the traditional relationship between ministers and civil servants placed under severe pressure. Thatcherites scorned Whitehall's consensual outlook and its departmental orthodoxies, and were therefore determined to teach the civil service a lesson in political control. Yet the dangers in downgrading the mandarins' traditional roles of problem-identification and policy-advice were clearly revealed in the poll-tax fiasco.

The 1980s had also occasioned controversy about the alleged 'politicisation' of the civil service, due to Thatcher's active role in appointing senior civil servants. There was never any evidence of party-political bias in her appointments and promotions, but she clearly wanted 'doers', rather than traditional mandarin types: civil servants who would help to solve problems, rather than merely identify them. Yet concern grew about the extent to which the Thatcherite expectation that officials should serve ministers with enthusiasm and unconditional loyalty conflicted with the traditional public-service values of impartiality and objectivity.

Many observers and civil servants expected (or hoped) that with Thatcher's replacement by John Major in November 1990, Whitehall reform would slip off the government's agenda. Yet Major had his own ideas about reshaping public services, and with key ministers – such as William Waldegrave and Michael Heseltine – also committed to further changes (and anxious for quick results), the reform of the civil service became increasingly radical, and the pace of change quicker, during Major's premiership.

THE NEXT STEPS: PROGRESS AND PROBLEMS

Executive agencies became a firmly established feature of the Whitehall landscape during the 1990s. At the time of Thatcher's resignation, only 34 had been established, employing 80 000 staff, thus causing scepticism about the government's claims that the Next Steps programme would eventually cover three-quarters of the civil service. However, John Major was strongly supportive of the programme, to the extent that by the end of his premiership, the Next Steps target had been met, and the programme was virtually complete.

Even by the 1992 election, 290 000 civil servants (half of the total work-force) worked in 72 agencies and cognate organisations, including the two big revenue departments, Customs and Excise and the Inland Revenue. By May 1997, the agency tally had reached 137, and – along with other bodies now organised along Next Steps lines, such as the Crown Prosecution Service and the Serious Fraud Office – employed nearly 384 000 civil servants. It was undoubtedly a remarkable achievement.

One of the main problems engendered by the Next Steps programme, however, was clarifying the relationship between ministers, departments and agencies. The aim – as delineated in the 1991 Fraser Report (Efficiency Unit, 1991) – was for Whitehall to move towards the private sector 'holding company' model, with core departments playing a more 'strategic' role, one which avoided over-detailed monitoring and intervention. Yet overlaps, confusions and tensions remained, as the 1994 Trosa Report found. Departments still tried to 'second-guess' agencies, and were reluctant to delegate, because they were loath to 'let go'. Furthermore, agency chief executives were frustrated by the various limitations which impinged upon their authority and autonomy (Cabinet Office/OPSS, 1994).

A crucial factor here was the absence of the sort of clear-cut distinction between 'policy' and 'operational' (or managerial) questions which Next Steps assumed. In practice, the line was blurred, with nearly 80 per cent of agency chief executives claiming to have a policy-advice input, while Departments frequently defined policy 'downwards' into the managerial sphere. Fraser had proposed countering this problem by cutting departmental headquarters staff by 25 per cent, but significant reductions only came after 1995 (see below).

The 'hands-off' principle could work only if the politicians were able and willing to make it work. Many agencies were small and low-profile, dealing with relatively uncontroversial matters, but in other cases, political pressures encouraged ministerial intervention. For example, although the Employment Service, headed by Mike Fogden, was one of the great successes of Next Steps, the chief executive had constantly to persuade Michael Forsyth, Minister for Employment, to confine himself to the big issues, and thereby permit him (Fogden) to deal with operational details and decisions (Lewis, 1997: 125).

Meanwhile, the political flak directed at the Child Support Agency in 1993–94 pulled social security ministers into detailed involvement with its business. The Child Support Agency was undoubtedly an administrative shambles, but it was also handicapped by poorly designed policy and legislation. Yet it was the high-profile chief executive, Ros Hepplewhite, who ended up carrying the can and resigning. On the other hand, Peter Lilley, as Secretary of State for Social Security, did try to stand back more from the day-to-day operations of the Benefits Agency (Greer, 1994: 55).

That the Next Steps arrangements could be subject to such immense strain when 'operational' decisions generated political controversy or ministerial embarrassment was demonstrated most vividly in the case of the Prison Service Agency, which was beset by riots and break-outs by prisoners, as well as criticism of the decision to transfer terrorist prisoners to Northern Ireland just days after the 1994 ceasefire had been announced by the IRA. The subsequent inquiries and their Reports – by Woodcock, and Learmont – drew attention to the confusion as to who was responsible for what, and the blurred accountability between the Home Secretary and the Director-General of the Prison Service. It became clear that certain ministers involved themselves in the minutiae of the day-to-day management of internal prison affairs (in one four-month period, over 1000 detailed briefing documents were submitted to them by the Prison Service HQ), yet Michael Howard, the Home Secretary, insisted that while he determined the policy, he was not responsible for its operation, thereby sacking (in October 1995) the agency chief, Derek Lewis, who had been brought in from the private sector to reform the Prison Service.

The 'Howard doctrine' was criticised for making 'passing the buck' into a convention of the constitution – centralising power but delegating blame – and opening up a 'bureaucratic Bermuda triangle' into which proper accountability disappeared (Treasury and Civil Service Committee, 1994, paragraph 165). Yet the Major government rejected a proposal by MPs to clarify responsibility by making agency chief executives directly accountable to select committees with regard to their annual performance agreements (Cm 2748, 1995: 31). The government claimed that this would be inconsistent with ministerial responsibility to Parliament, but the suspicion remained that the real reason was that ministers found the ambiguities politically convenient. Major's government made much of the distinction, elaborated by Sir Robin Butler, Head of the Civil Service, between ministerial 'accountability' and 'responsibility', with blame attaching to ministers only for actions and decisions in which they had some personal involvement. Although this was attacked as 'hair-splitting' and 'an artificial distinction' (Treasury and Civil Service Committee, 1994; Public Services Committee, 1996), there was a growing feeling that the traditional convention of ministerial responsibility was increasingly proving unworkable in the new world of agencies, and that an accountability gap was therefore opening up.

Meanwhile, whether the agencies were actually yielding the improved performance-gains which the government claimed is something of a moot point. There were certainly some dramatic improvements, such as the Passport Agency cutting the time taken to obtain a passport from three months to 7–10 days (*The Times*, 23 November 1995), while overall, agencies met 79 per cent of their performance targets in 1995–96. Yet behind these 'headline' figures, the pattern was uneven, with eight agencies – including the Child Support Agency – meeting only half or less of the targets which had been set for them in 1995–96 (Cm 3579, 1997). The hundreds of different performance indicators had to be interpreted carefully, with some measuring inputs, some measuring processes, and others – the majority – measuring outputs. Michael Heseltine was keen on aggregating them all into a single numerical index or agency league table, but the difficulties proved insurmountable (Talbot, 1997: 73–4).

THE CITIZEN'S CHARTER

John Major invested considerable political capital in *The Citizen's Charter*, published in July 1991 (Cm 1599, 1991), calling it 'the centrepiece of our policies for the 1990s'. Indeed, strong prime-ministerial backing was needed to overcome suspicion and resistance in Whitehall, and even among some ministers, to the initiative which had been dreamt up in the Number 10 Policy Unit (Hogg & Hill, 1995: 93–104; Seldon, 1997: 187–95).

Major had a genuine and deep personal commitment to improving the way in which officialdom dealt with the public, going back to his time as a local councillor in London during the late 1960s. Yet the *Citizen's Charter* also met a political need to come up with a 'Big Idea' which would signify continuity with Thatcherism while simultaneously marking out Major's own distinctive identity and agenda (Doern, 1993). Thus the commitment to securing 'value for money' and performance-related pay, while also extending privatisation, contracting-out and competitive tendering in the delivery of public services, continued the policies of the 1980s, but added a more positive gloss by placing a new emphasis on raising the quality of public services. The intention was to show that the Conservatives *did* care about public services, and were on the side of the ordinary person against anonymous bureaucrats and public-sector vested interests (although the Labour Party simultaneously dismissed the initiative as a public relations exercise, while claiming that they had invented the idea, and pioneered it in some Labour-controlled local authorities).

By 1996, 42 national charters had been published (including the Patient's Charter, the Taxpayer's Charter, and the Jobseeker's Charter) along with more than 10 000 local charters. There were 417 'Charter Mark' holders – organisations deemed to be delivering excellent services.

The basic Charter approach was to provide consumers of public services with more information about service-standards and targets; to establish independent inspectorates and monitoring of performance (including the publication of league tables); and to strengthen redress and complaints procedures.

Yet, however laudable, such initiatives as the 'Cones hotline' became a national joke, while cynics could point to the failure of the 'Charterline' telephone helpline service, which was closed down after just one year, having handled an average of only 25 calls per day, at a cost to the taxpayer of £68 for each enquiry. For its part, however, the Major government insisted that the various Charters had yielded significant improvements in service delivery, while also inculcating a fundamental change of culture in the public services (Cmnd 3370, 1996; Public Service Committee, 1997).

Rhetorically, the Citizen's Charter represented a populist assault on bureaucratic paternalism in the name of greater responsiveness to service-users, yet the Major government's concept of 'citizenship' was susceptible to criticism that it was too narrow and limited, focusing as it did on the individual consumer of services (Chandler, 1996a). The Charter(s) had not given citizens any new legal rights, and although organisations were thinking more about how they delivered services, and about the needs of their clients/ customers, the impact in practice was uneven.

The public and service-users played little or no part in setting performance targets, some of which were 'soft' or unambitious (Wilson, 1996). For example, no less than 47 per cent of Next Steps agencies' performance targets for 1995–96 were set at a lower level than the performance achieved in 1994–95. The Treasury, along with ministers themselves, insisted that there was no additional money available to fund the Charters; services had to be improved within existing resources, which effectively meant through greater efficiency and cost-effectiveness.

Yet critics could retort that the Government was seeking to distance itself from service-failure and the under-funding of public services. Could the Benefits Agency really deliver a better-quality service to claimants when the Department of Social Security's 'Change Programme' was heralding large cuts in staffing in order to achieve a 25 per cent reduction in running costs from 1996? Against the government's claims about the improved delivery of public services yielded by the *Citizen's Charter* is the fact that there were record increases in the number of complaints made to the Ombudsman, these tripling from 677 in 1989 to 1920 in 1996 (*The Independent*, 21 March 1996; 20 March 1997).

MARKET TESTING

During the 1980s, unlike the rest of the public sector, central government itself had been relatively untouched by the Thatcher governments' determination to introduce or extend market forces, competition, and contracting-out. By the beginning of the 1990s, therefore, only about £25 million of civil service work was subject to 'market testing'. However, this figure increased dramatically after the publication of the Treasury's *Competing for Quality* White Paper in November 1991, for this – along with the Citizen's Charter – signalled the Major government's determination to drive market reforms 'further into the core of the public services' and move towards a new model of 'government by contract'. Ministers talked of a new role for government, one which concentrated on what it really needed to do and no more, separating the purchaser and provider roles, and 'steering', not 'rowing', as the 1992 American 'cult' public management text *Reinventing Government* put it. In 1992, Stephen Dorrell, a Treasury Minister, spoke of a 'long march through Whitehall' involving the transfer to the private sector of activities which were not part of 'the inescapable core of government'. *Competing for Quality* was undoubtedly a Treasury policy, its own alternative to the Next Steps and the *Citizen's Charter*, both of which it feared would lead to higher public spending (Jordan, 1994).

There seemed to be competing agendas inside the Major government. With the Next Steps initiative, the Government had apparently acknowledged that civil servants could manage the service more efficiently, given the right structures. Yet – in the midst of the drive to create agencies – it was now declaring that competition (and, ultimately, privatisation), was the only way to make public services more efficient (Plowden, 1994: 14). Chief executives were resentful and disillusioned by this destabilising political interference, for having been promised more managerial freedom, central diktats now ordered them to meet targets for market-testing and contracting-out agency functions.

However, the ousting of Sir Peter Kemp in 1992 (the dynamo behind the Next Steps programme – sacked by William Waldegrave as Permanent Secretary of the newly-formed Office of Public Service and Science) marked a victory for John Major's new efficiency adviser, Peter Levene, in a behind-the-scenes conflict over policy-direction.

Between April 1992 and March 1997, £3.6 billion of activities across the whole of the civil service were reviewed under the auspices of the *Competing for Quality* initiative, with savings of £720 million being claimed – an average of 20 per cent (Cm 3579, 1997: 7). A further round of market testing covering £1.4 billion of work was announced for 1996–97, the main targets being ancillary services (such as catering, cleaning and security) and professional and white-collar support services (namely facilities and estate management, office services, payroll, libraries, financial and legal services, Information Technology and computing). Policy work and senior mandarins were largely unaffected, although in 1995, the Chancellor, Kenneth Clarke, insisted on private lawyers drafting parts of the Finance Bill (the cost of drafting 33 pages amounting to £130 000), and also appointed consultants to report on the feasibility of contracting-out the Treasury's economic forecasting.

For all the ministerial hype about a 'revolution . . . in public sector management' (Waldegrave, 1994), a report by the government's own Efficiency Unit on the market-testing initiative made sobering reading (Efficiency Unit, 1996). In the three years which it examined (1992–95), about one in eight of all civil service jobs had been subjected to review (69 283), and nearly a third of these (20 186) had been eliminated. The process had delivered innovations in service-delivery, along with financial savings averaging between 14 per cent and 30 per cent. However, nearly a fifth of all projects had yielded savings of less than 10 per cent, and the process of setting up tenders, preparing bids, and buying-in outside consultants accounted for 5 per cent of the value.

Contrary to the professed policy objective of the *Citizen's Charter*, service-quality was found to carry 'considerably less weight' than costs in decisions on contracting-out, thereby reinforcing the argument of outside critics that the real aim was not so much better management as a 'cost-saving jobs purge', or to 'dismantle the civil service altogether' (Plowden, 1994: 14). Even some insiders found it difficult to believe some of the government's claims about the savings yielded (Richards *et al.*, 1996: 32), and the Efficiency Unit (1996) reported doubts over whether the level of savings secured in the early years could be sustained in the longer-term, because in some sectors, competition might prove inadequate upon re-tendering (e.g. in the IT sector), and/or because many suppliers had pitched their initial bids too low. According to the Efficiency Unit's figures, 37 per cent of projects had been awarded 'in-house', 26 per cent had been contracted out after market-testing, and 16 per cent had been 'strategically contracted out' (i.e the work had been put out to the private sector without any competing in-house civil service bids). The Efficiency Unit also noted that the proportion of the programme subject to competition declined significantly after the first year, thus adding fuel to trade-union allegations about political prejudice in favour of the private sector.

The main source of the savings made turned out to be new working practices, and there was little difference in this respect between private sector and successful in-house teams, which clearly cast doubt on ministerial claims about the private sector's supposed special ability to bring about efficiencies in ways which the public sector could not. There was little doubt, however, about the overwhelmingly negative and demotivating effect on staff morale, and over half of the civil service came out on a one-day strike in protest against the policy, in November 1993.

While ministers played down the wider constitutional aspects of the market-testing policy, critics feared a loss of accountability, particularly as many contracts remained shrouded by 'commercial-in-confidence' restrictions. There were also worries that commercialisation might weaken the traditional public service ethos as private contractors brought a different culture and style of behaviour into government. Were private sector business practices really better? That these were not abstract considerations was shown by a widely-publicised Public Accounts Committee report in early 1994 which, citing instances of irregularities and improper spending, talked of a departure from time-honoured standards of public conduct (PAC, 1994). The Comptroller and Auditor-General, Sir John Bourn, complained that market testing made it more difficult to gauge whether public money was being spent efficiently or properly because the National Audit Office had no right to examine the books of private companies that had won contracts to deliver public services.

THE 1994 WHITE PAPER: *THE CIVIL SERVICE: CONTINUITY AND CHANGE*

Having introduced competition and contracting-out to civil service operations, it was only to be expected that there would be pressure to apply these methods to the central policy-making core of Whitehall, with Sir Peter Kemp arguing that: 'While the executive work of the civil service is getting better, the formulation of policy is deteriorating... at the centre, in Whitehall, old attitudes and the old guard prevail' (Kemp, 1993: 8). There were indeed fierce arguments inside Whitehall and among Ministers about the next moves. Kemp spoke of 'wayward barons' at the top of the civil service pulling in different directions, while a Cabinet committee on civil service reform was deeply divided. The Foreign Secretary, Douglas Hurd, tried to exercise a restraining influence, warning against an overly dogmatic or ideological approach to the role of the state and public servants (alluding to the dangers of a Mao-style 'permanent cultural revolution'), yet Kenneth Clarke and Michael Heseltine both pressed for more radical action, namely large reductions in the number of senior officials, universal fixed-term contracts, and the automatic open advertising of all top jobs.

Indeed, the very need for a single civil service was questioned, it being suggested that each Minister or Department could recruit its own staff. In the end, after Sir Robin Butler had apparently dug his heels in, John Major opted for a compromise between the radical reformers and the consolidators, as reflected in the 'continuity and change' subtitle of the 1994 White Paper on the civil service (Cm 2627, 1994). Thus was Sir Robin Butler able to comment: 'It could have been worse' (Talbot, 1995: 57).

The emphasis was now to be on managerial delegation and flexibility rather than central imposition. Departments and agencies were to draft annual 'efficiency plans' (scrutinised by the Efficiency Unit and the Treasury), and decide themselves on the mix of measures – including privatisation, market testing, and contracting-out – which would most effectively meet their own needs while delivering efficiency gains within tightly controlled running costs. Central targets for market testing would no longer be set, but it was not being abandoned as managerial tool. The financial squeeze would force Departments to take the hard decisions themselves. At the same time, the delegation of greater managerial flexibility from the centre of Whitehall (Treasury and Cabinet Office/OPSS) would continue. Already, 60 per cent of officials were covered by delegated pay bargaining arrangements at departmental or agency level, and from 1996, the responsibility for the pay and grading of all staff below the senior corps was to be delegated to the Departments and agencies themselves.

Meanwhile, the division between the top cadre of mandarins and the rest of the civil service would be further entrenched by the creation (from 1996) of a new Senior Civil Service, comprising the 3500 most senior officials, employed on individual contracts, and with pay reflecting individuals' responsibilities and performance. The 'fast stream' would remain as an inside track to posts in the elite corps (although there were worries about falling applications and perceptions of 'Oxbridge' bias in graduate recruitment). Responding to an earlier Cabinet Office report (the Oughton Report) on filling Whitehall's senior posts (Efficiency Unit, 1993), the government envisaged that more top jobs would be advertised and opened up to competition, although it appeared to rule out a large influx of 'imported' businessmen and managers by stating that most top positions would continue to be filled from within the civil service. A number of permanent secretaryships were advertised over the next few years, and in March 1995, the traditional mandarin mould was broken with the appointment of Michael Bichard (whose background was in local government and as chief executive of the Benefits Agency) as permanent secretary at the Department of Employment. Then, when the Department was merged with the Department of Education later in the same year, Bichard beat a regular career mandarin, Sir Tim Lankester, to the permanent secretaryship of the new Department of Education and Employment.

THE REVOLUTION 'WILL GO ON AND ON'

'The evolutionaries have routed the revolutionaries' was how *The Economist* (16 July 1994) interpreted the *Continuity and Change* White Paper, while Thatcherites viewed it as a fudge which did not go far enough in shaking up the senior mandarinate (Kemp, 1994). On the other hand, the Labour Party's Michael Meacher denounced it as 'a menu for the accelerated privatisation of the civil service, which threatens to destroy the constitutional principles on which the civil service has rested for 150 years' (HC Debates, 13 July 1994: cols 989–90). In fact, the dominant theme during the last two years of Major's premiership was that the pace and scale of change needed to be accelerated, with only lip-service paid to 'continuity' (*The Financial Times*, 24 January 1996). Reform 'will go on and on', warned Sir Robin Butler: '... however far we have come, we will have further to go' (*FDA News*, January 1996).

Much of the impetus for this drive came from Michael Heseltine, who carved out a powerful position at the centre of the government machine as Deputy Prime Minister after July 1995, taking on a wide-ranging political role, while also assuming effective charge of the Office of Public Service. Three main forces drove this new round of change in Whitehall: the stepping-up of the programme of agency privatisation, a Treasury-led assault on running costs (pay and administration), and the radical restructuring and reduction of departmental staffing.

Even back in 1991, some of John Major's Downing Street advisers had viewed the Next Steps agencies as an obvious target for a new privatisation drive (*The Times*, 22 April 1991). In 1993, the Government invited outside organisations to participate in the regular agency review exercises (the so-called 'prior options' tests), a move which suggested that it did indeed hope that the private sector would step in and take over agencies, or some of their operations. Yet it was only when Heseltine was appointed Deputy Prime Minister that the process of privatising agencies really gathered pace. Only one (DVOIT [Drivers, Vehicles and Operators Information Technology Directorate], the Transport Ministry's information technology agency) had previously been sold off, in 1993, but between November 1995 and the election in May 1997, a further ten were similarly disposed of, including HMSO.

While President of the Board of Trade back in 1993, Heseltine had wanted to privatise Companies House, and the Patent Office, but had been inundated with messages of opposition from their business and legal customers (Public Service Committee, 1997: 39). Once installed as Deputy Prime Minister, Heseltine turned his sights to key Cabinet Office agencies, with the Civil Service College one of his targets (*FDA News*, November 1995), However, this was spared, as was the Central Office of Information, although the latter had substantial job-cuts imposed, and its functions changed, so that it became an organisation procuring publicity and advertising services for Departments, rather than directly providing them itself (*FDA News*, January 1996). Meanwhile, the sale of the Recruitment and Assessment Service (RAS) – responsible for recruitment to the civil service's fast-stream – was pushed through in September 1996, in defiance of devastating criticism from peers in the House of Lords (including former senior mandarins, and ex-ministers from both sides of the House), who voted against the initiative by a two-to-one margin. As the RAS already worked efficiently, and the sale raised only £7 million, ministers were vulnerable to the accusation that they were jeopardising the traditional principle of fair and open recruitment by an independent body (the legacy of Northcote-Trevelyan) for the sake of Conservative party dogma and ideology.

Slashing running costs became a central feature of the Major government's civil service policy. The 1994 Budget announced cuts in the cost of central government of 10 per cent in real terms over three years, with the 1995 Budget subsequently seeking cuts of 12 per cent by 1998–99. The government insisted that 'efficiency savings' could be found in ways which did not affect the delivery of front-line services, but this was hotly disputed by civil-service unions. For example, the unions pointed out, plans for a 25 per cent reduction in the Department of Social Security's running costs over three years could result in 20 000 of the Department's 88 000 jobs being axed. Even the Secretary of State for Social Security, Peter Lilley, was concerned that 'the impact on operations will be devastating' (*The Independent*, 9 February 1996).

In its early years, the Major government did not enjoy much success in reducing the size of the civil service. Indeed, numbers rose by 12 000 in 1991–92, to a total of 565 000. By 1994, the number had fallen to 533 000, whereupon the government announced that it expected civil-service manpower to fall significantly below 500 000 during the next four years (Cm 2627, 1994: 30). Indeed, privatisation, contracting out, and the squeeze on running costs meant that by 1 April 1997, civil service permanent staffing had fallen to 476 000, with the blue-collar industrial civil service now numbering only 36 000 (compared to 61 000 in 1992, and 166 000 back in 1979). Yet the non-industrial civil service was still larger than it had been under the Conservative governments of the 1950s.

The senior civil service was subject to a number of 'senior management reviews' which resulted in large-scale reorganisations, 'delayering', and the elimination of some 23 per cent of top-level staff across the main Whitehall Departments (Mountfield, 1997: 309–10). The Treasury led the way, with a report published in October 1994 prompting a major restructuring of the Department, and a reduction of 25 per cent in its senior staff. There was also to be more delegation to other ministries, with the Treasury to play a more 'strategic' role, setting the framework and objectives, rather than getting involved in the nitty-gritty of departmental and agency business. Yet some critics were worried that this would weaken both the Treasury's control function, and the centre of government itself (Parry *et al.*, 1997).

These substantial cuts offered an opportunity to redefine the functions and role of departmental headquarters generally, marking the start of the process whereby the Next Steps revolution transformed the 'core' of Whitehall. A more critical view, however, suggested that by 1997, the senior civil service had been hacked back 'to the cusp of starting to have an effect on the ability to deliver policy advice' (*New Statesman*, 31 January 1997: 18). Yet there were no indications that the process would be terminated.

MORE OPEN GOVERNMENT

John Major's premiership evinced a number of limited steps towards greater openness in government. Having promised, after the 1992 election victory, to 'sweep away the cobwebs of secrecy which needlessly veil too much of government business', Major made the symbolic gesture of publishing details of the Cabinet committee system, de-classifying the *Questions of Procedure for Ministers* rulebook, and naming the security and intelligence chiefs at MI5 and MI6. Much was also made of the role of the *Citizen's Charter* in making available to the public more information about the performance of public services.

William Waldegrave's White Paper *Open Government*, published in July 1993, included a number of positive proposals, including commitments to publish Departments' internal administrative manuals, and to give reasons for administrative decisions to those affected. New statutory rights were promised concerning access to personal records, and to health and safety information. Yet Cabinet and departmental resistance meant that it fell far short of a proper Freedom of Information Act. The accompanying code of practice (which came into effect in April 1994) on the release of background information used in policy decisions included a range of exemptions, including 'internal advice and discussion', commercial confidences, and information relating to law enforcement, immigration and nationality, economic management, and defence and foreign policy.

This would be an exercise in 'openness' on the government's terms; there was no commitment to releasing actual documents, as opposed to information, and it would be those facts considered relevant by the government itself which would be made available.

CIVIL SERVICE VALUES UNDER THREAT?

John Major was not, in contrast to his predecessor, an 'anti-system' conviction politician. His consensual style extended towards relations with civil servants. There was certainly none of Thatcher's supposed 'is he one of us?' approach to senior civil service appointments and promotions. Indeed, Major left such matters largely to Sir Robin Butler, Head of the Civil Service, and other top mandarins (his backing for Michael Howard when he refused to accept Sir John Chilcot as his new Permanent Secretary at the Home Office, insisting instead on the appointment of Richard Wilson, was a very rare instance of prime-ministerial interference by Major (Seldon, 197: 739)).

At the same time, there were disturbing reports of things 'going wrong' with the relationship between Conservative ministers and civil servants during Major's premiership, and claims that the traditional values and understandings that used to underpin those relationships were breaking down. Plowden detected 'a worrying deterioration, in some cases at least, in the working relationship between ministers and officials' due to the unwillingness of a growing number of ministers to listen to unwelcome advice, and a consequent reluctance by officials to put their heads above the parapet and tell ministers things they did not want to hear (Plowden, 1994: 88–90, 104).

Michael Howard's relationship with his officials was particularly stormy and adversarial (Lewis, 1997), while two permanent secretaries – Sir Geoffrey Holland at the Department of Education and Sir Clive Whitmore at the Home Office – retired early amid reports that they had fallen out with their respective Secretaries of State.

The House of Commons' Treasury and Civil Service Select Committee (1994, paragraph 78) registered concerns about 'an unhealthy closeness between ministers and civil servants' after such a long period of one-party rule. There were also worries about alleged party-political interventions by civil servants, as evinced by the Opposition's anger when John Major defended Sir Duncan Nichol, the NHS chief executive (ranked as a senior civil servant), after he had offered a vigorous defence of the Government's policy on the health service, and attacked Labour, in the run-up to the 1992 election. In 1996, meanwhile, with another election looming, the First Division Association (FDA) – the top civil servants' union – disclosed that it had received a spate of complaints from officials who had been asked to undertake work that might compromise their party-political neutrality (*FDA News*, August 1996). It was also reported that Sir Robin Butler had to intervene to veto a plan by Michael Heseltine whereby officials would establish teams of 'cheerleaders' to champion government policy (*The Economist*, 16 November 1996).

Such episodes helped create an impression of the 'creeping politicization' of Whitehall (Kemp, 1994: 596), while a survey of 4000 senior officials found a widespread belief that the public service ethos was being eroded (Efficiency Unit, 1993: 108). The former Labour Prime Minister, James Callaghan, said that he was 'more worried about the civil service' than at any time in his 60-year association with it (Treasury and Civil Service Committee, 1993: 587), while John Smith (Labour Party leader 1992–94) argued that Whitehall's traditional impartiality was increasingly being compromised, and expressed concerns about a 'Conservative mind-set' among officials.

In response to such concerns, ministers, the Head of the civil service, and various Government white papers (for example, Cm 2627, 1994; Cm 2748: 1995), repeatedly insisted that the time-honoured core values of the civil service – impartiality, integrity, objectivity, appointment and promotion on merit, and accountability – were still safe, yet the very fact that these principles were having to be articulated so explicitly and frequently was suggestive of wider and deeper doubts. Indeed, in spite of its repeated insistence that civil service values remained intact, the Major government felt obliged, in January 1995, to introduce a new code of conduct for civil servants, which decreed that officials should act with 'integrity, honesty, impartiality, and objectivity' in their dealings with ministers, and not act in ways which were 'illegal, improper, unethical or in breach of constitutional convention'. An independent appeals route to the Civil Service Commissioners was also provided. Yet critics, including the FDA, felt that while this was a welcome step in the right direction, the initiative was neither comprehensive nor specific enough.

CONCLUSION

John Major's governments not only consolidated the Thatcher governments' reforms of the civil service, they radically extended them. Although Douglas Hurd had cautioned against 'a state of constant upheaval' (*FDA News*, August–September 1994), once Michael Heseltine had taken charge of the Office of Public Service in July 1995, and the Chancellor, Kenneth Clarke, was intent on remorselessly cutting running costs, 'macho ministerial management' (Gray and Jenkins, 1996: 246) became the order of the day. Civil-service unions, meanwhile, complained about 'a "scorched earth" policy of privatising as much of the civil service as possible, in as short a time as possible, in order to ensure that such privatisations were irreversible by the time of the next general election' (Public Services Committee, 1996, Vol. II: 14). There was speculation that if the Conservatives did win a fifth term of Office, then the next move might be the privatisation or contracting-out of policy advice (*The Independent*, 16 September 1995).

Major and his ministers presented their civil-service reforms as a comprehensive and coherent package, one which involved nothing less than a fundamental reappraisal of the role of government. Yet critics talked of destabilisation and dismemberment of the civil service, and of the substitution of ideology for strategic thinking. The White Paper *The Civil Service: Continuity and Change* had attempted a balancing act, affirming traditional values while insisting that managerial reforms would continue. In truth, it was no exaggeration to say, by the mid-1990s, that the civil service was 'in a state of crisis unprecedented in its history (Plowden, 1994: Foreword). Ministers had 'embarked on the fragmentation of government without knowing what they're doing' complained one insider. Plowden explained the Major government's reform of the civil service in terms of 'the frustration of a government at its failure to solve the substantive problems of the day', consequently 'turning to questions of administrative reorganization as a surrogate' (ibid.: 15).

Yet in contrast to their radicalism *vis-à-vis* the civil service, the Major government seemed remarkably cautious and conservative with regard to the constitutional implications raised by their reforms, as evinced in the arguments over the doctrine of ministerial responsibility, and the faltering steps towards more open government and a civil service code of practice. In a frank and controversial appearance before the parliamentary Public Service Committee in February 1996, Michael Heseltine dismissed the 'paraphernalia of so-called public accountability' as a 'bureaucratic overhead'. Yet the 'balkanisation' of the civil service into separately-managed units and contracted-out services, along with the individualisation of the service (individual contracts, performance-related pay, etc), was widely seen to raise serious questions about the preservation of the traditional public service ethos. The result was not just demoralisation among civil servants, but more fundamentally, increasing anxiety about the weakened policy-making and governing capacities of the understaffed, 'hollowed-out' and fragmented state (Rhodes, 1994).

'Whitehall ruined by Tory years' proclaimed a newspaper headline during the 1997 election campaign (*The Independent*, 31 March 1997). The story was inevitably more complicated than that, but there was no doubt that the Conservatives' civil service revolution had produced massive, and in many areas probably irreversible, changes. Broadly speaking, the early initiatives of John Major's premiership – agencies and citizens' charters – had bi-partisan support, but the changes carried out from 1992 onwards – market testing, contracting-out, privatisation – were not carried out on the basis of a cross-party consensus, with the Labour party attacking the 'commercialisation' of public services (yet having won the 1997 election, the Blair government announced that the drive for efficiency would continue, using the full range of methods and techniques inherited from the Major governments, albeit in a less dogmatic manner (Theakston, 1998)). It was perhaps not surprising, therefore, that whereas many within the civil service had been extremely relieved when John Major replaced Margaret Thatcher back in

November 1990, by the end of Major's premiership, no less than 77 per cent of Britain's civil servants yearned for a change of government. John Major's governments, like the Thatcher administrations which preceded them, had proved too radical for most of Britain's civil servants. In this sphere, as in various others, the Conservative governments of the 1980s and 1990s had alienated a key institution of the British state, to the extent that for many mandarins, the prospect of a Labour government was viewed favourably rather than with fear.

3 Centralisation and Fragmentation: John Major and the Reform of Local Government
John Kingdom

INTRODUCTION

John Major was no stranger to the world of local government. As a former councillor for the London Borough of Lambeth, he was part of a tide of lower-middle-class MPs swelling the party's ranks through the municipal route. Indeed, local government had not only assisted the journey to Westminster, it helped instal him in 10 Downing Street through the fiasco of the poll tax, and Margaret Thatcher's subsequent resignation.

Major kept a low profile during the troubled events. Even in the leadership contest, his opinion that the tax should go was voiced only privately (Norton, 1992: 60). He was effectively Thatcher's candidate, and most of her votes flowed his way on the second ballot so that on the three occasions it had been used, the party's electoral mechanism had spurned the traditional grandee figures. In contrast to his two main rivals (Heseltine, the Oxbridge-educated, self-made millionaire, and the patrician Hurd, with his landed background), Major had left school at 16, known unemployment, and advanced through the ranks. A beneficiary of the changing face of the parliamentary party, the self-made men and professional politicians recognised him as one of their own; a man who could be expected to know one end of a municipal drainpipe from the other.

THE CONTEXT

The Major era was not as tranquil as the prime minister, often characterised as grey, might have wished. Seismic changes in the state terrain raised issues extending well beyond the municipal world to address key themes of modern governance. In a process broadly characterised as hollowing out, the state moved from centralised provision of services towards the central regulation of a web of decentralised institutions created by various forms of privatisation, quasi-privatisation and agencification (Rhodes, 1994; 1997). Yet this had some very specific manifestations at the local government level, perhaps more so than in any other part of the state (Hogwood, 1997: 711–12)

The municipal landscape confronting Major in 1990 bore little resemblance to that he had left. The post-war consensus years had seen local government as a major arm of the welfare state apparatus working in partnership with central government. However, for Thatcher's New Right agenda, the territory concealed some dangerous landmines and became a key site for political action. Initially, as if obeying a kind of Newtonian law, the New Right force produced an opposing one in the form of a New Urban Left. Groups from the far left, churches, community organisations, women's associations, radical sections of the public-sector workforce, black rights groups, CND and environmentalists joined with left-wing councils to forge the kind of alliance that theorists such as Eric Hobsbawm had long advocated as a strategy for the British left.

In response, the Thatcher governments launched a legislative fusillade, aiming to weaken local government both financially and functionally. Consternation at the perceived unconstitutional 'politicisation' of local government led to the establishment of the Widdicombe Committee on the Conduct of Local Authority Business. Although no apologia for centralisation, its 1986 Report recommended various restrictions on local political activity, reminding any council that election

> may lend political authority to its actions within the law, ... but does not provide a mandate to act outside or above the law. Its continued existence ... depends on the contribution it can make to good government. (Widdicombe 1986: ch. 3, para. 49)

Hence, by the time Major became Prime Minister, the resistance of local government had been largely subdued (Lansley *et al.*, 1989). Many local firebrands had retired or moved on, some to fight in the Westminster arena. The 1990s was to see local politicians displaying more pragmatic styles under the guise of 'new realism'. Moreover, within the Labour party, the process of 'modernisation' begun by Neil Kinnock was gaining momentum in a quest for 're-spectability'. Local politics was no longer a domestic flashpoint, and thus not an area expected to promote sleepless nights.

Yet while John Major's premiership may not be widely remembered for its municipal pyrotechnics, lacking the fire and counterfire of the Thatcher years, it nonetheless witnessed the maturation of significant long-term developments and some important initiatives. When Major left, both apologists and critics could find grounds for agreement that something of a constitutional revolution had been wrought in the state territory beyond Westminster and Whitehall.

THE EARLY PORTENTS

Initially, the fact that the new occupant of 10 Downing Street had once served in local government was some grounds for optimism in Britain's council chambers. Those who had clung to their desks as the winds of change had gusted through the municipal corridors could have reasonably hoped for a new dawn of tranquillity.

Thatcher had shown ill-concealed contempt for the local government voice; the Consultative Council on Local Government Finance offering neither beer nor sandwiches and only a pretence of consultation. However, not only did Major speak of warm beer, on 27 February 1993 he told a conference of Conservative councillors: 'Let us stop battering one another around the head, and get on with good government' (*The Guardian*, 28 February 1993). Individual authorities and the associations could take heart from general expectations that Major's premiership would evince greater willingness to operate within policy networks.

However, Major was elected with two assets: he was not Thatcher; neither was he Heseltine. In office, both were to haunt him, one as welcome as Banquo's ghost, the other a more benign presence. Major had been Thatcher's favoured son for the succession and this was to prove a constraint; forever appearing before him, she was soon to declare that there was no such thing as Majorism. He showed no inclination to disagree (Norton, 1992: 60). Certainly many within the party wished to see in the new prime minister little more than an instrument for Thatcherism by other means. The imagery of carrying the torch was vivid and echoed by Thatcher herself: 'I wanted – perhaps I needed – to believe that he was the man to secure and safeguard my legacy' (Thatcher, 1993: 860).

As the more benign spirit, Michael Heseltine had been the enabler of Major's own ambition and could not be left in the cold. Indeed, Heseltine was to chart much of the Major era. Absent from office since January 1986, Heseltine was unmired by the fallout from the poll-tax calamity and, unlike some of his colleagues, had been alert to the political runes. He shrewdly made the fiasco a centrepiece of his leadership campaign, aiming to convince backbenchers that if it and Thatcher remained in place, their own parliamentary seats would be in jeopardy (Dorey, 1995a: 220). Well-placed to read the last rites on the unpopular tax, he re-entered government as Environment Secretary.

Thus Major had placed local government in the hands of possibly the most reformist minister of the era, one who had already presided over the Department of the Environment in the early Thatcher years when he had charted the passage of the 1980 Local Government Planning and Land Act; the harbinger of much of the agenda to come. Returning to his old empire, he was not slow to act and, although his tenure proved short, he set in motion wheels that were to revolve throughout Major's premiership, producing changes perhaps more fundamental than those secured under Thatcher.

EARLY BUSINESS – REPLACING THE POLL TAX

Some measure of the scale of the financial crisis was seen in Chancellor Norman Lamont's March 1991 Budget, which had to place an extra 2.5 per cent on VAT to ease poll-tax charges by an average of £140 per head. Of course, this exercise in robbing Peter to pay Paul could not mask the fundamental unacceptability of the tax. A few days after the Budget, Heseltine presented the House of Commons with his interim conclusions on various aspects of local government, including its finance. The poll tax would be laid to rest and replaced by a 'council tax'.

Here was the first important municipal action of the Major government. Did it suggest a new broom in Number 10? Did it do justice to the radical reputation of the Environment Secretary? The coincidence of an evident popular yearning for change, a reformist minister and a new prime minister could have been seen as an opportunity for Major to make his mark with a radical shake-up of local government finance. However, if there was temptation, it was resisted. The council tax returned to property values as its base, though these were banded to give it a progressive character.

However, the centrally administered Uniform Business Rate was retained, as was the capping regime, which was even tightened. The capping criteria for the financial year 1990/91 were announced before councils set their budgets, effectively putting a ceiling on expenditure. The Local Government Finance and Valuation Act 1991 extended capping to councils with budgets below £15 million, thereby bringing in the districts, most of whom had previously escaped. Almost half of all local authorities were forced to cut budgets or submit to capping. Linked to the grant regime, and the system of Standard Spending Assessments (SSAs) introduced in 1990, it produced a strong tool of central control. By April 1993, it was claimed that some £500 million had been squeezed from social service and education budgets (*The Economist*, 28 November 1992).

The system was roundly condemned by the Audit Commission (1993a) for failings in terms of economy, efficiency, effectiveness and accountability. With Byzantine complexity it confused officers as well as politicians. The Environment Select Committee added its voice to a critical cacophony with a report on the operation of the SSA system, noting failings in both methodology and implementation, and calling for more local discretion (HC 90, 1993/4).

Within the local government community, a groundswell of opinion among all political hues agreed that capping should have followed the poll-tax into oblivion. Support even came from some of Major's ministers, sensing that lifting restraints would expose 'profligate' Labour authorities to electoral censure as a consequence of council-tax rises.

By the mid-1990s, capping and the centralisation of the non-domestic rate meant that local tax covered only some 15 per cent of local government spending in England (only about 7 per cent in Wales), compared with some 53 per cent in 1989/90 (Wilson and Game, 1994: 161). This represented a huge reduction in local discretion, producing a gearing effect in that every 1 per cent rise in an authority's spending would require a council-tax rise of almost 7 per cent. A June 1997 meeting of European local government finance specialists in Rome revealed that local taxes in Britain, as a percentage of local authority revenue, were just one-fifth of those in France and Germany and less than half the level in Italy. The system would, in Tony Travers' view, have impressed Stalin, with a degree of detailed control which eluded even him (Travers, 1996).

WIPING AWAY THE TIERS

Other grounds for thinking local government might be granted a reprieve came in dramatic restructuring moves. Under Thatcher, the only reform had been negative: the abolition in 1986 of the GLC and metropolitan counties and of the Inner London Education Authority in April 1990. However, Heseltine argued that structural reform would be the *sine qua non* of a local government renaissance. The issue was by no means absent from the political agenda. The 1986 abolitions had left the metropolitan and Greater London districts as unitary authorities and these had been welcomed by some, including the Association of District Councils which, in 1989, advocated such a system for the whole country. The right-wing Adam Smith Institute (1989) produced its own radical plan in February 1989 to cover England, Wales and Scotland with a pattern of around 1000 single-tier authorities, delineating natural communities of between 60 000 and 100 000.

In April 1991, a consultation paper, *The Structure of Local Government in England*, was published, along with two others for Scotland and Wales respectively. In the case of England the government appeared to have learned from the poll-tax débâcle, with action now preceded by apparent attempts to find out what people thought. A Local Government Commission was set up in 1992 under the ex-chairman of the Audit Commission, Sir John Banham. Wales and Scotland were less favoured; here matters would lie in the hands of the respective Secretaries of State. Initially the commission was not asked for one single model, because Heseltine stressed the need for diversity in the light of local conditions. However, the *Policy Guidance to the Local Government Commission for England* stated unequivocally: 'The Government expects to see a substantial increase in the number of unitary authorities . . .'.

Wilson and Game adjudged the approach impetuous, failing to engage in 'meaningful debate about the role, constitutional position and function of local government in a democratic society' (1994: 300). However, as with the abolition of the GLC and metropolitan counties, there were political gains to be made; reform could end 'Labour's perpetual domination of the massive Strathclyde region of Scotland, of Derbyshire, Nottinghamshire, Humberside, and their ilk, and their replacement by either Conservative winnable, or at least smaller and less provocative, unitary councils' (Game, 1997: 6).

The commissioners took their remit to canvass local views seriously, with consultation and opinion-polling in a three-stage process:

Stage 1. Research to ascertain local feelings of community.
Stage 2. Production of draft proposals.
Stage 3. Further consultation.

However, the process gave an appearance of vacillation and in-decision, incurring increasing government displeasure. Sir John publicly accused ministers of interfering, allegations he repeated to the Environment Select Committee (HC 922, 1992/3). In May 1993 John Gummer, who had taken over as Environment Sec-retary, was reported to have asked the prime minister to wind up the commission. Although Major refused, tensions mounted as government preference for a unitary structure produced acrimonious exchanges. In 1993 Major had instructed Gummer to revise the guidelines to state that two-tier proposals should be the exception. However, these were challenged successfully by Derbyshire County Council, with the High Court ruling, on 28 January 1994, that he had acted unlawfully.

The 'stage 1' surveys entailed some 46 000 interviews in over 200 districts, and sought views on community feeling rather than struc-ture. Predictably the 'stage 2' proposals varied from area to area according to demography, local opinion and reorganisation costs; some were two-tier, some hybrid, but 99 were unitary. However, when returned to in 'stage 3', people reverted to a marked prefer-ence for the status quo. Further resistance to change came from Conservative MPs in the shires, concerned to preserve the coun-ties. Only the business community gave consistent support for the unitary model, but even this was not marked. As a result the com-mission cut its recommended number of unitary authorities first to 50 and then, in 1995, to 38.

Finally, in March 1995 Sir John (also subject to criticism from Labour, which backed the unitary model as more congruent with its regionalisation plans), was effectively sacked by Gummer. The process was reopened for 21 of the review areas under a new chair-man, Sir David Cooksey, like his predecessor a former chairman of the Audit Commission. Departing with an acrid taste in his mouth, Sir John advised his successor to listen to the people and not the politicians (*The Guardian*, 4 March 1995). However, this time less weight was placed on public opinion and the result was eight more unitary areas, sometimes flying in the face of local opinion and, to critical eyes, reflecting little logic beyond the principle that 'the Commission knows best' (Game, 1997: 8–9).

Yet for all the discord, the English process had at least permitted consultation. No such niceties were available in Scotland and Wales, where two deeply contentious Bills promoting the unitary model were pushed through the Commons. On 1 April 1996, 28 community authorities replaced the existing 65 in Scotland while, in the Principality, 21 unitary authorities replaced 8 county councils and 37 districts. Traditional Welsh counties, such as Gwent, and Scottish regions, such as Strathclyde, disappeared overnight, in a process described by Sir David Steel (former leader of the Liberal Party) as the most corrupt he had ever encountered.

For England, the resulting structure was more disparate, if not messy, and materialised gradually. It was expected that by 1998 there would be 34 counties, some of which would be hybrids, divided into 238 districts and 46 new unitary authorities. Critics described the process as a mishandled and highly expensive policy mess, presaging more than 7000 job losses (*Local Government Chronicle*, 29 March 1996). The new pattern would also add to a perceived democratic deficit by reducing the number of serving councillors and comparing unfavourably with other European countries. Moreover, despite its prevalence in western Europe, the government remained resolutely set against regionalism, Major attacking opposition parties' plans for devolving powers to Scotland and Wales, and for any suggestion of devolution to the English regions.

The process had provided an insight into central–local networks under pressure (Wilson, 1996: 442). There had been little rationality; goals, and the means of achieving them, were fuzzy, and clouded further by the vast and changing number of participants (Stoker, 1993: 4). The outcome could hardly be counted a Major success story. One commentator pondered whether the whole exercise was a smoke-screen produced by Whitehall to obscure more fundamental changes in its relationship with local government (Leach, 1993: 35). Certainly, the reform linked in with another seismic change in the local government landscape.

THE ENABLING AUTHORITY: (LOCAL) GOVERNMENT BY CONTRACT

The Conservative regime was to question the traditional rationale of local government: its responsibility to provide services. Through a process of compulsory competitive tendering (CCT) these were to be 'contracted out' to the private or voluntary sectors. This reflected the Major government's view that while

> local authorities have historically seen the direct provision of services to the community as one of their major tasks . . . now is the time for a new approach. The real task for local authorities lies in setting priorities, determining the standards of service which their citizens should enjoy, and finding the best ways to meet them. (Cabinet Office, 1991: 34)

The implications of this new approach went to the very nature of local democracy. Though by no means new, the practice became central to an ideological crusade with a battery of analysis and rhetoric from the New Right think-tanks. Although assets were not necessarily transferred to the private sector, and customers did not purchase services individually, CCT shared the same roots as privatisation (Greenwood and Wilson, 1994: 406). Indeed, the initiative had the potential to change radically the ethos of British public administration, and was a foretaste of a market-testing wave to hit civil servants (see Chapter 2).

The Major governments made significant advances on this front, compared with the relative caution evinced by Thatcher (in spite of her adversarial style). The 1980 Local Government, Planning and Land Act had introduced CCT for only a limited range of services (construction, building maintenance and highways), to be extended via the 1988 Local Government Act to six further services (cleaning, refuse collection, street cleaning, building cleaning, vehicle and ground maintenance, catering and leisure services management). Under Major, a 1991 consultation paper, *Competing for Quality*, pushed CCT into the core of local administration, while the 1992 Local Government Act embraced professional, technical and accounting responsibilities. Perhaps more significantly, it gave the Secretary of State discretionary power to add further services.

The government sought to tie this advance to its structural reform, its *Policy Guidance to the Local Government Commission for England* declaring that 'there should be no presumption that each authority should deliver its services in house' (1992: 3). Although some critics noted the failure of the commission to take account of the new public management movement (Leach and Barnet, 1997: 52), there could be little doubt that smaller unitary authorities, less able to reap the economies of scale and with a reduced financial base, would be less well equipped for the direct provision of key services.

The policy encountered massive opposition from local authority associations and bodies such as CIPFA, which argued that it would threaten corporate management and undermine professionalism (Mitchell, 1992). There were also fears that the search for profit would lower the quality of services and increase the risk of fraud and corruption (see Doig, 1995: 104). Moreover, the role of the officers would be radically recast – for, now that they were no longer required to undertake professional tasks or manage large workforces, the skills needed would be those of purchasing, contracting, quality control and regulation. A reduced role for elected representatives was also threatened, because with legislation emphasising the importance of commercial criteria in awarding contracts, and with little room for social or democratic considerations, the job could more easily be seen as a part-time one.

Local responses varied with political disposition. Conservative flagships, such as Bromley, Berkshire, Wandsworth and Westminster, were enthusiastic. In East Cambridge the district council even contracted out the collection of council tax and the payment of benefits. Other authorities resisted the loss of functions, awarding contracts to the 'in-house' teams. Many private contractors, though expressing considerable initial interest, fell away; the actual number of bids was low, particularly in metropolitan areas under Labour control. The option of management buy-out, which had also been canvassed, never proved popular (Robbie and Wright, 1996).

Local authorities could not avoid the culture shock. Even where in-house tenders were awarded, workforces became leaner and management structures placed officials in more competitive relationships, with some cast in the role of contractors and others as providers (Audit Commission, 1993b). A Local Government Management Board study (1993) contrasted old and new ways of thinking: the former largely producer-driven, paternalistic, comfortably financed and subject to only slow changes; and the new, including many previously leftist authorities, employing management-speak, talking of consumers rather than citizens, working with tight and declining cash-limited budgets, and accepting accelerated patterns of change.

The Major government maintained the momentum to the end. In 1996 it promised draconian measures to drive authorities further into areas such as finance, information technology, housing management, social services and personnel, as well as setting higher targets for work contracted out and making changes in previously agreed rules (*Public Finance*, 24 May 1996; 15 November 1996).

MANAGEMENT AND LEADERSHIP

The internal management of local authorities was not the exclusive concern of the Conservative government. An unceasing subject of post-war debate, it had been addressed in the 1967 Maud and 1972 Bains reports. However, these had assumed local government to be a provider of services and the central issue had been their coordination through corporate management.

In the new climate there was some feeling that mere tinkering with the age-old machinery would not suffice (Hambleton, 1996: 94). 'New Public Management' was an accepted term, recognisable as an international movement (Lowndes, 1997). In September 1990 the Audit Commission published a report, *We Can't Go on Meeting Like This*, its punning title focusing on labyrinthine committee structures and laborious decision-making procedures.

In June 1991, Heseltine followed up with another consultation document, *The Internal Management of Local Authorities*. Its broad thrust fitted snugly with the enabling vision, arguing that the control of large workforces would no longer be the central management task. Paragraph five of the paper envisaged the key skills in the areas of standard setting: specifying service requirements, assessing tenders, awarding contracts, monitoring and taking action where performance was unsatisfactory. In this new environment traditional committee structures would be cumbersome. The paper looked for speedy decision-making at the top with local cabinets, appointed council managers or directly elected US-style mayors with high public profiles and thrusting leadership styles. Most councillors would be devoting rather more time to their constituency roles, if not their families.

For critics, this divide between the decision-making and constituency roles was artificial (Wilson and Game, 1994: 318). Moreover, there seemed little argument to show why speedy decisions would be better decisions. As with the structural consultative paper, there was no discussion on the fundamental aspects of democracy and local accountability.

Soon, though, the Heseltine steam was taken out of the engine as Major's post-general election Cabinet reshuffle (on 11 April 1992) elevated him to President of the Board of Trade. His successor, Michael Howard, set up a working party comprising representatives from the local authority associations, the Audit Commission, the Local Government Management Board, and also including some academic opinion. This was to consider the response to the Heseltine document and establish trials in selected authorities. However, progress was inhibited by the fact that of more than 600 replies, most supported the status quo.

Howard was replaced by John Gummer on 12 May 1993, and a report, *Community Leadership and Representation: Unlocking the Potential*, appeared the following month. The potential was to be unlocked variously; ordinary councillors were to receive more training and develop their roles as consumer watchdogs, while leaders were to spend less time on detail, concentrating instead on providing clear policy direction.

While recognising that diversity and innovation could be accomplished within the existing legal framework, the government opened the possibility of forms of management not possible under current legislation which might be tested in pilot authorities. Four possibilities were canvassed: the single-party executive committee with delegated powers of strategy and policy formation subject to full council scrutiny; the leader-member system with power delegated to individuals rather than a collective executive; the cabinet system formed by the leaders of the majority party acting with collective and individual responsibility; and the legally separate political executive, perhaps directly elected and with power held independently of the council.

The last of these pointed to elected mayors, the option that had enthused Heseltine, envisaging central leadership, clear mandates and perhaps more popular interest. The *Municipal Journal* (14 June 1996) reported an astonishing 70 per cent public support for the principle. The Greater London area, without an elected authority since GLC abolition, was seen as a particularly suitable launch-pad and figures such as Tony Banks, Jeffrey Archer and Ken Livingstone were speculatively canvassed. However, the working party fought shy of this; the prospect of all-powerful Ken Livingstone clones in the town halls was hardly attractive to Major and his colleagues. Yet there could be little doubt that the direction was towards a more elitist system.

A NEW MAGISTRACY?

Reforms set in train under Thatcher, and continued under Major, saw the emergence of a parallel universe: an informal system of local governance where power fell into the hands of non-elected office-holders. The effect was to reduce the role of elected representatives, creating a 'democratic deficit'. John Stewart recalled the days before modern local government when bigwigs had dominated municipal life through an array of *ad hoc* boards. He dubbed the emerging local elite the 'new magistracy' (Stewart, 1992; 1995). It began to hold sway over a wide front, as a brief perusal of four specific policy areas – housing, health and social services, urban development, and law-and-order (a fifth key policy area, education, is omitted here because it is discussed in Chapter 8 – illustrates.

Housing

From the outset, the Thatcher government had challenged local government's central role in social housing, the 1980 Housing Act making substantial cuts in government subsidy while giving tenants a 'right to buy' at a considerable discount. When the Major era opened, some 20 per cent of public housing had been purchased in this way. Legislation in 1988 sought to reduce the role further by giving council tenants a right to choose an alternative landlord from the voluntary or private sectors or a housing cooperative. 'Tenants' choice' was made on the principle of a ballot, but the rules worked against the local authority (with abstentions deemed to be 'yes' votes in favour of an alternative landlord). In fact, the policy did not work as planned; housing associations worked with rather than against local authorities, many of which transferred their housing stock voluntarily. The 1989 Housing Act brought all housing authorities under central control, enabling Whitehall to set minimum rent levels in a quest to reflect the market value, thereby providing a further incentive to buy.

The Major governments maintained the approach with the 1992 Housing, Land and Urban Development Act extending the possibility of home ownership to more council tenants through rent-to-mortgage schemes. The power to extend CCT, conferred upon the Secretary of State by the 1992 Local Government Act, became apparent in June 1992 with the publication of a consultative paper, *Competing for Quality in Housing*, which introduced CCT into housing management. Local government was left to contemplate the prospect of a severely depleted housing stock, and a residual responsibility for only the most awkward cases, including the homeless and problem families.

Health and Social Services

Although no longer responsible for health care, local councils had still been able to exert some NHS influence through representation on health authorities. However, a much publicised White Paper, *Working for Patients* (Department of Health *et al.*, 1989), which sought to introduce market disciplines into the NHS through the 'internal market', ended this representation in favour of local business interests. The same pattern emerged for the self-governing NHS trusts created to run hospitals and community health care services.

However, at first sight, local authorities gained through the 'care in the community' initiative. Although nurtured under Thatcher by adviser Sir Roy Griffiths, this experienced no impediment under Major, and thus came into force in April 1993. Local government was to assume responsibility for a range of patient categories, including the chronically sick, the aged and the physically and mentally handicapped. Yet this was but another step along the enabling road. In what was termed a 'mixed economy of welfare', authorities were to plan and purchase 'packages of care' from state, private and voluntary providers. The result was highly fragmented services at the point of delivery but tight resource constraints at the centre, enhancing the role of managers at the expense of elected representatives and replacing electoral accountability with accountability through markets (Radcliffe, 1996: 166).

By 1996, the Major government was aiming to extend the enabling principle to social services through privatisation of domiciliary care and local authority residential homes. The prospects for children's services evoked particular criticism; private companies lacked the specialised staff for child care and child-abuse investigations and even the children's charities showed reluctance (*The Guardian*, 13 March 1997). As a result the March 1997 White Paper, *Social Services – Achievement and Challenge*, confined tendering to services for the elderly and the physically or mentally disabled. However, critics pointed out that these were often as complex and challenging as child care.

Urban Development

Until 25 years ago local authorities played little part in economic development. The role was one they created for themselves in the face of rising unemployment and regional imbalance (Haughton and Strange, 1997: 105). However, Thatcher was not happy with this and the area subsequently became a major breeding ground for 'quangocracy'. The 1980 Local Government Planning and Land Act established Urban Development Corporations (UDCs) on the model of the New Town Corporations to take over the urban programme. A further player entered the game in 1989/90 when the training policy under the Manpower Services Commission was decentralised into a system of centrally financed Training and Enterprise Councils (TECs) working under a Training Agency of the Department of Employment. These ended local authority involvement in training provision and policy. Various other initiatives emerged, including city grants, housing corporation grants, city action teams, derelict land grants and English Estates (a government agency building factories in rundown areas).

Much emphasis was placed on local government working in partnership with the private sector. However, some centrally created economic bodies were given an explicit remit to challenge many of the working practices of local government. For both UDCs and TECs, the emphasis was on making the market more effective as a creator of wealth rather than of jobs (Haughton and Strange, 1997: 89). The TECs were employer-dominated, with local government and trade unions given only weak representation. Signs of a more conciliatory approach seen under Major were misleading. While local authorities were given a lead role in the 1992 City Challenge scheme, the object was always to win central approval (John, 1994a: 424). Hence the partnership arrangements made to access both government and EU grants often masked 'a battle for ideological and policy supremacy over an ever dwindling resource base' (Haughton and Strange, 1997: 105). In July 1992 the government created an Urban Regeneration Agency (URA) to coordinate the range of urban programmes. A Single Regeneration Budget extended the competitive bidding through the public–private partnerships model of City Challenge, yet, despite its innovatory appearance, it proved a vehicle for Treasury domination (Tilson *et al.*, 1997).

Law and Order

During the Thatcher era it was recognised that a neo-liberal government needed the strong arm of the state. However, failing to display the 'adulation towards the police demonstrated by Mrs Thatcher' (Loveday, 1996: 23) the Major government found tensions rising. Paradoxically, this was part of her legacy. The key lay in rising crime rates, a matter of some embarrassment to a party priding itself on its law-and-order reputation. Critics – including the opposition parties, the liberal press and the churches – linked the issue to economic policies which subjected society to the vagaries of the market, generating social problems such as inequality, unemployment, drug abuse and demoralisation, particularly among the jobless young. Not surprisingly the government rejected the thesis and blame was apportioned variously: upon 'soft' judges, the police and leftish police authorities, and assorted 'trendy do-gooders'.

The issue of 'soft judges' yielded various direct criticisms of the judiciary, sometimes voiced at party conferences. Home Secretary Michael Howard's 'prison works' approach culminated in the 1996 Crime (Sentences) Bill introducing mandatory prison terms for certain offenders, including life terms for those aged 18 or over convicted for a second time of a serious violent or sexual crime. The judiciary were outraged, alleging that the government, with soundbites such as: 'If you can't do the time, don't do the crime', was taking more notice of tabloid newspapers than judges.

The police service itself was also targeted. Former Home Secretary Kenneth Baker was to reveal how the government felt that the police, the recipients of generous increases in both expenditure and powers, had let them down (Baker, 1993). Consequently, the cure-all medicine of managerialism was to be administered. Ostensibly promoting efficiency, the measures threatened seriously to 'destabilise established police interests' (Loveday, 1996: 23). The starting-point was the report commissioned from businessman Sir Patrick Sheehy in 1993. This castigated what were regarded as excessively cosy practices: recruits could expect a job for life, there was little performance appraisal and the service was top-heavy with senior grades. Proposals included performance-related pay, fixed-term contracts, the abolition of certain senior ranks, limitations on pension rights, compulsory redundancies, cuts in allowances and a ban on overtime. There was also to be a reduction in starting salaries.

Predictably, the package aroused widespread police wrath. Major's Home Secretaries, Kenneth Clarke and Michael Howard, were subject to a barrage of unprecedented criticism from police associations and decidedly uncordial receptions at conferences. On 30 July 1993, a protest rally of 20 000 officers gave notice of the strength of feeling, and in October 1993 Howard agreed to drop certain key recommendations. However, Major had presided over an historic realignment in the party's position within the establishment. To complete the transformation, Tony Blair, as Shadow Home Secretary, promoted his 'Tough on crime and tough on the causes of crime' message, relieving the police of blame for rising crime rates and winning the plaudits of the Police Federation.

In allowing his Home Secretary to take such liberties with bastions of the establishment, John Major demonstrated a distinct lack of touch. In attacking the local government dimension of the issue he was perhaps on safer ground. Policing had traditionally lain within the ambit of local government; the counties and joint bodies formed from the metropolitan districts; Police Committees comprising two-thirds councillors and one-third Justices of the Peace.

The 1993 Police and Magistrates Court Bill aimed to change this. Police authorities were no longer to be local authority committees, but independent bodies on which councillors were no longer to constitute a majority. Regardless of population served or area size, each would be standardized at 16, with only eight local authority representatives, while the chair, and one-third of the membership, were to be subject to the Home Secretary's patronage. However, amid considerable hostility, the House of Lords forced some concessions. Size was increased to 17, with nine local councillors, three JPs, and the remaining five appointed from a short-list vetted by the Home Secretary. Authorities would select their own chairpersons. Yet despite the compromise, the Act heralded a clear shift of power from local government.

A Constitutional Revolution?

The new pattern could be seen as a revolution by stealth. A July 1996 report by the constitutional scrutiny group Democratic Audit detailed a vast expansion in Whitehall's control of basic local services through the quangocracy of at least 5750 bodies controlling local services. Between 1994 and 1995, expenditure rose by £9 billion to reach £60.4 billion, so that 35 per cent of public money was managed by bodies appointed by, and answerable only to, ministers (Hall and Weir, 1996). Moreover, this 'new magistracy' had no particular reason to satisfy the communities they served. Members looked to central government for their reappointment, promotion, or even inclusion in the Honours List.

Was the cost in accountability matched with other improvements? One study of the diverse pattern found some were making sincere efforts to remedy their democratic deficiencies. However, 'performance has not been unambiguously enhanced: it has simply been reformulated and, in many cases, narrowed' (Rouse, 1997: 74). Moreover, the agencies were operating with little coordination – the very thing nineteenth-century municipal reformers sought to eradicate.

What kind of people formed this shadowy elite? Estimated at around 66 000, they outnumbered elected councillors by three to one (Hall and Weir, 1996), although they shared many of their characteristics. Indeed one study found that one in 10 had stood in a local election (Skelcher and Davies, 1996: 20). However, with a preponderance coming from local business communities, they had a lower level of correspondence with the populations served. Politically, many claimed to be independent, yet 'patronage through the appointments system, as well as the desire by the government to see greater private sector involvement, all contribute to the possibility of one set of political interests predominating' (Skelcher and Davies, 1996: 20). With Lord Nolan's inquiry into standards in public life, and widespread concern about 'jobbery', critics complained that Conservative patronage had reached new heights – or plumbed new depths – at the expense of local democracy.

THE EUROPEAN UNION CONNECTION

The EU was, of course, Major's *pons asinorum* (see Chapter 5) in many respects and, not surprisingly, little was done on the local government front to assist the integration into the wider community. The structural reforms actually limited the ability of local government to take full advantage of EU involvement (Barber and Millns, 1993). There was also continuing resistance to the idea of regional government, even though this tier was recognised by the EU for economic development purposes. Indeed, the creation by Whitehall of unified regional offices could be seen as an attempt by central government to 'seize the regional ground' for itself (Martin and Pearce, 1994: 19).

Yet the growing body of European legislation demanded that local authorities become engaged through greater responsibility for implementing legislation, monitoring standards and conforming to requirements (in areas such as consumer protection, the environment and competitive tendering). Left to themselves, some authorities were content with a minimalist response, but others sought to overcome their weakness and 'Europeanise' (John, 1994b). Many came together in regional or subregional partnerships to prepare EU funding bids. Some even forged transnational regional partnerships to lobby national governments and EU institutions over shared objectives. Generally, the European Commission, needing both cooperation and advice in formulating and implementing policy, became increasingly attractive to local authorities. Tangible incentives emerged in the form of grants from both the European Social Fund and European Regional Development Fund, the importance of which was increased because of the constraints on central government support (Martin and Pearce, 1994: 14).

With some irony, Major's 'game, set and match' diplomacy at Maastricht was inadvertently to champion the local government cause though his advocacy of the subsidiarity principle. The assertion that functions should remain with the lowest tier of government compatible with efficiency (argued to protect UK sovereignty against a 'European superstate'), could equally be cited in favour of an increased role for local (or regional) government. It could even justify authorities seeking Brussels' support in central–local conflict, thereby hoisting the Major government by its own petard. This possibility was increased through the creation (under the Maastricht Treaty) of the Committee of the Regions, comprising representatives from regional and local bodies, with rights to be consulted and give opinions (Hebbert, 1993).

THE ELECTORAL VERDICT

When the council tax slid into place, it appeared to herald the end of the Thatcher era for local government. However, it was not enough to avert electoral nemesis for her successor. On 6 May 1993, in one of the worst local election nights in its history, the party lost almost 500 councillors. The 1994 result saw another 429 of Major's footsoldiers fall as 18 more councils slipped away, with the Conservative vote share at 27 per cent. The low barometer of the

Major years fell further in May 1995, with a loss of some 1800 seats and 59 councils. The Conservatives were left with control of only 59 authorities, including just one metropolitan district and four London boroughs.

The 'tartan judgement' was even harsher. In April 1995, a judge banned the showing of a BBC *Panorama* interview with John Major because of possible influence on the forthcoming local elections (though sceptics might have wondered which way this influence might operate). In the event, the Conservatives won only 81 of the 1159 Scottish seats contested, thereby failing to secure control of any of the 29 new councils they had created (20 going to Labour, three each to the Nationalists and Independents and the remaining three left with no overall control).

The 4 May 1996 local elections were particularly significant, being the last before those coinciding with the general election verdict. Essex Man, the symbol of the go-getting 1980s, spoke with a new voice. As Labour and the Liberal Democrats made sweeping gains, Labour took control of Basildon, a totem seat in Major's 1992 general election triumph. The Conservatives were bereft of any representation whatsoever on more than 50 councils, including several former Tory strongholds, while on many others, including six metropolitan authorities, the party was down to one member. The outcome left Labour controlling 212 of the 465 authorities in England, Scotland and Wales (including 13 new shadow unitary councils), the Liberal Democrats controlling 55 and the Conservatives three.

A modest recovery from the previous year's record low contradicted the more extreme predictions of a total Conservative wipeout. There was talk of Major being a political survivor. Yet not only did the results augur badly for the general election, there was fear that the collapse would sap the party's campaigning strength. Normally among the party's most effective activists, there was some feeling among the defeated that they had been scapegoats for the sins of their Westminster cousins. When the party won power in 1979, some 12 143 of its stalwarts had populated the council chambers (*The Times*, 4 May 1996).

The local elections on 1 May 1997 were eclipsed by the national contest. The structural reforms had emphasised the rural–urban divide and helped return some of the shires to the Conservatives. However, the 240 victorious Conservative in the 56 councils holding elections were the only members of the party with grounds for contentment that night. At a nadir of 165 Westminster seats, a modest recovery in the town halls could bring little cheer to a prime minister to whom had fallen the task of closing an era. There was serious doubt that the depleted and disillusioned party would be in any shape to take advantage of the inevitable post-honeymoon fall in Labour popularity. This would leave the door ajar for a Liberal Democrat surge to effect an historic shift and become the 'official' municipal opposition (Rallings and Thrasher, 1997a).

CONCLUSION: SAFEGUARDING THATCHER'S LEGACY?

A salient feature of post-war politics has been the erosion of local government autonomy. When Britain was a world power, Westminster was occupied with great affairs of state and world diplomacy, content to leave local authorities to attend to the municipal minutiae of drainpipe and blackboard. However, with the loss of empire and the diminishing international role new tasks were needed for the fabled Rolls Royce minds of Whitehall; 'Cumbria and Coventry . . . replaced Asia and Africa as the object of the imperial government's attention' (Travers, 1996). Moreover the post-war welfare package demanded social justice; government would wish to monitor standards and secure equality of provision across the country (Rose, 1985). Latterly, the coming of the computer has opened new doors to control and monitoring, particularly in the crucial area of finance.

Yet the Major premiership saw the consolidation of quite new levels of centralisation. Despite her warlike rhetoric and detestation of local government, this had not proved so easy for Thatcher (Jenkins, 1996: 41). Rhodes has explained this with a power-dependence model of the central–local relationship, stressing that local authorities, like other interests, were actors in complex policy networks and possessed a number of powerful bargaining counters (expertise, organisation, information, and a crucial role in policy implementation). There was no reason to assume the wishes of the centre must invariably prevail.

Utilising this approach, Marsh and Rhodes (1992) were able to explain the limited impact of Thatcherism across a wide front, particularly with respect to local government. Hence the mass of local government legislation demonstrated not central dominance but a continuing need to correct policy failures. Chandler (1996b: 109–23) criticized this model for over-emphasising local autonomy, seeing councils as analogous to stewards of an estate, given discretion by virtue of being on the spot, but no real autonomy. Ultimately the steward must defer, or face removal.

Although some new initiatives foundered in the manner documented by Marsh and Rhodes, straightforward policy instruments such as the sale of council houses worked well for Thatcher. This leads John (1994a) to argue that the power-dependence model tended to ignore central government's capacity to learn. Thus the Major premiership, coming after a long period of Conservative rule under Thatcher, witnessed a more effective marginalising of local government because, after various policy failures of the 1980s, central government had sharpened its tools of control. This is supported by Hogwood's thesis that a party's duration in office is a key factor in explaining radical change (Hogwood, 1997: 715).

The lengthy term enjoyed by the Conservatives enabled government to contemplate a time-span beyond the four/five-year political cycle and effect fundamental shifts in local government, increasing business involvement, changing the management culture, and restricting the role of elected representatives. Under such circumstances, short-term policy failures could be absorbed. Strong evidence for this comes in the all-important area of finance where, after various problems including the poll-tax furore 'the government retreated from the idea of arm's length control that had informed the reform of local government finance in 1988' (John, 1994a: 424).

While the Major government appeared to pay more attention to views from within policy communities, seeking to win support and build coalitions, and including local authorities in local economic initiatives through City Challenge and later Urban Development Corporations (UDCs) and Housing Action Trusts (HATs), central direction remained the motive power. The Training and Enterprise Councils provided a particularly powerful form of intervention, 'a nation-wide multi-functional decentralised central administration . . . like a prefecture in embryo' (John, 1994a: 425). Indeed, it could be argued that the central–local relationship looked similar to that between government and the Next Steps agencies of the civil service (King, 1993: 196).

On the other hand, structural reform, and the extension of CCT to various local-level public services, still corresponded to the power-dependence view. A practical reaction to chronic centralisation and structural reform came via the three-into-one transformation of the local authority associations into a single Local Government Association (LGA). Sir David Williams, leader of the growing Liberal Democrat force on the association said: 'There is a growing awareness among senior councillors at a national level that we either hang together or hang separately' (quoted in Meikle, 1997a).

While Margaret Thatcher (who told the House of Lords on 8 June 1993 that *she* would not have signed the Maastricht treaty) could not hide her disappointment with her protégé on the European front, local government was an area where John Major largely carried on her torch. Indeed, in many respects, he appeared more effective and successful than Thatcher herself in this area.

However, it is uncertain how far developments can be attributed to Major himself, given that he did not project any great vision. The appointment of Michael Heseltine to the Department of the Environment injected much energy into the system, and there were also influences from wider reforms in train, some driven by civil servants, some by efficiency advisers and some by right-wing think-tanks, all using the rhetoric of 'reinventing government'. Even John Major's own 'Big Idea' of the *Citizen's Charter* was largely seen to emanate from the brain of policy adviser, Sarah (now Baroness) Hogg.

Yet the changes probably fitted within his cast of mind. Major seemed to be a constitutional conservative. Elevated from humble origins to the highest post in the land and without the benefit of a leisured education or opportunity for constitutional reflection, he played safe as a devout defender of the status quo. According to one cabinet colleague, the issue for Major before the 1992 general election was 'preserving the integrity of the kingdom from the threat from without and the threat from within' (*The Economist*, 17 December 1994). The threat from without was European federalism, while that from within was the break-up of the UK. Such a position left him a natural preference for government at nation-state level and discomfort with power shared with regions or town halls. Hence, and not without paradox, the not insignificant 'reinvention' of local government during the Major premiership served an essentially Conservative end.

Note: Thanks to Dr Jim Chandler for helpful comments.

4 Renewed Consultation or Continued Exclusion? Organised Interests and the Major Governments

Rob Baggott and Victoria McGregor-Riley

INTRODUCTION

Most observers agree that the 'philosophy of consultation' (Stewart, 1958), a key feature of government–group relations in the heyday of consensus politics, was first undermined during the 1970s, and increasingly eroded throughout the following decade by the authoritarian and confrontational policy style of successive Thatcher governments. Following Margaret Thatcher's departure, a return to a more consensual style of politics was widely anticipated, with John Major being portrayed as a more conciliatory and pragmatic leader. The 1992 general election – which left Major with a much-reduced majority – was seen as reinforcing this policy style by making it more difficult for government to steamroll legislation through Parliament as it had often done in the 1980s. It was widely expected that the parliamentary calculus – along with other factors, such as deteriorating party discipline, and the impact of by-elections on the government's majority – would place added emphasis on negotiation, compromise and consultation with organised interests. In short, it was believed that the 'philosophy of consultation' would once again be a dominant force in British politics.

This chapter assesses the actual relationship between organised interests and the Major government, as opposed to government posturing and rhetoric. It begins with an analysis of the baseline situation – the Thatcher legacy – and then moves on to analyse various aspects of government–group relations in the Major period.

THE THATCHER LEGACY

The impact of the Thatcher governments on the representation of organised interests can be summarised as follows (see Baggott, 1992, 1995; Richardson, 1990 for a more detailed analysis). First, the Thatcher governments' policy style undermined certain representative procedures that had acquired legitimacy in the post-war era. Second, some of the policies initiated by the Thatcher governments damaged relationships between the executive and particular interest groups which had previously enjoyed a privileged position in the policy process. Third, there appeared to be a considerable variation in the experience of organised interests during the Thatcher era, with certain groups actually enjoying an improvement in relations with government. We shall now examine these points more closely.

Policy Style

Although relations between government and some organised interests, notably the trade unions, became increasingly turbulent during the 1970s, the accommodation of groups through consultative procedures remained the dominant policy style (Richardson and Jordan, 1979). However, the Thatcher governments took a rather different view, whereupon strong government was emphasised, corporatism was despised, and less value was placed on the traditions of consultation, negotiation and compromise. The Thatcher governments were guided by the New Right mantra, which decreed that interest groups undermined effective government, the public interest and economic efficiency (Brittan, 1975; Olson, 1982; Pirie, 1988). Politically, Thatcher's governments were reinforced with large parliamentary majorities, a feeble political opposition, and a supportive popular press.

The result was a decline in 'institutions of compromise' and other processes aimed at accommodating interest groups. No new Royal Commissions were created during the Thatcher era (compared with an average of one per year in the period 1950–79), while the number of departmental committees of inquiry declined from an average of ten new committees a year during 1979–80, to around seven in the 1980s (Hennessy, 1986). Meanwhile, the number of advisory committees fell by a third between 1979 and 1990.

Some of the institutions that survived were downgraded, as was the case with the National Economic Development Council (NEDC), a forum for business, trade unions and government, whose meetings were cut from ten to four per year, with the Chancellor of the Exchequer attending only one meeting. Furthermore, the number of NEDC subcommittees, focusing on particular industrial sectors, was cut by half (the NEDC subsequently being abolished by the Major Government).

The Thatcher governments were openly hostile to corporatist forms of decision-making, particularly in the industrial sphere, although it did create some new quasi-governmental bodies that incorporated outside interests, such as the National Curriculum Council (now part of the Schools Curriculum and Assessment Authority), created by the 1988 Education Act. This body included people from a variety of backgrounds on its subject committees, though there was some bias in the selection of members: representatives of local education authorities and teachers' unions seemed to be less favoured than representatives of the independent sector and right-wing educational pressure groups (see Graham and Tytler, 1993).

Most of the procedural formalities of the consultative process were, however, retained during the 1980s, leading some observers to argue that the practice of consultation actually grew in the Thatcher era (Maloney, Jordan and McLaughlin, 1994). The Thatcher governments continued the practice of issuing Green Papers and other consultative documents. Indeed the overall number of consultative documents increased substantially (from 38 a year under the Callaghan government to 290 a year in Thatcher's third term) reflecting in part the growth in legislation and the expansion of policy initiatives in the 1980s.

Perhaps more important, though, than the reported rise in the number of consultative documents, were the purposes to which they were put and the government's willingness to modify its proposals in the light of comments. It is here that we find the main criticisms of the Thatcher governments' approach to consultation. It has been said that the Thatcher governments failed to allow sufficient time for comments to be made on their proposals. Certainly, the submissions to the Hansard Society Commission on the Legislative Process (Hansard Society, 1993) contain many criticisms of this nature, to the extent that the Commission concluded that, overall, there was 'substantial, objective evidence of failure to consult, inadequate time for consultation and subsequent unworkability of legislation' (ibid.: 30).

The second feature of the Thatcher period was a deterioration in the relationship between government and certain groups which formerly had enjoyed a privileged position in the policy process. These included trade unions, some professional organisations – particularly those representing public sector professions, such as teachers and doctors – and local authorities. These groups fell out of favour partly because of their opposition to specific policies in their sphere of interest, but also due to the manner in which the government formulated these policies.

The trade unions suffered the most from the change of government. In addition to economic, financial and legislative constraints imposed upon them during the 1980s (see Dorey, 1995b: Chapter 7), they were increasingly excluded from the consultation process. Trades Union Congress (TUC) contacts at prime ministerial level and all forms of government-initiated contact declined sharply after 1979 (Mitchell, 1987). Nonetheless, the trade unions were consulted on a narrower range of issues, such as training policy for example, and did retain membership of tripartite bodies such as the Health and Safety Commission and the National Economic Development Council.

Professional associations also suffered from a deterioration in their relationship with government. The British Medical Association (BMA) is a case in point (see McGregor-Riley, 1997). In 1989, the government announced the introduction of an internal market in the NHS, following a review which had deliberately excluded the BMA, as well as other prominent professional associations in the health field. The BMA was deeply offended, traditionally having been used to full consultation on health policy issues (see Eckstein, 1960). This was part of a broader change in the relationship between the government and the medical profession which evolved throughout the 1980s. Contact with government was maintained, but relationships with Ministers deteriorated considerably. The situation is described by a former senior civil servant at the Department of Health as follows:

> The relationship never foundered, there was never a situation in which we weren't talking to one another, it was rather a situation in which an old sort of consensual relationship broke down and became much more of a relationship between a government and a producer organisation. . . . [C]onversations still took place but on a rather more distant basis than had been the case previously. (McGregor-Riley, 1997)

An analysis of contact between the BMA and the Department of Health reveals that the average frequency of contact fell from 14.4 to 12.4 episodes a year between 1975–79 and 1980–90 (McGregor-Riley, 1997). However, in contrast to the TUC's predicament noted earlier, BMA-initiated contact with the Department of Health remained stable in the Thatcher period (59 per cent of recorded contacts were initiated by the BMA in both the 1975–79 and 1980–90 periods).

Another set of organised interests, the local authorities, were also frozen out during the 1980s. While communication with government, through the local authority associations, was maintained in this period (Wilson and Game, 1994), local authorities were, for the most part, excluded from prior consultation on policy (Isaac-Henry, 1984; Rhodes, 1986), despite their experience and expertise. As the poll-tax fiasco clearly illustrated, their views were often simply ignored, in this case with disastrous consequences (Butler, Adonis and Travers, 1994).

The teaching unions were similarly disgruntled by the failure to consult on major reforms such as the 1988 Education Reform Act. Other traditionally well-connected lobby groups, such as the brewers, the broadcasting industry and the legal profession also complained about the announcement of radical reforms. However, in these cases, the government did subsequently seek to maintain a close and relatively constructive relationship, enabling these groups to exert considerable influence over the reforms in question.

This leads on to the third point about government–group relations in the Thatcher era: a variation in the experience of different groups. Survey evidence reveals that many groups – just under half in one survey (Baggott, 1992) – did not perceive any change in the frequency or effectiveness of contacts with Ministers and civil servants during the 1980s. Indeed, some groups claimed to have benefited from the Thatcher regime by way of greater access to government and more influence over policy. These included business organisations (with the exception of the CBI, still tainted by its involvement in the corporatist politics of the 1970s), moral-cause groups and right-wing think tanks. Their privileged, 'insider' status arose largely because their objectives were highly compatible with Thatcher's agenda and to a certain extent they were pushing at an open door.

There was also a considerable variation in ministers' handling of particular groups. Kenneth Clarke, for example, acquired something of a reputation for antagonising organised interests, especially during his time at the Department of Education, the Department of Health, and the Home Office. Other ministers, most notably John MacGregor, Wiliam Waldegrave, and Chris Patten, were applauded for their more constructive approach. Yet even where Ministers were hostile and antagonistic towards organised interests, groups were often able to maintain good links with civil servants. Survey evidence suggests that many of the groups that experienced a deteriorating relationship with Ministers in the 1980s actually retained effective links with civil servants (Baggott, 1995). This suggests that the strength of established networks had a protective effect which prevented a complete breakdown of group–government relations.

Relationships between groups and government in the 1980s also varied at different stages of the policy process. At the policy-formation stage the Thatcher governments restricted consultation and excluded certain interests. However, organised interests often counter-attacked at the legislative stage, whereupon the threat of an embarrassing defeat, particularly in the House of Lords, occasionally led the Thatcher government to seek a compromise, such as the amendment to the 1988 Education Bill on parental ballots for school 'opt-outs' (Welfare, 1992). Similarly, the Thatcher governments found it difficult to ignore organised interests when it came to implementing legislation. As Richardson (1990) observed, traditional processes of consultation and negotiation were reasserted at this stage, as the government had to compromise in order to secure cooperation from those responsible for implementing policies and enforcing legislation. Consequently, radical reforms in both health and education were diluted in the light of criticisms from professional interests at the implementation stage.

Hence, although the Thatcher government did have a significant impact on group–government relations, this impact was not as straightforward or as uniform as some have assumed. Having established this baseline, we can now analyse how these relationships fared under Major.

The Major Governments' Impact

The replacement of Margaret Thatcher by John Major in 1990 was widely expected to herald a significant change of style. Despite uncertainty about his ideological position, he was portrayed as a 'one-nation Tory'. Moreover, he appeared to be a pragmatist, intimating a more flexible approach to policy-making and a greater commitment to compromise and consensus.

The early signs were that a philosophy of consultation might once again predominate (Richardson, 1993). The Major government indicated a desire to build bridges with those interests which had been alienated during the previous decade – such as the teachers, doctors, trade unions generally, and local authority associations.

A survey of over a hundred groups undertaken a year after Major became Prime Minister indicated that many groups believed the climate was changing for the better. Almost 40 per cent claimed that the new government was more sympathetic, showed a greater willingness to listen and grant access to senior decision-makers. The vast majority of the remainder did not perceive any significant change. This was, however, something of a honeymoon period. Moreover, as the next General Election approached, the Major government – like all governments – was aware of the need to placate interests. Pre-election 'sweeteners' totalling almost £3 million were authorised – much of this being spent as a response to specific pressure-group campaigns – including a plan for nature conservation, compensation for haemophiliacs infected by HIV-contaminated products, and increased resources for the Social Fund, a part of the social security system heavily criticised by the poverty lobby.

The 1992 Election result brought a much-reduced majority for Major. Although it was ostensibly a working majority, growing indiscipline within the parliamentary Conservative party suggested that the government would have to place greater emphasis on persuading its own MPs to support its proposals. In addition, it was believed that more effort would have to be expended on consulting organised interests at the policy-formulation stage, in order to pre-empt problems at the legislative stage.

Hence the belief that the philosophy of consultation would be restored under Major. But did this happen? Again, as with the Thatcher period, there are difficulties of generalisation. Yet it is possible to estimate the impact of the Major governments, firstly by looking at general data on consultative processes, secondly by examining its treatment of those organised interests whose relationship with government deteriorated in the 1980s, and finally by analysing how the Major government handled other domestic policy issues arising in the 1990s.

How did consultative processes alter under the Major government? Certainly there was a notable departure in the establishment of a Royal Commission (on Criminal Justice) in 1991, and although the Major government did not establish any further Royal Commissions, it did establish high-profile consultative bodies on other issues, such as the Local Government Commission in 1992 (see below), and the Nolan Committee in 1994 to investigate standards in public life.

However, the number of committees of inquiry continued to fall during Major's premiership. Only twelve such inquiries were set up between 1991 and 1994, an average of only three per year. This was about half the level of the 1980s and a third of that of the 1970s. Committees of inquiry were generally used for two main purposes – to investigate shortcomings of policy and/or practice, and to review policy options. In the 1980s, and even more so in the 1990s, committees of inquiry and Royal Commissions were increasingly replaced by other methods.

One such method was the appointment of a task force comprising experts in the field to recommend new policies and practices. Alternatively an 'independent review' was launched, often by an individual appointed from outside government, in some cases assisted by expert 'assessors'. Both alternatives offer opportunities for organised interests to make comments and influence policy debates, but in contrast to committees of inquiry and Royal Commissions, such forums are more geared to promoting immediate action than to the building of consensus and the painstaking collection of views and evidence. Furthermore, these alternative mechanisms lack the high profile enjoyed by a committee of inquiry or Royal Commission, and consequently, though having an effect on public policy, appear to have had less impact on public debate.

As the number of committees of inquiry declined, so did the number of advisory committees. During John Major's premiership, the number of such committees fell from 971 (1990) to 674 (1996), a decline comparable to that of the 1980s. Major continued to attack particular intermediate institutions, and in some respects his government went further than its predecessor (for example, abolishing that vestige of post-war corporatism, the National Economic Development Council).

Again ever, though, the official figures do not tell the whole story. Government departments developed other arrangements to achieve similar ends. *Ad hoc* working parties and expert groups were established to investigate problems and sound out organised interests, yet because these committees are not permanent, formal

Table 4.1   Green Papers and Consultative Documents under the Major governments

Year	No. of Green Papers	No. of Consultative Documents in total
1991	6	261
1992	8	293
1993	17	336
1994	10*	346
1995	13	270
1996	15	199
Total	69	1705

* In 1994, 30 consultative documents were published by HMSO on local government reorganisation, each relating to specific local authorities. These have been counted as one 'high profile' Green Paper.

arrangements, they are not classified as advisory committees in the official statistics.

One can compare the record of the Major government on consultation with its predecessors in a number of other respects. First, the number of Green Papers and other consultative documents can be regarded as an indicator. Second, the length of consultation periods illustrates the extent to which government values an adequate response from organised interests. The Major governments' record on Green Papers and consultative documents is shown in Table 4.1.

Table 4.2 suggests that the Major governments had a comparatively good record on issuing consultative documents compared with their predecessors. The average number of Green Papers and consultative documents overall during the Major governments is higher than those of the Callaghan and the Thatcher governments. However, care must be taken when interpreting these figures, not least because one has to bear in mind that a quantitative analysis fails to show the extent to which government has modified proposals following comments.

The length of consultation periods, however, does shed some light on the value placed by government on this process. In Figure 4.1 we reveal the results of an analysis of consultation periods taken from documents received by the House of Commons Public Information Office. The first sample was taken from a six-month period during Thatcher's third term. The second was taken from the same

Table 4.2   Green Papers and Consultative Documents, 1976–96

Years	Average per annum Green Papers	Average per annum all Consultative Documents
1976–78 (Callaghan)	9.6	38.3
1979–90 (Thatcher)	10.3	171.0
1991–96 (Major)	11.5	284.2

six-month period five years later, when the Major government was in office. The third sample was taken from the same six-month period, two years later.

The analysis revealed that the average consultation period in the Thatcher sample was slightly less than 40 working days. Virtually two-thirds (65 per cent) of the documents requested comments within a period of 40 working days. The first sample from the Major period found that the average consultation period was only 1.5 days longer, but that the number of documents requesting comments within 40 days had fallen to just over half the total (53.5 per cent). The third sample (the second from the Major period) suggested some further lengthening of consultation periods: the average consultation period for this sample was 43.9 days (though this may have been slightly affected by the extra day arising from a leap year). Also, the percentage of documents giving deadlines of 40 days or less was lower than the previous two samples (at 50 per cent). Clearly this research is not conclusive, but it does suggest some relaxation of consultative periods between the Thatcher and Major periods, with a significant movement away from the relatively short deadlines of the 1980s, particularly towards the end of Major's premiership.

A further approach to gauge the impact of the Major governments on organised interests is to examine the experiences of groups which lost their privileged status in the policy formation process during the 1980s: the trade unions, local authorities, doctors and teachers.

In general there was a slight thawing of relations between the trade unions and the Conservative government post-Thatcher. There was greater dialogue between the two sides and more talk of cooperation than in the recent past. Indeed, David Hunt, Secretary of State for Employment between 1993 and 1994, spoke of the prospect of a 'close working relationship' between government and the trade unions. There were also a few concrete examples of an

**Documents issued 1 Dec. 1998–31 May 1989
(Thatcher Government)**

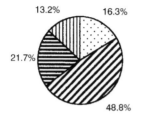

No. of Documents = 129
Average Consultation Period = 39.2 days

**Documents issued 1 Dec. 1993–31 May 1994
(Major Government I)**

No. of Documents = 157
Average Consultation Period = 40.7 days

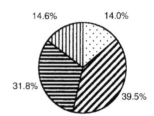

**Documents issued 1 Dec. 1995–31 May 1996
(Major Government II)**

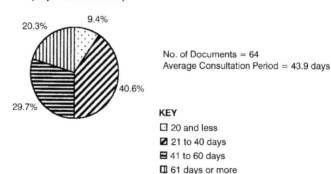

No. of Documents = 64
Average Consultation Period = 43.9 days

KEY
☐ 20 and less
▨ 21 to 40 days
☰ 41 to 60 days
⊞ 61 days or more

Figure 4.1   Consultation Periods under Thatcher and Major

improved relationship, such as the new apprenticeship scheme announced in the 1993 Budget, which was hailed as an example of what could be achieved through cooperation. Nonetheless, as Taylor (1994) has observed, in spite of the more conciliatory image of the Major governments, there were strong continuities of purpose and action with its predecessor, which reduced the scope for any new relationship to flourish.

Indeed, the Major governments continued to pursue and extend policies opposed by the unions (see Chapter 10). These included further restrictions on strike action, and greater regulation of trade unions' internal affairs. Various economic and social policies also antagonised the unions, especially the abolition of wages councils and the refusal to adopt the Social Chapter of the Maastricht Treaty. The announcement of a public-sector pay freeze, and further privatisations – including coal, rail and the Post Office (which was defeated – see below) – also caused consternation in the union movement.

The trade unions continued to find themselves frozen out of the decision-making process. They did meet with the Prime Minister on a few occasions, and in 1993 they also met the Chancellor of the Exchequer for the first time in five years. Yet such meetings were few and far between, and in other respects the trade unions' position deteriorated further. The National Economic Development Council on which they were represented was abolished in 1992. A year earlier, the tripartite system of decision-making in training had been replaced by Training and Enterprise Councils, bodies dominated by employers. Old-style corporatism was still therefore still in retreat during Major's premiership.

Elsewhere, in spite of early expectations of a more conciliatory style, the Major governments experienced battles with various professional groups, not least in the sphere of health. Although relations with the BMA had initially appeared to improve following the departure of Margaret Thatcher and the replacement of the combative Kenneth Clarke as Secretary of State for Health, first of all by William Waldegrave and subsequently by Virginia Bottomley, these perceptions began to erode during the 1990s. While there was a definite change in attitude – Secretaries of State seeing the profession in a less antagonistic light – the government's relationship with the doctors continued to suffer from the legacy of the 1980s. Indeed, disputes between the government and the profession continued throughout the Major premiership. Issues such as local pay agreements, GP deputising services and the review of London's health services highlighted the continuing disharmony in this relationship. Moreover, according to senior BMA sources, there was a continuation, to some extent, of the previous government's failure adequately to consult the profession. This complaint was raised by BMA representatives on a number of occasions during this period, and with some justification, for a quantitative analysis of contact between the BMA and the Department of Health shows a decline from 12.4 recorded meetings a year in the period 1980–90 to nine a year between 1991–95 (McGregor-Riley, 1997). Furthermore, meetings initiated by the Department of Health decreased between the two periods from 41 per cent of the total to only 30 per cent.

However, as the next General Election approached, a more conciliatory approach appeared to return, coinciding with the arrival in 1995 of Stephen Dorrell as Secretary of State. Compromises were reached on the local pay issue and GP deputising, while the government also responded to complaints from GPs regarding excessive paperwork and administration. Furthermore, there was evidence of an increased willingness to seek out views on future health-care reforms. For example, in 1995 the government launched a 'listening exercise', consulting those involved in primary care about future developments in this sector, which paved the way for legislation in 1997.

A similar picture was revealed in education policy. After Thatcher's departure, it appeared that the government and the teaching profession would be able to work together in a more constructive way. However, following initial efforts to rebuild relationships, hostilities resumed (see Chapter 8). This culminated in the teachers' boycott of the standard assessment tasks (SATs), externally prescribed assessments for schoolchildren introduced by the 1988 Education Reform Act. Teachers' representatives complained about these tests, and the national curriculum introduced by the 1988 Act. Both had been modified at the implementation stage in an effort to overcome practical problems partly resulting from poor consultation at the policy formation stage. For example, SATs tests for 7-year-olds were radically modified after their introduction in 1991. But these concessions did not go far enough for the teachers, who threatened to boycott the tests for secondary school children in the summer of 1993. Initially the government stood firm and refused to countenance further change. The teaching unions' position was bolstered by membership ballots in favour of industrial action, a failure by the Conservative borough of Wandsworth to obtain an injunction against the boycott, and growing support for reform among head teachers, parents, school governors, some independent schools and even some of the government's own education advisers.

Further concessions included the establishment of an independent review (with full consultation) of both the curriculum and the assessment process (by Sir Ron Dearing) and the offer of a more simplified system of tests for the following year. The boycott nevertheless went ahead, only 5 per cent of secondary schools administering the tests. When the Dearing review was published in December 1993, the result was seen very much as a victory for the teachers. The government accepted proposals to simplify the curriculum and assessment systems. It also agreed to involve teachers nominated by teacher and subject associations in new working parties established to shape the new curriculum.

The teaching unions' strategy was successful in two respects. First it had an impact on policy. Secondly, it led to a review (and a structure for further revision of the curriculum) that enabled the teachers' views to be heard. But in other areas of education policy the government continued to ignore the views of the profession and other interested parties at an early stage in the policy process. A proposal to introduce a 'mum's army' of untrained teachers in primary education was withdrawn after widespread criticism. In 1994, a further Education Bill was introduced amid complaints of insufficient prior consultation. Then in 1995, the Major government announced a nursery vouchers scheme despite warnings from a whole range of groups in the field that it would have an adverse impact on standards of pre-school education and on smaller private pre-school play groups.

The local authorities had a similar experience to the doctors' and teachers' associations during the 1990s. The initial signs were favourable as the Major government initiated consultations on three areas of reform: the internal workings of local government, its structure, and finance. In addition a Local Government Commission was established in England in 1992 to consult on, and recommend, structural changes to local government. Notably, in Scotland and Wales new arrangements were imposed without appointing a Commission. However, the Local Government Commission was heavily criticised. Academic commentators have been sceptical of the inconsistency of its proposals, the lack of coherence of the whole process, and central government's efforts to manipulate the outcome (see Kingdom, this volume; Leach, 1994; Wilson, 1996). The latter point is particularly important. Despite the initial emphasis on consultation and local self-determination, central government began to impose solutions of its own – clearly favouring a unitary solution to reorganisation. The chairman of the Commission, Sir John Banham, complained of ministerial interference in the review. Subsequently, a further review was initiated with the intention of proposing reorganisation on the lines favoured by central government.

Aside from this issue, there does seem to have been some general improvement in the relationship between the local authority associations and government. In 1992, meetings between local authority associations and the Secretary of State for Environment were convened, taking place on two or three occasions a year. The associations (which have since been merged into one umbrella organisation – the Local Government Association) reported that the Major government did appear to be more willing to listen than its predecessor (Baggott 1995). They pointed out examples where the government was prepared to change its mind following representations. For example, the associations were able to delay and dilute plans for extending compulsory competitive tendering during the 1990s. Even so, there is little to suggest that the local authorities' position improved with regard to prior consultation. As with the teachers' and doctors' associations, their influence was mainly confined to the legislative and implementation stages of policy, when ministers were more vulnerable to pressure and more dependent on their cooperation.

These cases demonstrate a similar pattern. Although the Major government initially expressed its willingness to rebuild relationships with organised interests, prior consultation did not appear to improve significantly. Indeed in some areas, a confrontational style continued. However, lacking the political resources of its predecessor, the Major governments were often forced to compromise and negotiate with organised interests to a greater extent at subsequent stages of the policy process, most notably during implementation.

This pattern was evident in other policy areas, even those where, throughout the 1980s, government had maintained a relatively good relationship with the main producer and professional groups. One example of such a policy area is law and order. During the 1980s, the Thatcher governments had enjoyed a fairly good working relationship with associations representing the police and the legal profession (even the battle with the lawyers over the future development of the profession was conducted with a certain civility and a considerable amount of consultation). Yet during Major's premiership, these relationships deteriorated considerably.

Although the Major government began with a highly consensual approach by appointing a Royal Commission in 1991, to examine the criminal justice system, only 30 of its 352 recommendations were immediately accepted. In addition there was considerable delay in implementing others – such as the establishment of a body to investigate miscarriages of justice. The government also rejected one of the key recommendations of a majority of the Commission – the retention of the suspect's right to silence.

Subsequently relationships with key groups in this policy area began to deteriorate. The repeal of certain provisions of the Criminal Justice Act 1991 in particular relating to the 'unit fine' scheme, provides a good example of this. This scheme, intended to relate fines to offenders' ability to pay, raised a large number of practical problems. Law and order groups, including the Magistrates' Association, lobbied for reform of the scheme and discussed with the Home Office ways of improving it. Further consultations were then suddenly cancelled and the scheme was abolished without explanation (BBC, 1993).

Poor consultative processes were also evident when the government backed the 1993 Sheehy Report on police pay and conditions. Subsequently, however, pressure from the police associations obliged the government to dilute some of the more contentious proposals, including fixed-term contracts and performance-related pay.

A further example of poor consultation related to the creation of a victims' helpline in 1994. It was envisaged that victims would be able to register views on a range of issues relating to the perpetrators of crime, including home visits for prisoners, parole and release. However, it transpired that ncne of the victim support groups had been consulted about the scheme, nor had the associations representing probation officers and prison governors. Victim support groups were later outraged by the government's decision in 1993 to introduce a new compensation system in an effort to reduce the amount paid out in claims. Subsequently, legal action (which ruled the Home Secretary's actions unlawful) forced the government to revise the scheme yet again.

The Criminal Justice and Public Order (CJPO) Act and the Police and Magistrates' Courts (PMC) Act of 1994 further illustrated the

Major governments' approach to policy-making in this area. Both pieces of legislation were heavily criticised by the police, the legal profession and penal lobby, which complained of a lack of prior consultation. The legislation was attacked in both the Commons and the Lords and Ministers were forced to compromise by introducing amendments to head off defeat (Klug *et al.*, 1996; Loveday, 1994). As Morris (1994: 313) has observed, the number of concessions to critics suggests that both bills were drafted under pressure and without 'sufficient anticipatory intelligence gathering' as to the strength of opposition, suggesting inadequate consultation processes.

Organised interests lobbied strongly against the provisions in the PMC bill aimed at changing the composition of police authorities, forcing the Home Secretary to move away from his original plans to create new bodies dominated by Home Office appointees. The CJPO bill attracted wider public protest. Among the most heavily criticised clauses related to the abolition of the suspect's right to silence, the creation of special secure units for young offenders and new rules aimed at giving police greater powers to control mass protests. Despite the level of opposition, the bill became law, although as with the PMC Bill the government had to make several concessions.

Regardless of these battles on law and order, the Major government continued to introduce policies at odds with the views of organised interests and often failed to consult on key issues in advance of policy decisions. In 1995, the Home Secretary announced a range of measures that would, in effect, remove discretion from judges when sentencing offenders. These included minimum sentences for repeat offenders and mandatory life-sentences for persistent violent and sexual offenders. These measures were strongly opposed by the judiciary, including the Lord Chief Justice.

Turning now to the groups that benefited from the Thatcher era, it appears that most of these groups consolidated their position during the 1990s. Right-wing think-tanks and moral groups were initially concerned that they would exert much less influence over the Major government than its predecessor. This proved not to be the case. The think-tanks continued to influence policies such as market-testing, private financing of public projects and consumerism in public services. Meanwhile the Major government's endorsement of 'Back to Basics' in 1993 revealed its support for the political agenda of the moral right (Lister, 1994).

Similarly the business lobby in general continued to benefit from a government that favoured business solutions to policy problems. Closer relations with business associations were encouraged by Michael Heseltine's policy of 'dialogue' with industrial sectors, although the actual impact of this initiative was less than envisaged (Bennett, 1997). The government continued to coopt business people to advise on policy. For example, its deregulation initiative led to the appointment of business people on special task forces to recommend changes in regulatory practices. One business group that sometimes had an uneasy relationship with the Thatcher governments – the CBI – seemed to enjoy a far more harmonious relationship with the Major governments. However, some other business organisations claimed to have fared less well during Major's premiership – including some of the privatised corporations which faced both tougher regulation and increased competition in this period.

CONCLUSION

Although there are difficulties in assessing the impact of the Major governments on group–government relationships, one can make a number of general observations. First of all, in spite of the rhetoric, the Major governments often demonstrated a combative and confrontational approach to policy-making, combined with a reluctance to consult widely and fully with interested parties prior to announcing policy initiatives. Despite the media portrayal of Major as a pragmatist (and Thatcher's own public criticism of his style of leadership), the Major governments were not afraid to take on organised interests, though they perhaps did so with less hostility toward the organisations involved than Thatcher herself had previously displayed.

However, the Major governments had fewer political resources at their disposal compared with their predecessors. They were weakened by a small – and steadily disappearing – parliamentary majority, successive by-election defeats, relatively poor party discipline – including the defection of some Conservative MPs to other parties and the suspension of others (see Chapter 1) – and an increasingly hostile media. Hence Major and his ministers were often forced to compromise and negotiate with organised interests both at the legislative and implementation stages of policy. The continuing failure of consultation processes, particularly relating to prior consultation, clearly demonstrated that the lessons of the 1980s had not been learned. The Major governments did not significantly respond to the catalogue of problems identified by the Hansard Society Commission (Hansard Society, 1993). The result was familiar: ill-thought-out policies and practical difficulties of implementation. In spite of the initial rhetoric, the Major premiership did not see a restoration of the philosophy of consultation *vis-à-vis* organised interests.

5 Strategic Errors and/or Structural Binds? Major and European Integration
Daniel Wincott, Jim Buller and Colin Hay

INTRODUCTION

If the disintegration of the Major government, which culminated in massive electoral defeat at the hands of 'New Labour', is associated with any single issue, it is 'Europe'. In this chapter, we explore the manner in which European integration constrained and channelled Conservative politics and the Major government's policies. The key question in evaluating the impact of 'Europe' on Major's premiership is 'might things have been different, and if so, how?' To what extent was the Conservative government caught in a structural bind (or, better, bound by the intersection of several 'structures') over which it had little control? Conversely, how far did John Major and his government make strategic errors? At root, these issues concern the relationship between structure and agency, a central concern of social analysts, which poses them with some of their most difficult analytical and theoretical tasks.

For 'Eurosceptics', the nature of the European Community (EC), the European Union (EU) created by the Maastricht Treaty, and the Exchange Rate Mechanism (ERM) of the European Monetary System (EMS), were all structurally flawed and needed to be either fundamentally recast (in the case of the EC and EU) or scrapped (ERM/EMS). At the same time, however, both these critics and those sections of the media (traditionally supportive of those in positions of power within the Conservative party) which took on a Eurosceptical hue, berated Major for his failures of 'leadership', an attack which had considerable resonance.

Those of a less sceptical turn of mind either blame the Major government for making particular strategic errors or, if more closely associated with Major, hunt for other actors to blame. Prime suspects include the German Bundesbank (for undermining the British position in the ERM) and notorious 'bastards' – disruptive Eurosceptics within the Cabinet and the parliamentary Conservative party (for making the party ungovernable). These views may give precedence to either structures or agents, or oscillate unhelpfully between the two.

In place of these views we wish to develop a perspective which is (1) grounded on the view that, in principle, structures and agents are inextricably intertwined with one another and; (2) more detached from the debate in practical politics, in order to gain critical distance. As far as the first issue is concerned, we argue that while structures appear as impersonal constraints on and facilitators of agents, in turn they are constructed and maintained by the activity of agents. Many existing analyses of the relationship between the UK and Europe are structuralist, voluntaristic (agency-centred) or oscillate between these two positions. We emphasise the 'duality' of structure – the interaction of structure and agency (Giddens, 1984; Hay, 1995). We acknowledge that while structures are often difficult or impossible for a particular actor, or indeed actors in general, to control, the ways in which actors produce and maintain structures is crucial. Thus, key aspects of the structural context within (and against) which the Major government operated were the product of earlier action.

For example, the problems the ERM posed for Major were exacerbated by the decision to free up capital markets as part of the internal market programme – a decision in which earlier Conservative governments had played a central role. Another feature of the structural context for British European policy – the strength of the Franco-German alliance – was cultivated and sustained by the two states involved. A British strategy to de-centre this alliance would probably need to operate indirectly, by cultivating new alliances with France, Germany and other states. In principle, our position on structure and agency also leads to the adoption of a longer historical perspective, in order to draw the creation of structures into the field of view. Thus, for example, we suggest that the process by which, and the terms on which, the UK came to participate in the ERM are crucial questions, which may have very deep roots. Other structures include the organisation of financial markets, and the Franco-German alliance.

Turning to the second issue, we argue that few British politicians (and certainly very few Conservatives) have faced up to the dramatic changes which membership of the European Community entails (alongside other geopolitical and economic trends) in terms of the nature of the British state, economy and society. This failure, we argue, is common to politicians on both sides of the divided Conservative party. No British prime minister has fully confronted the scale of these changes. A consideration of the conduct of exchange-rate policy during the fateful summer of 1992 shows that Major does not seem to have appreciated the constraints imposed on Britain by membership of the ERM. Of course, it would not have been easy for him to do so. He was largely trapped by the existing mystifying and elitist terms of discourse within Britain on Europe – in itself an important form of structural constraint, setting the parameters of the possible. This approach to the management of the European issue in Britain was a particular, and peculiarly awkward, reflection of the general elitism of European integration. With roots in some national governments and the structure of European institutions (going back to Jean Monnet, Europe's 'founding father'), a widespread ethos existed that European integration should be left to those in power, and that the general population would 'wake up' one morning in a 'United States of Europe'. While mostly ignoring or occasionally resisting the final 'European' destination, when in government most British politicians have attempted to keep discussion of the European issue out of the limelight, while presenting the population with the platitudes of Parliament and sovereignty.

This elitist and obfuscatory position has proved remarkably useful to British politicians in power since Britain joined the EC. Aside from the Major case, and the deposing of Margaret Thatcher (both, admittedly, very important), the European issue seems rarely to have prevented a British prime minister from doing what s/he wanted. Arguably, it may even have helped those in government to achieve unpopular goals that they might otherwise have found it hard to attain. Meanwhile, the British public seems to have remained largely unmoved by the European issue, and even Members of Parliament (aside from the left of the Labour Party in the early 1980s) appear for the most part to have little interest in the issue (Wincott, 1991).

WESTMINSTER IN WONDERLAND: HOW EUROSCEPTICS
AND THE GOVERNING ELITE IMPOVERISHED THE
DEBATE ON EUROPE

To an increasing extent during the 1990s, the position of British
governing elites cannot be understood in isolation. In an important sense, the positions of the Eurosceptics and their opponents
became relational and mutually reinforcing – they were constructed
in opposition to one another. If the mainstream view of Europe
was based on, at best, an economy with the truth, it encouraged
the Eurosceptics to adopt an impossible position as well. Unencum-
bered by state power, they were able to adopt a critical and
oppositional position on the European question. They made it clear
what they were opposed to (a centralised federal European
'superstate', probably imbued with an 'outdated' socialist agenda –
a construction which was largely chimerical) but never presented a
plausible vision of what they were for. In 1994 Norman Lamont
did suggest that the UK repudiate its membership, but he was largely
a figure of fun by then. It is remarkable that, aside from Lamont,
no Eurosceptic during Major's period as Prime Minister seriously
suggested that Britain should leave the European Union. Short of
leaving, other projects for reforming the EC or EU would need
the agreement of other countries, which could only be constructed
through a process of negotiation and alliance-building. This, if it
was to have any chance of success, would presumably place Britain
at the 'heart of Europe'.

Moreover, although useful in the construction of an oppositional
position critical of the government, most of the proposals which
the Eurosceptics might have made – for example, for the transformation of the EU into a free-trade area, would simply not have
been taken seriously anywhere else in Europe. In turn, of course,
the existence of this Eurosceptical position made it still more difficult for the government to acknowledge the degree to which collective decision-making in Europe already encroached on the
decision-making process in Whitehall and Westminster.

MAJOR'S EARLY STRATEGY ON EUROPE

Ironically, Major took office – and indeed negotiated the Maastricht
Treaty – with what seems to have been a clear strategy of engage-

ment with Europe. To be sure, since British accession to the EC, most incoming governments have *claimed* that they would replace intransigence and ineffectiveness – attributed to the previous administration – with enthusiasm, albeit usually of a tough variety. Major's variant of constructive engagement, the strategy described as putting Britain at the 'heart of Europe', was relatively sophisticated. Had it been played out in more auspicious circumstances, the strategy might well have paid political and economic dividends. Indeed, in the run-up to the General Election of 1992, some headway was made in Europe, while Conservative Eurosceptics remained relatively quiet, perhaps owing to the difficult election campaign they were about to face.

However, the strategy did contain internal contradictions, which, although often a partial legacy of earlier Conservative decisions, do not seem to have been acknowledged or recognised by Major. Of course, under other conditions, these might have been eliminated through processes of evolution or policy-learning. During the difficult summer of 1992, however, they tore the heart out of the Major administration.

The strategy had at least two important aspects. First, it had a European dimension, including some accommodation to perceived European realities and institutional and structural constraints. In particular Major probably believed that monetary union would go ahead, and that Britain could not afford to remain outside of it, but also that the internal market had, and would continue to have, an important social dimension. Yet he also seems to have believed that if Britain was more fully engaged in European Community policy-making, it would be possible to limit the influence of the Franco-German alliance. Britain could make common cause with other states on a series of particular issues – especially the French (for example on defence) and the Germans (on economic issues concerned with 'free movement').

Secondly, strategy within his own party was already equally important to Major. The Conservative party was in a catastrophic condition when Major came to power. Margaret Thatcher's symbolic presence in the party, the country, and Europe, had been enormous. She was the most potent leader of the Conservative party in the twentieth century. Yet many of the most senior politicians in the party were instrumental in removing her from office. In other words, she had become isolated – and was increasingly perceived as an electoral liability. While other factors or policies – notably the poll tax – contributed to her isolation and status as a dubious electoral asset, it was around the European issue that opposition to her condensed within the Conservative party, at a level (involving Howe, Lawson, Heseltine) and to an extent necessary to compromise – and eventually to terminate – her leadership.

Against this background, Major made his first moves on the European issue. He adopted a two-fold strategy, which, on the one hand emphasised new openness – a change of attitude and tone towards Europe, while on the other, stressed the continuing need for tough negotiation of British interests. This strategy should be understood as an attempt to bind together a Conservative party comprising the pro-European 'barons' who had unseated Thatcher, and mourning Thatcherites, who seemed increasingly to regard themselves as Eurosceptics.

MAJOR AND MAASTRICHT

The Maastricht Treaty was the first great challenge for this new European strategy. The widespread perception at the time was that John Major handled the negotiations extremely well. He himself claimed to have won 'game, set and match' for Britain. Within the Conservative party itself, praise for the prime minister was expressed in most quarters, with any criticism that was offered emanating primarily from those most enthusiastic in their support of further integration in Europe, including Edward Heath. Even Margaret Thatcher famously declared herself 'delighted' with the outcome, albeit while looking rather less than thrilled.

The most important British objective concerned the structure of the proposed European Union. It was to keep important areas of Union activity outside of the European Community, thus restricting the role of the European Commission in these areas and confining the jurisdiction of the European Court of Justice to them. In other words, rather than including all new areas of European competence within what came to be known as a single 'tree trunk' of the European Community, three distinct 'pillars' – (1) the Community, (2) Common Foreign and Security Policy and (3) Justice and Home Affairs – would have distinct patterns of authority and policy-making, with the 'supranational' element much less significant in the latter two than in the first. However, the failure of the single 'tree trunk' proposals, championed by the Benelux countries,

occurred in the Inter-Governmental Conference (IGC) which negotiated most of the content of the Treaty long before the final negotiations in the town of Maastricht. It was not solely (or indeed
unambiguously) a British victory.

It was at Maastricht itself that the role of heads of government/
state in the negotiations became crucial. John Major had four main
objectives in these negotiations: the excision of the term 'federal'
from the Treaty; the inclusion of a tough conception of 'subsidiarity';
the inclusion of opt-outs on EMU; and ensuring that the provisions of the so-called 'Social Chapter' of the Treaty would not apply
to the UK. Major succeeded in the first of these objectives – the
notion of the European Union having a 'federal vocation' was removed from the Common Provisions, replaced by the older formulation which characterised it as an 'ever closer union of the peoples
of Europe'.

Now, some commentators, particularly elsewhere in Europe, regard the notion of federalism as less centralising than an ever closer
union (see the discussion in Wincott, 1994; 1996). Moreover, although the Common Provisions provide important political guidelines for Union policy-making, and have been used by the European
Court of Justice as an aid to the interpretation of Community law,
strictly they are not legally binding. This victory was mainly of political
significance, although we by no means want to diminish its importance by identifying it as such. Whether or not they were justified,
given the negative associations which had developed around the
world, its removal was crucial if the Treaty was to be acceptable
within the Conservative party.

Major claimed the inclusion of the principle of 'subsidiarity', as
well as a toughening of its wording in the final negotiations, as a
victory won by British negotiators. It is certainly true that this provision was tightened up at the last minute, so as to highlight the
fact that fundamental policy competence remains with the member
states, and Community policy-making is only justified where its
objectives or purpose cannot be achieved by the states themselves
(at least aside from the undefined category of policies in which the
Community has 'exclusive competence'). However, whether this
change can be attributed to the British negotiating team is a more
difficult question.

As a contemporary constitutional principle, subsidiarity is mainly
associated with German federalism, and to some extent with Dutch
consociationalism (van Kersbergen, 1995, discusses subsidiarity in

these states). Both the inclusion of the principle in the Treaty, and the change in the negotiations at Maastricht, probably owed more to German experience and the German delegation than to the British. Moreover, given its roots in German federalism, the fact that the European Community does not have a clear ('federal') division of competences, means that subsidiarity has the potential to spread confusion in the Community, a fact reflected in the endless, and largely fruitless, debate on its meaning which developed subsequently.

Third, the British delegation succeeded in negotiating an opt-out from the Monetary Union for the UK. Generally countries whose economic performance qualified them to do so would have to join the Monetary Union, while Britain could adopt a 'wait and see' policy, deciding whether or not to join at a later date. However, Major had wanted to change the policy more fundamentally. In order to prevent Britain from appearing isolated, and perhaps also to reduce the impression that Monetary Union was inevitable, he argued that all states (which qualified economically) should be allowed to decide whether or not to join at a later date. He failed to achieve this objective – only Britain and Denmark (the latter conditional on a referendum) were granted an 'opt-out' at Maastricht.

Major's most dramatic substantive negotiating achievement at Maastricht concerned social policy. The part of the draft Treaty initially presented at Maastricht covering the European Community contained a 'Social Chapter', which extended Community competence in several aspects of 'European social policy', an area mainly concerned with the regulation of employment. Although at the time, Major's personal attitude to European social policy was not wholly clear, under considerable pressure from Michael Howard, the then Secretary of State for Employment, he made refusal to accept the extension of social policy competence a central plank of his negotiating position. His initial strategy was to dilute the Social Chapter as much as possible. However, even after he had achieved a significant watering-down of its contents, Major refused to accept that the Social Chapter should apply to the UK. In a last-minute concession to the UK, the entire Social Chapter was removed from the main body of the Treaty. The substantive new text on social policy was placed in a 'Social Agreement' accepted by the other eleven states, aside from the UK.

The concession on social policy created an extraordinary and unique structure of dubious status – it is not clear what legal force or normative status the Social Agreement enjoys. The Agreement is attached to the Treaty by a protocol (the 'Social Protocol' which has a clear – binding – legal status) signed by all 12 states which were then members of the Community. This Protocol does not concern the substance of social policy. Instead it says that all member states agree that the 11 can 'borrow' the institutions and procedures of the Community in order to make social policy, as set out in the 'Social Agreement'. In other words, although it is often described as the 'Social Chapter' or the 'Social Protocol', strictly speaking, the UK opted out of (and the other 11 states opted into) the 'Social Agreement'. The 'Social Chapter' no longer exists and the 'Social Protocol', which *is* binding on the UK, is a technical mechanism, rather than concerning the substance of social policy.

Moreover, it is crucial to understand that the UK merely opted out of the new policies initially proposed under the 'Social Chapter', not the extensive pre-existing body of social policy, nor the competence to make new social policies under existing Articles of the Treaty, nor even from other new aspects of the Treaty of Maastricht which had some sort of social element. Finally, the attempt to reintroduce measures which had been removed from the 'Social Chapter' during the initial phase of negotiations at Maastricht into the Social Agreement was a failure. The extent of potential or latent support for the UK position on social policy is indicated by this failure.

A general assessment of Major's much-vaunted negotiating 'success' at Maastricht suggests that it was (perhaps unsurprisingly) somewhat overstated, although still 'not inconsiderable'. The main achievement seems to have been to find a position on the Treaty which it seemed that both the pro- and anti-European wings of his party could live with. The direction in which Major wanted to lead the Conservative party is revealed by the conduct of British 'European Policy' in the early months of 1992, the period immediately after the summit at Maastricht. The 'change of tone' towards the EC, placing Britain at the 'heart of Europe', which was detected when Major first became Prime Minister, could be heard once more, even more clearly. Particularly in the area of European social policy, the Major government appeared to have been trying to minimise the division between the UK and the rest of Europe marked by the Social Agreement. Michael Howard, who had pressured Major on the social policy issue during the immediate run-up to the Maastricht negotiations, was replaced as Secretary of State for Employment by Gillian Shephard, thereby facilitating a renewal of enthusiastic cooperation (Howard was moved to Environment, which thereby removed him from a significant day-to-day role in European policy-making).

Shephard and Major emphasised the crucial role of the 'social dimension' in European integration, and stressed the fact that Britain had the best record of all member states as far as the *implementation* of 'social dimension' policies was concerned. Large areas of European social policy which were mainly concerned with employment law, were presented in pragmatic, commonsense, non-ideological terms – hardly the backdoor socialist threat evoked by Margaret Thatcher in her Bruges speech of September 1988.

MAJOR'S STRATEGY STARTS TO UNRAVEL: THE DANISH REFERENDUM

Despite her initial 'delight', little more than six months after the final negotiations of the Treaty on European Union, Margaret Thatcher had publicly attacked it, in a speech in The Hague on 15 May 1992. What explains this 'change' of heart? First, her initial statement probably owed more to the fact that a general election was looming than to her true feelings about the Treaty. In addition, the increasing warmth which the Conservative government expressed for Europe may have influenced her – allowing her to express her 'true' views. Placing her views in the context of the wider political debate in the UK, however, it is the limited nature of voicing of Conservative opposition to Maastricht that is most striking – only one event of any real significance occurred – Richard Shepherd's abortive attempt to introduce a national referendum on the Treaty. The emergence of a powerful and articulate Danish opposition to the Treaty in the build-up to the referendum vote in June 1992 was the most important element catalysing British/Conservative opposition to Maastricht. After the agreement at Maastricht, a powerful aura of inevitability surrounded the idea of European integration.

However, given that, in principle, the whole Treaty would be destroyed if a single state refused to ratify it, when opinion-poll evidence made it clear that the Danish population was likely to reject the Treaty, the sense that further integration was inevitable evaporated. Mrs Thatcher's attack on Maastricht might be regarded as much as an intervention in the Danish debate as an attempt to influence opinion in the UK. She was not alone – a number of British (Conservative) Eurosceptics travelled to Denmark to support the 'No' campaign. This indirect approach to undermining the Treaty appeared to have been successful when, within 10 days of the Danish referendum rejecting the Treaty, the Major government suspended further parliamentary debate on it indefinitely.

However, the Treaty was partly re-vitalised on 18 June by the Irish referendum, in which nearly 70 per cent supported it. In this context, the Danish government decided to hold a second referendum, to attempt to salvage the Maastricht Treaty, a move whose normative justification was questionable, to say the least. In order to provide some justification for the second referendum, the Danish government sought to renegotiate, or at least to clarify, the Treaty. On 25 June the European Council met in Lisbon and the first important steps towards reversing the Danish result were taken.

The atmosphere of this meeting was extraordinary. Jacques Delors, the continuation of whose position as President of the Commission needed to be confirmed at the summit, brought forward a list of European policy competences which might be re-patriated, that is returned to the sphere of autonomous state activity. (Subsequently, little was heard of this strategy from the Commission, as other ways of making Maastricht less unacceptable to the Danes were pursued.) It is worth noting that John Major supported the re-appointment of Jacques Delors as the President of the Commission during this meeting.

THE SUMMER OF 1992: MAJOR'S ELITIST POLITICAL STRATEGY

During the summer of 1992, a chaotic atmosphere built up in the European Community. Its main origins were in the Danish referendum campaign, subsequently spreading to other parts of Europe, particularly the UK and France. It was both massively deepened and spread to the whole of Europe by the result of the referendum. However, rather than viewing the further intensification of the chaotic atmosphere as natural or inevitable, the ways in which political and economic actors constructed and projected particular views of Europe and 'the European crisis' needs to be analysed.

On the political side, British politics played a key role in fomenting the atmosphere of crisis. It was at this stage that the effectiveness of dealing with 'Europe' by attempting to depoliticise it and remove it from the political debate began to break down. The Major government continued to pursue this approach, presumably believing that the public would eventually accept the rules and institutions created at the European level, or at least be unwilling to carry the costs and risks of trying to change them.

The elitist strategy depends on the mass of the public, and perhaps even politicians outside of the core executive, remaining relatively uninterested in the European issue. This assessment of a lack of interest in Europe was probably correct into the early 1990s, even among many members of the parliamentary Conservative party. Although the strategy has been remarkably successful across Europe since 1958, it does contains a potentially fatal flaw. By refusing to engage in a general debate on Europe and restricting discussion to the cognoscenti, the field of debate was left wide open to other actors.

In Britain, Major essentially allowed the Eurosceptics to define the terms of debate within the parliamentary Conservative party, yet Euro-enthusiasts appear to have been convinced that the government remained broadly on their side of the argument, and were therefore loyally quiet. Throughout June 1992, Margaret Thatcher publicly attacked the Maastricht Treaty, and her hostility (and the conflict with Major) deepened in her maiden speech to the Lords on 2 July. Public evidence that Thatcher's view of Maastricht might motivate a wider rebellion was provided three days later when a group of Conservative MPs announced their intention to see a referendum on the Treaty. The momentum of rebellion grew gradually during the summer.

Major's reaction to the chaos was to seek the path of least resistance. If the Maastricht Treaty was decisively rejected in any other member state, then there was no point in Major investing any further political capital in the increasingly problematic process of getting it ratified in Britain. Despite pressure from other governments and members of the Commission to proceed with ratification in order to increase the momentum behind the Treaty, Major failed to do so. However, while dropping hints throughout the summer and autumn that the Bill would not be reconsidered until the last quarter of 1993, or until after the result of a second Danish referendum, he refused to provide details of the parliamentary timetable for the ratification of Maastricht.

The idea that the Eurosceptics defined the terms of the debate on Europe must be treated with some caution. Even the most cursory analysis of the 1997 election reveals that a good proportion of the British electorate remains uninterested in the European Union. The Eurosceptics do not seem to have been successful in mobilising popular opinion. Even within the Conservative party itself, a significant element remains more concerned with traditional Conservative loyalty and election-winning.

However, it seems likely that in the late 1980s a large proportion of the parliamentary Conservative party was broadly agnostic on the European issue. During the 1990s, the size of that agnostic group has diminished, albeit partly due to changes in the composition of the Conservative party in parliament (an increasing number of 'Thatcherites'). Where the rebels have had some impact is on changing the terms of political discussion, influencing the views of the Party and dragging the leadership along behind them.

THE SUMMER OF 1992: ECONOMIC CHAOS

The second strand contributing to the chaotic summer and autumn of 1992 was economic. If a single moment encapsulates the failure of the Major government, it is 16 September 1992. Immediately dubbed 'Black Wednesday', this was the day on which sterling was suspended from the Exchange Rate Mechanism (ERM). In retrospect, 'Black Wednesday' came to be seen as the moment when the Government abandoned its economic strategy and the electorate lost faith in the competence of the Conservatives to govern the United Kingdom. These events cast the Major government as 'helpless', faced by seemingly irresistible forces or uncontrollable structures. Of course, political issues are inevitably raised in the evaluation of the events of that day, and the period leading up to it (see Thompson, 1995). Those who want to defend the ERM and the decision to take Britain into it usually argue that some course of action might have saved it, while those opposed to the ERM, including out-and-out Eurosceptics, generally argue that the disintegration of that system was inevitable. In order to consider these issues fully, it is necessary to provide an outline of the events of that day.

By mid-September 1992, sterling was at its lowest permissible level within the ERM. The government had become closely associated with the view that the condition of the British economy required interest rates should probably fall. Certainly, they should not rise. In the absence of a major cut in German interest rates, which were set at an unprecedentedly high level in order to contain the inflationary costs of unification in 1990 (as well as French preparedness to match the high German rates in order to keep the franc strong and control inflation, whatever the cost in terms of domestic economic growth), the British government was caught in a bind – it was committed to maintaining the level of sterling within the ERM, but controlled no policies with which it could do so. In these circumstances, those who work on the foreign exchange markets can generate a self-fulfilling pressure on a currency. Everyone was selling the pound at 2.778 D-Marks (its 'floor' within the ERM), except the Bank of England (and other central banks) who were required to buy it. By selling massive volumes of sterling, the actors within the markets were inflicting huge – unsustainable – losses on the government, thus forcing it in effect to 'devalue' the pound (the option against which it had set its face).*

The collapse of the pound has been attributed to a variety of factors. Some analysts suggest that the ERM was either basically flawed structurally, or had come to be flawed by changes in the relative positions of various European economies. Others argue that errors were made in the operation of the system by the British government and/or by others, particularly the German central bank, although, in keeping with the general position on structure and agency adopted here, we would expect strategic choices made at earlier stages to become part of the structural context for later ones. Thus, the factors identified as 'strategic errors' here tend to be immediately associated with the management of sterling during the summer of 1992.

The view that the system was fundamentally misconceived is particularly associated with Alan Walters, who had formerly been Margaret Thatcher's controversial economic adviser. Many economists regard the dispute over the ERM as a version of the venerable dispute over the relative merits of fixed as against floating exchange rate regimes (see Walters, 1990; Lawson, 1992). Walters, however, argued that the ERM was structurally flawed – 'half baked' as he put it – because it was not a pure version of either system. It had, he believed, the disadvantages of both, from the point of view

---

* Once the value of the currency had fallen, sterling could be bought back at its new, cheaper price. The foreign exchange market had found (a situation in which it could create) a 'sure thing', an infallible way of making money.

of the conduct of state policy. Others, particularly those close to Major after 'Black Wednesday', criticised the system for what they saw as its lop-sided character. They believed that the burden of adjustment fell disproportionately on the weaker economies. Germany, in particular did not seem to carry heavy adjustment costs. However, this characteristic of the system may have been a reflection of the fact that other states were using it to 'import' German anti-inflationary discipline into their economies.

The view that the system was structurally flawed gains some support from its subsequent breakdown in August 1993, when even the French franc came under severe pressure, and the size of the 'bands' within which currencies were allowed to fluctuate was increased dramatically, loosening the whole system. While this change does suggest that the system was flawed, it is important not to overplay the significance of these events. They do not necessarily show that the system was already generally flawed at the earlier date, as the events of 'Black Wednesday' may have weakened it. Moreover, given the role of credibility, sentiment and 'animal spirits' in financial markets, it may be that one major currency crisis may subsequently provoke others.

Those less convinced that the system had been basically misconceived could still point to changes in its operation and the economic conditions within which it operated to argue that it had become structurally flawed. Probably the most important change came from the transformation of the position of the German economy resulting from unification. The process of unification had created significant inflationary pressure for Germany, which the Bundesbank, acting as a classic conservative monetary authority, sought to counteract through increases in interest rates. This inflationary pressure is usually attributed to the policy of swapping the East German currency for D-Marks at a rate of 'one for one', although it was also partly due to the fact that the reconstruction of the East was largely deficit-financed (Stephens, 1996; Davies, 1997: 1124). As a consequence, the currency which had served as the 'anchor' for the ERM had unprecedentedly high interest rates at a time when most other European countries, and particularly the UK, were mired in recession, escape from which required lower rates. In these circumstances, the 'asymmetry' of the system alluded to in the previous paragraph which had been perceived as a tough mechanism for reducing inflation became a means of trapping these countries in an economic slump.

This characteristic of the system was exacerbated because the member states had moved away from the frequent adjustments between the currencies which had been a characteristic of the earlier period of its operation towards greater rigidity. The increasing rigidity of the system was closely associated with its increasing anti-inflation discipline and with the use of the system as a stage in the process of monetary union. This latter use of the system has often been criticised as a flaw, although from another point of view the usefulness of the system as an anti-inflationary device for many countries (especially France) may have been associated with the credibility of their commitment to further European integration, particularly monetary union. On this view, the credibility of the overall system would have taken a severe blow when the Danes voted against Maastricht and thus called the inevitability of monetary union into question.

A further change, less remarked upon, is that the shift to a more rigid system occurred at the same time as the Single Market Programme removed capital controls, removing a weapon many of the states had traditionally used to defend weaker currencies. The position of the pound was particularly vulnerable because it had been taken into the ERM in 1990 at the rate of DM 2.95, a level widely regarded subsequently as too high. Partly this parity was a product of the desire to use the ERM as an anti-inflationary device. Certainly the fact that revaluation of the relative levels of currencies within the system had been largely ruled out by this stage was largely due the feeling that the inflation-combating credibility of several states (particularly France and the UK) would be undermined if their currencies were devalued.

If 'Black Wednesday' was produced by strategic errors rather than the structure of the system then, again, several factors are pointed to. Major and his allies point in particular to the role played by the Bundesbank in refusing to support the pound (at least to the extent that it support the franc – both at the time and a year later), in refusing to cut domestic interest rates and even in various comments made by senior officers of the Bank at sensitive times which suggested that there was a need for sterling to be devalued.

Others tend to blame the conduct of policy by Major and Lamont themselves. Some suggest that the pound should have been devalued within the system earlier in the year, even going so far as to insist that the 'failure' to do so was due to a hubris – a pride in the pound – on the part of the government (Stephens, 1996). However, although the British economy benefited from the *de facto* devaluation which followed 'Black Wednesday' it is by no means clear that those on the financial markets would have accepted a deliberate devaluation, or that such a devaluation would not have provoked inflation.

From another point of view, it might be argued that the UK government had not accepted the full implications of participation in the ERM, as it was then constituted, when they joined in 1990. According to this view, participation in the system required a commitment to follow German interest rates, however harsh the consequences for the domestic economy – the position adopted by France. Certainly Major and Lamont stood out against German rate-rises in 1992. According to one version of this argument, the very fact that the UK was equivocal about its future participation in monetary union made it vulnerable within the ERM.

Perhaps the clearest example of an 'error' in the conduct of policy during the summer of 1992 was Norman Lamont's bungling of economic diplomacy with Germany. One incident stands out particularly – Lamont's mishandling of a meeting of European finance ministers and central bankers in Bath in early September. In the chair of the meeting, owing to the UK's Presidency of the Council of Ministers, Lamont attempted to brow-beat Schlesinger, the Bundesbank's President, into lowering German interest rates. In doing so, Lamont broke with protocol by using the Chair in an overtly controlling manner.

Moreover, his approach was one that was extremely unlikely to succeed, as anyone with knowledge of the cultural and structural position of the German Central Bank should have known. If Bundesbank representatives later acted in ways which were not sensitive to British needs, their actions may have been due to the hostility built up as a consequence of this meeting. Although most officials were horrified by Lamont's handling of the Bath meeting, the crassness of his approach could be regarded merely as an extreme version of the general failure of the Treasury to cultivate allies in other finance ministries in Europe (Stephens, 1996).

AFTER 'BLACK WEDNESDAY': THE DIE IS CAST

After 'Black Wednesday', John Major's position became much more difficult politically. Ironically, it provided the UK with a substantial, apparently non-inflationary, export-boosting devaluation (something which might well have been difficult to achieve had it been consciously engineered). He had cleverly managed to spread the blame for 'Black Wednesday' among all his senior ministerial colleagues – they all spent most of the day itself with him. In the immediate aftermath of 16 September, apparently with Major's support, Lamont remained at the Treasury.

Although Major came in for severe criticism in the autumn of 1992, particularly in previously loyal pro-Conservative newspapers, Lamont did serve as something of a lightning rod for him. The significant decision that Major made during this period was to continue the attempt to salvage the Maastricht Treaty. In the face of continued determination from Paris and Bonn to complete the monetary union, his calculation seems to have been that the UK would be less successful in any future negotiation of these issues than it had been at Maastricht. Moreover, the Danish referendum result might make it possible to squeeze out further concessions favourable to the UK, especially as the UK was in a particularly strong position to influence the EC's agenda, given that it was holding the Presidency of the European Council.

Arguably, Major again showed his adroitness in the Edinburgh European Council meeting in December 1992, which managed to create the conditions in which the Danes could go back to their electorate and, eventually, gain a positive result in the second referendum. Moreover, in doing so, he seemed to strengthen those aspects of the Treaty which played best in the UK.

1993 was dominated by the long and difficult process of parliamentary ratification of the Maastricht Treaty, although the detail of this process need not detain us here. What is more important is that the ratification process exacerbated, rather than ameliorated, the image of an administration desperate to remain in government, but lacking a strategic vision. Moreover, the government was shown to be accident-prone, although it did, in the end, manage to achieve its goal of Treaty ratification.

Subsequently, however, Major's attempts at interventions in Europe seemed to have been successful only when they were largely symbolic rather than substantive. Major attempted to keep the number of votes required to achieve a 'blocking minority' in the Council of Ministers at the same size after the 'Scandinavian/Alpine' enlargement, despite the fact that the total number of votes increased (effectively making it easier to block legislation). He failed, despite the fact that he found a form of words partially to disguise this failure. Perhaps the most famous of Major's 'victories' was the blocking of Jean-Luc Dehaene from becoming the President of the European Commission.

For domestic purposes, he seems to have regarded as an asset the fact that he was in a minority of one, antagonising other European leaders. Substantively, however, it is hard to see significant differences between Dehaene and Jacques Santer, the man Major accepted for the job. However, Major also suffered substantial defeats in Europe, the most notorious of these being that surrounding BSE and the beef industry. Although the issue of BSE had deeper roots, and was handled ineptly, by the time it erupted in Europe, the Major administration had backed itself into a corner from which it could not escape – the earlier action of its Ministers meant that it had become structurally constrained.

John Major's overall strategic orientation towards Europe remained largely unclear even several years after Black Wednesday. His attempts to construct a strategic vision of Europe seem deeply confused, partly reflecting the confusion which we have already seen is deeply engrained in UK European policy. Most of Major's broad statements about Europe, particularly in the campaign for the European elections of May 1994, suggested that a wider Europe was necessary, one in which different groups of states might cooperate on matters of common interest, without necessarily involving all the states of the Union – so-called 'variable geometry'. Of course, there were elements of insight in these speeches; the argument that the European Union needs to change in the context of the post-cold war world, and the break-up of the 'Eastern bloc' has considerable force.

However, in his Leiden Speech in September 1994, although again stressing many of these themes, John Major reacted against a policy paper of the German Christian Democrats which suggested that an inner core of countries might move ahead together towards closer union, leaving more reluctant countries behind. Although politically understandable, Major's criticism of the idea of an 'inner core' was weak. On what grounds could an advocate of 'variable geometry' (a position which Major's opt-outs on EMU and social policy promoted) veto other countries' use of it to deepen cooperation among themselves?

It is worth underlining the relative quiescence of pro-Europeans in the Conservative party during most of the period under examination

here. To some extent their quiet reflected the past patterns of behaviour of the 'wets' or 'one-nation' Conservatives during the 1980s
(Dorey, 1996). However, this wing of the party adhered – at least
implicitly – to the discreet elite consensus on the European question, based on the view that there was little to gain by engaging/
enraging popular opinion on it. This orientation was blostered by
the reassurances that Major offered them, albeit often *sotto voce*.
If the pro-European voice was raised in public debate it was usually done by proxy – by 'captains of industry' or Conservative MEPs
– rather than by Westminster parliamentarians. In the 1990s, there
were, however, some signs that the pro-Europeans were becoming
more vocal as the creation of the Positive European group in 1993
and, more important, of the Action Centre for Europe in 1994
testify (see Ludlam, 1996: 115–16).

Throughout the last years of Major's administration, the European issue was a running sore within the Conservative party. Even
the most bold of domestic strategies failed to cure it, and only
managed to salve it temporarily. In June 1995, Major resigned from
the leadership of the Conservative party, pre-empting the challenge
to him which seemed to be waiting in the wings. Although he won
the subsequent election, perhaps partly due to the fact that rivalry
among Eurosceptics meant that a coordinated campaign could not
be mounted, and that John Redwood, an icily intellectual character, emerged as his challenger, it failed to silence Major's critics.

However, Major's victory did mean that he could not be challenged as party leader before the 1997 general election. As all of
the other potential leaders were powerfully associated with one or
other of its wings, his victory may have held the party together,
but the tensions over Europe within it had certainly not been
eliminated.

Indeed, squabbles in the Conservative party re-emerged almost
from the moment that Major's victory in the leadership election
was confirmed. These difficulties were exacerbated by regular swings
in the economic fortunes of European states, which provoked discussion about which countries would qualify for EMU and the likely
strength of the monetary union if and when it was formed. These
discussions meant that the opposing sides on Europe in the Conservative party were provided with multiple opportunities to air
their differences. Eurosceptic criticism of the EU and Britain's place
within it was sustained right up to the 1997 general election, cul-
minating in a declaration of opposition to EMU by two junior

ministers little more than two weeks before the election itself. Euro-enthusiasts largely reverted to the traditional tactic of allowing others – leaders of industry and, to some extent MEPs – to articulate their case, rather than getting fully embroiled in a public debate on the European issue. Throughout the election campaign then, the Conservative party remained fundamentally and fatally divided over Europe. If the party does not fracture, its 'cohesion' will probably owe more to the scale of its electoral defeat in 1997, rather than to any agreed 'solution' to the 'European problem'.

AN EPILOGUE

In his December 1997 *Spectator* interview, Major himself provided an epilogue to our discussion of the European issue during his administration (interview with Petronella Wyatt, 1997). The general tone of that interview is pragmatically pro-European. Major insists that his refusal to rule out a single currency was not dictated by Kenneth Clarke or any other pro-European cabinet colleague, but was his own position. Moreover, he asserts that the Conservatives would not have gained additional support in the 1997 election had he ruled out British membership. Nevertheless, the interview is dominated not by alternative visions of European integration, but by recrimination, albeit of a relatively genial variety, against his own party. However, he seemed to accept that his own position had shifted towards Euroscepticism. His explanation for this shift was not convincing – he claimed that he had become 'more and more doubtful of the economics of a single currency' – although the various economic perspectives on monetary union were well established when he first became prime minister. Despite Major's attempts to avoid being cast in a bitter role, the impression left by the interview is of a man obsessed by the politics of the Conservatives, whose premiership had been dominated by the internal divisions within his own party.

6 Renewed Hope for Peace? John Major and Northern Ireland

Christopher Norton

INTRODUCTION

In 1994, it appeared that John Major was coming close to attaining what is probably the most elusive prize in British politics: the peaceful resolution of the centuries-old 'Irish Question'. The joint strategy of both the British and Irish governments to bring all parties together in inclusive negotiations (what became known as the 'peace process') and the announcement by Republican and Loyalist paramilitary groups of a 'complete cessation' of their military campaigns (in August and October 1994 respectively) raised hopes that an agreed and peaceful settlement in Northern Ireland was possible.

Such an unprecedented achievement would undoubtedly have been the crowning glory of Major's premiership, and regardless of his government's landslide electoral defeat in 1997, would have assured him his place in history. However, by the time he left office, this glittering prize was seen to have slipped from his grasp: the IRA ceasefire collapsed in August 1996, and thereafter the 'peace process' stalled. Moreover, while Sinn Fein/IRA was not absolved of blame for its decision to end the ceasefire, there were many at the time who considered the Major government's handling of the 'peace process' to have been a contributory factor leading to the collapse. More recently, the Major government has been criticised for its failure to 'constructively' exploit the opportunity created by the Republican and loyalist ceasefires in 1994 (O'Leary, 1997: 672).

This 'failure' in Northern Ireland was an ironic dénouement for John Major's premiership; unlike his predecessors who had served in Number 10 since the outbreak of 'the Troubles', Major was initially regarded by all sides as having a deep personal commitment to achieving a lasting settlement. He has latterly provided evidence of this commitment, recounting how in his first few days as prime minister, he drew up a four-point list of aims to be achieved during his premiership; 'Ireland' came second on the list. As he was later to explain to his biographer: 'It had been on my mind for a long time.'

Major's interest in Northern Ireland was motivated not by a detailed knowledge of Irish affairs, but by a long-held conviction that the endless cycle of death and destruction in Northern Ireland was an unacceptable situation which demanded and deserved more attention from the British government (Seldon, 1997: 134, 263). However, his determination to do something about Northern Ireland had to take account of the unpropitious circumstances left behind in the wake of Margaret Thatcher's resignation in November 1990.

THATCHER'S LEGACY

Margaret Thatcher had introduced a characteristically radical dimension into the British government's handling of Northern Ireland when – along with the then-prime minister of the Irish Republic, Garret Fitzgerald – she signed the Anglo-Irish Agreement (AIA) in October 1985. The AIA was a significant departure from the strategic parameters of the Northern Ireland policy which both Labour and Conservative governments had followed since the introduction of Direct Rule in 1972. In practice, this policy had involved the search for an accommodation between moderates within Northern Ireland's main constitutional parties; an accommodation that would facilitate the setting-up of a power-sharing, devolved administration in Northern Ireland (Arthur and Jeffrey, 1996: 126).

However, in the absence of accommodation, and with the rise in the early 1980s of Sinn Fein, which challenged the constitutional nationalist Social Democratic and Labour Party, Thatcher was persuaded of the advantages of an Inter-Governmental approach to Northern Ireland. In the course of London–Dublin negotiations between 1983 and 1985 the Irish government pushed strongly for the introduction of a substantial Irish dimension as part of any future settlement. Only this, they argued, could halt the rise of Sinn Fein and tie Northern nationalists to a devolved power-sharing assembly. This Irish dimension, a consultative role for the Irish government in the affairs of Northern Ireland, was enshrined in the AIA, and embodied in an Intergovernmental Conference with a permanent Anglo-Irish secretariat, staffed by British and Irish civil servants, and based on the outskirts of Belfast (Bew and Gillespie, 1993: 189).

THE EFFECTS OF THE AIA

It is clear that Margaret Thatcher expected certain benefits to accrue from her radical initiative. High on her list of priorities were the defeat of the IRA and a halt in the electoral fortunes of Sinn Fein. But Thatcher was to be disappointed. At the 1987 general election, Gerry Adams, the President of Sinn Fein, retained his Westminster seat (first won in 1983) and Sinn Fein registered a vote that was only slightly down on their pre-Agreement level. It was evident that the AIA had failed to erode the Republican support base. Furthermore, boosted by a sizeable delivery of Libyan-supplied arms, there was a notable increase in the IRA's campaign of violence.

The AIA did however have a far-reaching effect on the main constitutional parties in Northern Ireland. Negotiated 'over the heads' of these parties, the AIA was greeted with undisguised outrage by all shades of Unionist opinion. Unionists saw the Agreement with its Irish dimension as a vehicle to transport them into a united Ireland against their wishes. As such, it was perceived as an act of betrayal by the British government. This perception led to a growing rift between Unionism and the British government, with Unionists refusing to enter into talks held within the framework of the AIA. More disturbingly, it encouraged the extremists in the Loyalist paramilitaries to intensify their campaign of violence.

On the nationalist side, meanwhile, expectations of the AIA were high. John Hume, the leader of the SDLP, had in fact made a major input into the Irish government side of the Agreement negotiations, and it did appear that the Agreement favoured the 'solution' offered by Hume (i.e. a devolved power-sharing settlement with a strong Irish dimension (O'Leary and McGarry, 1993: 238)). Yet nationalists were also to be disappointed. Hume's prediction that Unionists would soon come to the bargaining table to discuss this 'solution' turned out to be naively optimistic. Nor did the AIA marginalise the SDLP's main competitor for the nationalist vote, Sinn Fein, in the manner intended.

However, the AIA was profoundly to affect future SDLP strategy. Thatcher's decision to sign the Agreement convinced Hume not only of Britain's neutrality on the question of the Union between Great Britain and Northern Ireland, but also of a general drift in British policy towards acceptance of sharing 'joint authority' in Northern Ireland with the Irish government. Hume now found the prospect of entering into negotiations with Unionists over what he considered a purely 'internal' settlement (i.e. one without a dynamic Irish dimension) increasingly unattractive (Bew, Gibbon and Patterson, 1995: 217–20). By 1988, rather than participating in talks with the main Unionist parties, he had instead engaged in his first round of talks with Gerry Adams. Hume was unsuccessful in his attempt to persuade Adams both of Britain's neutrality and that the IRA's campaign of violence was preventing the prospect of an all-Ireland settlement, but the makings of the 'pan-nationalist front', which would increase Unionist fears and uncertainties, was beginning to take shape (Routledge, 1997: 218–22).

THE BROOKE/MAYHEW TALKS

Towards the end of the 1980s the steady rise in the level of political violence and the evident lack of progress on the security front led to Mrs Thatcher's own disenchantment with the AIA. She was now 'disappointed by the results' and prepared 'to consider an alternative approach' (Thatcher, 1993: 413–15). This 'alternative approach' was a talks process involving the British and Irish governments, and all of Northern Ireland's constitutional parties, but excluding Sinn Fein. Launched by the Secretary of State for Northern Ireland, Peter Brooke, in January 1990 it was clearly designed to end Unionist isolation, for it offered the Unionists the prospect of a negotiated alternative to the despised AIA, if this could secure all-party support. This was the policy inherited by John Major on his entry into 10 Downing Street in December 1990.

The three-stranded talks process (Strand 1: talks between the constitutional parties in Northern Ireland; Strand 2: talks between the Northern parties and the Irish Government; and Strand 3: talks between the British and Irish governments) was inevitably going to be one fraught with difficulties. Unionists were, after all, seeking to scrap the AIA, while the SDLP considered it 'a minimum and irreversible base line from which to negotiate' (O'Leary and McGarry,

1993: 316). The process proceeded hesitantly under the stewardship of Brooke up until the 1992 general election, from which Major
emerged victorious but with a much-reduced majority.

Following the election, and under the direction of the newly
appointed Secretary of State, Sir Patrick Mayhew, the pace quick-
ened, with Northern Ireland's four constitutional parties (Ulster
Unionist Party, Democratic Unionist Party, SDLP, Alliance Party)
entering the Strand 1 talks in April 1992. However, the talks process was to collapse without agreement in November 1992. Was
this inevitable? It was clear that seven years of the AIA had produced an uneven effect on Unionist and Nationalist attitudes. Here
the positions of the main constitutional unionist and nationalist
parties, the Ulster Unionist Party (UUP) and the SDLP, at the
conclusion of the failed talks were revealing, for they demonstrated
both the possibilities of, and obstacles to, agreement.

The UUP favoured the rebuilding of structures of government
in Northern Ireland through an elected Ulster Assembly. Interestingly they ceded ground on a number of issues, most notably the
acceptance of power-sharing in any future government and an Irish
dimension – they proposed a consultative body without executive
powers, the 'Inter-Irish Relations Committee', to be composed of
representatives of an Ulster Assembly and the Irish Dail (parliament). There were other signs of Unionist flexibility. Before their
collapse, the talks had proceeded to Strand 2 and the UUP had
been prepared to go to Dublin to negotiate with the Irish government; in Irish terms a gesture of some considerable symbolic importance. However, despite these signs of movement, which have
been described by some writers as 'minimalist' (Arthur and Jeffrey,
1996: 108), the SDLP were not prepared to accept any erosion of
what they considered to be the major benefit of the AIA: the Irish
government's role in Northern Ireland.

In fact the SDLP sought to extend and strengthen this role. The
SDLP's main proposal before the talks – a six-person executive to
govern Northern Ireland (three of whom would be elected in Northern Ireland and three appointed by Dublin, London and the EU),
and a purely advisory role for a Northern assembly – reflected their
rejection of an 'internal solution'. It also suggested a movement
beyond the 'base line' of the AIA towards a greater executive role
for the Irish government and the establishment of some form of
joint authority with a European dimension. (Bew, Patterson and
Teague, 1997: 76). The AIA had raised nationalist expectations,

but had it brought the prospects of an agreed settlement any closer? The other three parties, who all sought to maintain the Union with Britain, rejected the SDLP's proposals.

A NEW DEPARTURE

The breakdown of the talks, which took place against the backdrop of a deteriorating security situation, was a severe disappointment for John Major and his government. To most observers there now seemed little prospect for any dramatic breakthrough in Northern Ireland. Throughout 1992, levels of paramilitary violence increased dramatically. The IRA intensified its deadly and costly bombing campaign on the British mainland (the Baltic Exchange bomb in the City of London in March 1992 killed three people, and caused an estimated £800 million of damage), while the Loyalist paramilitaries killed more people in Northern Ireland than the Republicans did.

As this grim trend continued into 1993, Major called for a resumption of inter-party and inter-governmental talks. Speaking on a visit to Northern Ireland in April 1993 Major claimed that the previous round of talks had in fact made 'tremendous progress' and spoke of a renewed opportunity 'to achieve a political accommodation' (Bew and Gillespie, 1993: 295). Yet the Major government was not about to return to the Brooke/Mayhew talks format, but were, instead, to shift the whole focus of their approach to finding accommodation in Northern Ireland. For whereas previously the government sought to encourage agreement between the constitutional parties, it was now to adopt the very different position of attempting to bring into the talks process those who had been engaged in political violence: the Republican and Loyalist paramilitaries.

TALKING TO THE IRA

Was there any basis to the belief that this was a policy that could succeed, that the paramilitaries were prepared to give up the gun and accept constitutional politics? Certainly one did not have to go back very far to hear the fundamentalist message of Irish Republicanism delivered by leaders of the Republican Movement. In 1986 Gerry Adams, the President of Sinn Fein, had stated:

The tactic of armed struggle is of primary importance because it provides a vital cutting edge. Without it the issue of Ireland would not even be an issue. (Adams, 1986: 64)

Had there been a dramatic change in Republican thinking in the years between the mid-1980s and 1993? In a secretive and conspiratorial organisation like the Republican Movement it was difficult to establish with any certainty its capacity for change and compromise, but it was known that there was a debate within Sinn Fein/IRA as to the continuing relevance of the 'Armalite and ballot box' strategy. Adopted after Sinn Fein's entry into electoral politics, by the late 1980s the contradictions of this strategy were becoming apparent to some within the Republican Movement. Elements within the leadership now identified the 'armed struggle' as an obstacle to Sinn Fein's political advancement in both Northern Ireland and the Irish Republic. Sinn Fein had reached its electoral watermark in the North and had polled abysmally in successive Southern elections in the late 1980s. It was obvious that the majority of the nationalist electorate on both sides of the border were not prepared to condone the activities of the IRA.

It was in this context that John Hume initiated his first round of talks with Gerry Adams in 1988. At this stage Adams was not convinced by Hume's analysis of Britain's declining commitment to the Union. However, Adams was attracted by the prospect of Sinn Fein being part of a coalition of nationalist forces (along with the SDLP, Fianna Fail and Irish America) which could both exert pressure on Britain to withdraw from Ireland and rescue Sinn Fein from political marginalisation. For Republicans, the realities of the new political situation were translated into a more benign rhetoric in their policy documents (*Scenario for Peace*, 1987; *Towards a Lasting Peace in Ireland*, 1992) in which the search for peace rather than military victory appeared to take precedent. However, although the Republican leadership acknowledged the negative impact of the armed struggle on Sinn Fein's progress (graphically demonstrated by Adams' loss of his West Belfast seat in the 1992 general election) there was little evidence at this stage that Republicans were prepared to abandon the 'armed struggle' and accept the sort of compromises that a purely political path would bring (Patterson, 1997: 209–20).

The Major government, aware of the debate on future strategy within Sinn Fein/IRA, took steps to encourage what they perceived to be the 'revisionists' within the movement in the hope that this could lead to a Republican break with militarism. Publicly, this was demonstrated in Peter Brooke's statement of November 1990 that Britain had no 'selfish strategic or economic interest in Northern Ireland', while behind the scenes, Brooke authorised the opening of a channel of communication between himself and the IRA. Statements of British neutrality and contacts with the IRA were both continued under Mayhew during the period of the three-stranded talks process.

The Major government's strategy of engaging in secret talks with the IRA carried high risks. Mayhew consistently denied rumours of talks, but revelation of their existence in the *The Observer* in November 1993 called Major's political judgement into question. There was also an issue of personal integrity. In the weeks before the *The Observer* story, Major had been emphatic, while replying to questions in the House of Commons, that he would not talk to Adams and the IRA. The very thought of it he stated, 'would turn my stomach' (Seldon, 1997: 423–4). Major would later claim in a BBC documentary (*Provos*) in 1997 that the imminence of a breakthrough with the Republicans necessitated the discrepancy between his public and private position:

> When I was certain that someone was genuinely seeking a peace I would have spoken to Beelzebub if it would have delivered peace because that was my objective.

Interpreting the ambiguous and often contradictory messages coming out of the Republican Movement with certainty was in the event an unlikely prospect. It now seems that the alleged IRA statement – 'The conflict is over but we need your advice on how to bring it to an end' – which was passed to the British government in February 1993, was in fact an intermediary's optimistic assessment of Republican thinking (Taylor, 1997: 330). While it may have raised British hopes, it was not representative of the then strategic considerations of the Republican Movement. A very different assessment of Republican strategy is now available.

This points to the fact that British statements and actions impacted on the Republican Movement in a way not anticipated by the British government. Republicans did not accept that Brooke and Mayhew's gestures towards them were indicative of the British government adopting a position of neutrality on the question of Northern Ireland's constitutional position. They were, however, encouraged to believe that there were elements within the British establishment who favoured withdrawal and who could be pushed further in this direction. There was also a Republican reappraisal of the timing and manner of that withdrawal. Whereas previously their demand had been for withdrawal within the lifetime of a parliament, Republicans now considered a longer time-scale during which Britain would continue to provide economic support and deal with any Protestant backlash. Finally, Republicans began to talk of the possibility of a ceasefire (not a total cessation of violence) to enable talks with the British government in order to negotiate their withdrawal (Patterson, 1997: 238–41).

However, Major was not alone in detecting positive signs emanating from the Republican Movement. In parallel with the British government's contacts with the IRA, the government of the Irish Republic had also initiated a secret channel of communication with Republicans. As a result of these contacts, the Irish prime minister, Albert Reynolds, who had replaced Charles Haughey in February 1992, was similarly convinced in early 1993 that the conditions for a major breakthrough on Northern Ireland were in place, and that the IRA could be 'persuaded to lay down their arms' (Duigan, 1996: 96).

The mechanism devised by the Irish government to achieve this was a proposed joint Anglo-Irish declaration that would lay down a framework for an inter-governmental approach to an inclusive all-Ireland settlement to the Northern conflict. This, it was believed, could move past the deadlock of the constitutional talks and advance the political process to a stage where Republicans would be convinced that progress could be made without recourse to the 'armed struggle'. Originally drawn up by John Hume, the draft declaration (which became known as 'Hume–Adams') went through a process of numerous rewritings with contributions from the Irish government, Hume and the Republican leadership. In June 1993, Reynolds passed the draft declaration to Major as a basis for discussion between the two governments.

THE DOWNING STREET DECLARATION

Reynolds was later to acknowledge that the draft contained some 'extreme' proposals. It would appear that there was much in the document that appealed to Republicans, including a timeframe for British withdrawal and a recommendation that the British should 'persuade' the Unionists that their future lay in a united Ireland. This latter proposal effectively countered the document's commitment to obtaining the consent of the majority in Northern Ireland for any change in the Province's constitutional position (Taylor, 1997: 335–6).

The declaration in this form was totally unacceptable to Major. The political fall-out from the AIA had taught the British government that no initiative would work without the agreement of the Unionists. Major was insistent that the British would not be the 'persuaders' for Irish unity, that 'consent' should underpin any future political settlement in the North, and that no agreement would be forthcoming on the basis of 'Hume–Adams'.

However, in the light of the collapse of the inter-party talks, and in the belief, held by both British and Irish governments, that the IRA was contemplating an end to its military campaign, Major was prepared to pursue an initiative that held out at least the prospect of success. There now followed an intense and often heated round of negotiations between the two governments during which Major resisted both Reynolds' and Hume's assertions that British acceptance of the draft declaration would deliver an IRA ceasefire. Major argued that without substantial amendments to the draft declaration there could be no movement forward (Seldon, 1997: 421–6).

The outcome of these negotiations was the announcement in December 1993 of the Downing Street Declaration. The Declaration laid down the guiding principles on which both governments would advance their search for a political settlement. For their part, the British restated their neutrality *vis-à-vis* Northern Ireland's constitutional position:

> The Prime Minister, on behalf of the British Government, reaffirms that they will uphold the democratic wish of a greater number of the people of Northern Ireland on the issue of whether they prefer to support the Union or a sovereign united Ireland. On this basis, he reiterates, on behalf of the British Government, that they have no selfish strategic or economic interest in Northern Ireland . . .
>
> The role of the British Government will be to encourage, facilitate and enable the achievement of . . . agreement. . . . They accept that such agreement may, as of right, take the form of agreed structures for the island as a whole, including a united Ireland achieved by peaceful means on the following basis.

> The British Government agree that it is for the people of the island of Ireland alone, by agreement between the two parts respectively, to exercise their right of self-determination on the basis of consent, freely and concurrently given, North and South, to bring about a united Ireland, if that is their wish. (Joint Declaration: para 4)

The Irish government in turn clarified its position on the consent principle, acknowledging that:

> it would be wrong to attempt to impose a united Ireland, in the absence of the freely given consent of a majority of the people in Northern Ireland. He [Reynolds] accepts, on behalf of the Irish Government, that the democratic right of self-determination by the people of Ireland as a whole must be achieved and exercised with and subject to the agreement and consent of a majority of the people of Northern Ireland. (Joint Declaration: para 5)

The rhetoric of the Declaration was nationalist in tone, and retained parts of the original 'Hume–Adams' phraseology. However, the British government was satisfied that Reynolds had moved considerably from the position of the 'Hume–Adams' document (Seldon, 1997: 429).

The Declaration did contain the concept of an 'agreed Ireland' but there was no timetable for a British withdrawal and no commitment for the British government to become the 'persuaders' for Irish unity. Furthermore the right of self-determination for the Irish people was now inseparable from the consent principle. The Irish government accepted that Irish unity could only come about if the greater majority in Northern Ireland gave their active consent.

Reactions to the Declaration varied; constitutional nationalists broadly welcomed its inter-governmental approach as a move in the right direction, but Unionists were wary. However, although the British government's restatement of 'no selfish strategic or economic interest' was not welcomed by Unionists, James Molyneaux, the leader of the UUP, saw this as a necessary 'smokescreen' for what he considered the most significant part of the Declaration (Seldon, 1997: 429). This was paragraph 10 in which both governments affirmed that 'the achievement of peace must involve a permanent end to the use of, or support for paramilitary violence', and confirmed that only those 'democratically mandated parties which establish a commitment to exclusively peaceful methods . . . are free to . . . join in dialogue in due course between the Governments and the political parties on the way ahead'. Molyneaux (though not Ian Paisley, the leader of the DUP) was prepared to accept the Declaration on the grounds that only a total renunciation of violence would secure entry into talks on a settlement.

THE CEASEFIRES

The response of the Republicans to the Declaration was crucial; the whole initiative was, after all, primarily aimed at bringing them into political talks, yet there was now much that was objectionable to them in the document. The Declaration's requirement of a commitment to a permanent end of paramilitary violence as a prerequisite to entering talks was particularly galling to the IRA, and the initial response of a significant element of that organisation (IRA prisoners in the Maze prison) was to reject it (Taylor, 1997: 343). However, Sinn Fein did not outwardly reject the Declaration, for there was a real danger that the 'peace process' would move forward without them had they done so. A negative response would also have endangered Sinn Fein's recently assumed position as part of the pan-nationalist alliance of the Irish government, SDLP and Irish America, all of whom were urging acceptance upon the Republican Movement. The Republican leadership believed that the powerful political leverage of the alliance could force the British government closer to a nationalist agenda.

Significantly, the Republican leadership was encouraged in this belief by the Irish government's contribution to the Joint Framework Document – proposals drawn up by the two governments to act as guidelines for future discussion between the parties. The Irish government's proposal of cross-border administrative bodies with executive powers, which Adams was given sight of, was not Irish unity, but it did suggest joint authority which Adams now regarded as an acceptable transitory stage. Working on the assumption that the conditions existed in which the Republican Movement could advance its political demands, and against the expectations of its own rank-and-file, the IRA declared its 'complete cessation of military operations' on 31 August 1994.

The 'peace process' now moved into a highly complex phase. The triumphalist Sinn Fein celebrations in West Belfast that accompanied the IRA announcement raised hopes on the Republican side, and fears on the Unionist side, that a secret deal had been

struck between the Republican leadership and the British government. However, within six weeks of the IRA ceasefire, the Combined Loyalist Military Command (CLMC), an umbrella organisation
for the Loyalist paramilitaries, announced they were to cease 'operational hostilities' having been convinced by Major's statements
that the Downing Street Declaration did not undermine Northern
Ireland's constitutional position within the United Kingdom (Rowan,
1995: 126–7).

The CLMC claim that 'The Union is safe' was unsettling for
republican supporters. Their unease, and that of the Republican
leadership, was further added to by the slow pace of political progress
following the IRA ceasefire. Sinn Fein, who had anticipated early
entry into talks on the future of Northern Ireland, were later to
speak of British 'bad faith', but the British government evidently
saw the 'peace process' evolving over a longer timeframe than that
anticipated by the Republicans.

An immediate difficulty for Major, and one which prevented him
moving the 'peace process' along, was the ambiguity of the IRA's
statement and its reluctance to affirm the permanence of its cessation. IRA unwillingness to begin the decommissioning of its illegal
arms also raised doubts as to the durability of the cessation. The
decommissioning issue was one that was to haunt the 'peace process', and this, along with the demand for clarification of permanence, came to be seen as examples of British obstinacy, unnecessarily
placing obstacles in the path of progress. Consequently, the British
government was criticised not just by Sinn Fein but also, towards
the end of 1994, by the Irish government. Yet the requirement for
the IRA to hand over their arms was one that both governments
had been in agreement on in 1993. Also, in the weeks before the
ceasefire, both Albert Reynolds and his Deputy Prime Minister,
Dick Spring, had insisted that Sinn Fein would not be admitted
into the political process without the IRA calling 'a permanent
cessation of violence' (*Irish Times*, 2 September 1994). The decision
by the Irish government to abandon decommissioning, and an unambiguous declaration of permanence, were indications of its greater
acceptance of the IRA's commitment to purely peaceful means.

There was a high level of British scepticism about the IRA cessation in some quarters (Sir John Wheeler, the Northern Ireland
Office security minister, considered it to be a sham), but John Major
continued to believe that there was cause for optimism. Speaking
in the House of Commons in October 1994, he declared that 'there

is greater hope that peace may now be permanently achievable than we have seen at any time in the last quarter of a century' (Bew and Gillespie, 1996: 75). This optimism appears to have been based on the assumption that Gerry Adams was committed to political dialogue, and in control of those in the IRA who did not share his views. It now became incumbent on the British government to support Adams, a position acknowledged by Sir Patrick Mayhew in what was meant to be an unpublicised address to sixth-form students in January 1995:

> to some extent, we have got to help Mr Adams carry with him the people who are reluctant to see a cease-fire, who believe they might be betrayed by the British government. (Sharrock and Devenport, 1997: 371)

This 'help' consisted of a number of measures – the lifting of the broadcasting ban on Sinn Fein, the opening of border roads – designed to increase Republican confidence in the political process. But a much more significant confidence-building measure was the publication by the two governments of the Framework Document in February 1995.

THE FRAMEWORK DOCUMENT

The Framework Document had, prior to its publication, been used as an inducement to encourage the IRA to bring about its cease-fire (Bew, Patterson and Teague, 1997: 210). When the document finally appeared, after yet another interminable round of intense Inter-Governmental negotiations, it largely retained its nationalist flavour and all-Ireland character. In particular, its proposed 'harmonising' role for cross-border bodies with executive powers and an 'open dynamic' made it possible to interpret the proposals as a transitory phase towards an eventual united Ireland. This was Adams' reading of the document, the very publication of which he claimed was an acknowledgement that 'partition has failed, that British rule in Ireland has failed'. It would appear that this interpretation was actively encouraged by British officials anxious to keep the cease-fire alive and the IRA on the political track (Sharrock and Devenport, 1997: 376).

However, the Framework Document did not represent a 'greening' of the British position on Northern Ireland's constitutional status.

In the course of the Framework negotiations, Major had attempted to persuade the Irish prime minister, Albert Reynolds (at an EU summit meeting in Corfu in June 1994), to drop the Republic's territorial claim over Northern Ireland contained within articles 2 and 3 of its constitution (Seldon, 1997: 525). Had he been successful, Unionists may have responded more positively to the concept of cross-border bodies. As it was, an Irish offer of constitutional change to incorporate the principle of consent did not prove enough to offset mounting Unionist suspicions that the cross-border bodies were an Irish dimension too far, and the Framework Document a nationalist agenda.

The notorious complexity and obscurity of the document raised questions as to whether it could ever form the basis of a lasting settlement between the parties. Neither did the very different readings of the Framework Document bode well for the 'peace process'. Unionists displayed a mood of increasing paranoia, the most damaging manifestation of which was the sectarian confrontations between Protestants and Catholics at the Orange parades at Drumcree in July 1995 and 1996. Republican expectations were raised to an unrealistic level. At the very least, Adams wanted joint authority, but this was not on offer. Michael Ancram, the Northern Ireland political affairs minister, was later to express surprise at Adams' favourable response to the Framework Document. From the British government's perspective, Ancram explained, the document was in fact 'predicated on the continuation of the union', any change in which 'can only be achieved with the agreement of an assembly in Northern Ireland'. Furthermore the 'dynamic' role of cross-border bodies was to be developed only with the consent of the Northern Ireland Assembly (Sharrock and Devenport, 1997: 375).

Had the Framework Document been written in language of such clarity, it is doubtful if the IRA ceasefire would have ever been called. However, obfuscation had become an integral part of the precariously balanced 'peace process'.

THE COLLAPSE OF THE CEASEFIRE

From 1993, the Major government's Northern Ireland policy was guided by a belief that the Republican Movement was genuinely committed to breaking with militarism, and a calculation that involvement in a political process would have a positive educative effect on them. This was a high-risk strategy. So, too, was the strategy pursued by Republicans. They had entered the ceasefire in the belief that a coalition of Nationalist forces existed which could secure in a relatively short period of time what they failed to achieve in 25 years of armed struggle: the coercion of Unionists into a united Ireland. It was not a strategy that explicitly abandoned militarism. From the outset the Republican leadership had assured its supporters that a return to violence was an option in the event of failure. Nor was it a strategy that involved the demilitarisation of the IRA.

While the declaration of August 1994 called for a cessation of 'military operations' it did not call for a cessation of violence and IRA training; surveillance and 'policing' activities continued unchecked after the ceasefire (Patterson, 1997: 285). A positive response to what was originally the basic requirement of both governments for inclusion into an all-party talks process – the decommissioning of illegal arms – was never an option considered by the Republican leadership.

The abandonment of the decommissioning requirement by both Dublin and John Hume towards the end of 1994 left Major isolated. Adams now talked about a 'British demand to surrender weapons' which had been introduced as a 'precondition' after the IRA ceasefire declaration in an attempt to delay peace talks. But was IRA surrender a British objective? Despite the popular perception of a hardening of British attitudes, Major's government showed signs of flexibility on the decommissioning issue. In a speech delivered in Washington in March 1995, Sir Patrick Mayhew outlined a three-point plan that made it clear that the British government did not expect the IRA to decommission its entire arsenal before Sinn Fein's entry into talks with the other parties. Instead it sought a 'willingness in principle to disarm progressively', an agreement on the 'modalities' of decommissioning, and 'the actual decommissioning of *some* arms as a tangible confidence-building measure'. This was all-important, for as Michael Ancram pointed out at a meeting with Gerry Adams and Martin McGuinness in July 1995, the government was faced with the task of creating 'confidence to bring others around the table' (Sharrock and Devenport, 1997: 391). What this required was some gesture from the IRA to send a signal to Unionists that it was in accord with the commitment to 'a permanent end to the use of . . . violence' contained within the Downing Street Declaration. The 'Washington Three' condition (as it became known) incensed Unionists and Conservative backbenchers who detected a climbdown by the British government, but the Republicans rejected the new minimalist decommissioning requirement out of hand.

In a further attempt to remove the decommissioning obstacle, both the British and Irish governments, with the support of the United States President, Bill Clinton, launched the twin-track strategy in November 1995. This placed the resolution of the decommissioning question in the hands of an independent, international body under the chairmanship of the former US Senator George Mitchell. It also set a date for all-party talks (the end of February 1996). The Mitchell Commission Report of January 1996 concluded that the British government's requirement of the decommissioning of some arms prior to all-party talks (Washington Three) was not feasible, and offered the alternative of decommissioning in parallel with talks. It also proposed that all participants in the talks would have to sign up to six principles of 'democracy and non-violence'.

The report of the Commission was undoubtedly a disappointment for Major. The six Mitchell principles did not require an unambiguous acceptance of the consent principle, and the dropping of the requirement for some prior decommissioning raised the possibility of Unionist refusal to participate in the talks process. In recognition of this, Major's acceptance of the report in the House of Commons was qualified by his announcement that in the absence of prior decommissioning, an electoral mandate would be a guarantee to entry into the talks (a formula acceptable to the new leader of the UUP, David Trimble). Republicans responded that Major, reduced by Westminster arithmetic to relying on the Ulster Unionists for the survival of his government, had 'binned' the Mitchell Report. Ironically, given the IRA's refusal to comply with the parallel decommissioning proposal and its own rejection of the six Mitchell principles in 1998, it was to claim that Major's allegedly negative response to the Mitchell Report was the principle reason for the ending of its ceasefire.

However, the bomb that exploded at Canary Wharf in London, killing two people on 9 February 1996, had been planned in advance of the publication of the Mitchell Report and Major's response to it. The failure to achieve concessions on their minimum political demands (joint authority and the British becoming 'persuaders' for a united Ireland) and the requirement of parallel decommissioning was more than the militants in the IRA were prepared to accept; the 'peace process' had not lived up to their expectations.

John Major's handling of the 'peace process' was not without fault, but whether he can be accused of mishandling the process to the point of collapse is questionable. The whole 'peace process' strategy was highly complex and unpredictable. Once the paramilitary ceasefires had been announced in 1994, the logic of the strategy meant that both governments would do all in their power to sustain the 'peace'. This led to an often public disagreement between London and Dublin over what was necessary to achieve this. Major was perceived at the time as being intransigent and obstructive, both in political negotiations and on the arms question, but evidence available now points to a mixture of flexibility and judicious caution governing Major's actions both before and after the resumption of IRA violence on 9 February 1996. Major realised that a balanced settlement required sensitivity towards Unionist opinion. The question of how this opinion was to be represented and conciliated formed the basis of his differences of opinion with the Irish government. On the decommissioning issue, he was prepared to give ground, but in return this required some evidence of good-will on the side of the paramilitaries. However, Major was prepared to fudge decommissioning after the collapse of the ceasefire in an effort to bring about its restoration. The Republicans refused Major's offer in the belief that he was hostage to the Unionists, and that a more advantageous deal could be struck after the May 1997 general election with the leader of a Labour government with a commanding majority (although by early 1998, Republican accusations that Tony Blair was guilty of playing the 'Orange card' proved what a miscalculation this had been).

Major failed in his attempt to deliver a historic settlement in Northern Ireland, but towards the end of his time in office the possible outline of a solution was beginning to take shape. Ulster Unionist acceptance of an Irish dimension, and Irish nationalist recognition that a settlement based on the principle of consent would mean no foreseeable change in Northern Ireland's constitutional position, would be an integral part of this.

A permanent settlement on these lines was not possible during John Major's premiership. The leaders of the constitutional parties were unwilling or unable to reach agreement and the paramilitaries remained uncommitted to democratic politics. However, if a breakthrough does emerge, based on the principle of consent and a balanced settlement acceptable to both governments and the majority of Unionists and Nationalists, then history may record the Major premiership in a more generous light.

7 Devout Defender of the Union: John Major and Devolution

J. Barry Jones

INTRODUCTION

Scottish and Welsh devolution was never a dominant issue on the political agenda of the two Major governments. Between November 1990 when Major became Conservative party leader and May 1997 when he was overwhelmingly rejected by the British electorate, devolution was at best a marginal and intermittent issue. Europe dominated Conservative party politics, deepened the split within the parliamentary party and, eventually, brought it down to catastrophic defeat. Nevertheless the two issues – devolution and Europe – were not totally different. Both related to the supremacy of parliament, and both raised fundamental questions about the character and role of the Conservative party.

In retrospect one could argue that Major should have been more radical and pragmatic on devolution. On those rare occasions when Major addressed the issue, particularly in the context of Scotland, he clearly regarded it as of fundamental importance to the balance of the British constitution. However, by any objective measure, Major's devolution policy was a total failure. In the 1997 general election, the Conservatives lost all their MPs both in Scotland and in Wales. Their vote in Wales fell to 19.6 per cent, while in Scotland it was only 17.5 per cent. After the election the Conservatives, the self-styled party of the Union, had become in terms of their representation in the House of Commons an English regional party.

The incoming Labour government, having placed Scottish and Welsh devolution at the top of its legislative priorities, gained the approval of the Scottish and Welsh electorates in devolution referenda in September 1997, and subsequently introduced legislation setting up a Parliament in Scotland and a National Assembly in Wales. The balance of the British constitution which Major had sought to maintain was fundamentally changed.

The intention of this chapter is to explore and explain the reasons for the failure of Major's policies on Scottish and Welsh devolution. Three factors require consideration: the traditional and ideological commitment of the Conservatives to a unitary state in which sovereign power is located in the Westminster parliament; the Thatcher legacy which was particularly profound and painful in Scotland and Wales; and John Major's personal commitment and leadership.

THE CONSERVATIVE UNIONIST IDEOLOGY

The Dicean tradition

The roots of the ideology, if ideology it be, are to be found in the views of A. V. Dicey, the Vinerian professor of law at Oxford from 1882 to 1909. He moved out of the realms of academia into practical politics because of Gladstone's policy of Home Rule for Ireland. Dicey (1885) argued that such a move would destabilise the British constitution based on a sovereign parliament unconstrained by a written constitution. It is this Dicean view of the constitution which determined the Conservative party's position first on 'Home Rule' and subsequently on devolution. Although the rhetoric changed during the century the party's formal commitment to a 'sovereign Westminster parliament' has been virtually constant.

This interpretation of the British constitution by successive generations of Conservative politicians is very limiting. While ritual nods in the direction of 'constitutional evolution' were regularly made, there was an underlying presumption that the constitution was the outcome of the workings of natural Providence. Accordingly the constitutional settlement of 1688 marked the victory of English nationalism, which was very defensive when confronted with proposals to amend constitutional institutions, usages and habits (Blake, 1972: 273). Thus the Conservative party in defending the constitution could be regarded as the party of English nationalism, an identification which created difficulties when amendments to the constitutional position of Scotland, Wales and Northern Ireland were raised (Mount, 1992: 8).

There are difficulties in tracing the Conservatives' ideological stance on constitutional issues (Johnson, 1980: 126). The party is nothing if not pragmatic and at various times, on both Irish home rule and

Scottish and Welsh devolution, one can find evidence of the pragmatic tendency.

Conservatives and Federalism

Federalism, imperiously rejected by the Royal Commission on the
Constitution in 1973, has a respectable parliamentary history in
Britain. The Westminster parliament approved federal constitutions
for Canada (British North America Act 1867) and Australia (Com-
monwealth of Australia Act 1901). Even at the peak of the Irish
Home Rule crisis in 1912, Dicey's interpretation of the British constitution was not universally accepted within the Conservative party.
F. S. Oliver, addressing the competing demands of Irish nationalists and Irish unionists, concluded that Westminster should become
a federal parliament:

> [It is] the only solution to the Irish question because it is the
> only means which enables nationalists to realise their ideal of
> Irish unity, which allowing unionists to keep inviolate the Union
> of the Three Kingdoms. (quoted Bogdanor, 1979: 36)

The federal idea had been raised by Joseph Chamberlain during
the first Irish Home Rule crisis in 1886. He never retracted the
federal option. His campaign for 'Imperial Preference' was the trade
and commerce answer to the question of how Britain could co-
exist with the rising superpowers of the United States, Germany
and Russia. The political aspect was reflected in the sentiments
expressed by conservatives in Britain as well as in Canada and
Australia for 'Imperial Federation'. It was never to be but it does
show that the federal concept was not alien to Conservative thinking.

The federal option reappeared on the political agenda during
the devolution debates leading up to the 1979 referendum. Francis
Pym, destined to be Margaret Thatcher's Foreign Secretary during
the 1982 Falklands War, was critical of the constitutional *ad hoc*
nature of Labour's proposals for Scotland and Wales. He was particularly sensitive to the ambiguities attendant on the 'West Lothian
Question' and argued for a properly thought-out federal scheme
which would establish a more stable constitutional framework for
the whole of the United Kingdom (quoted in Bogdanor, 1979: 223).

The Labour government's failure to carry its devolution proposals
and Margaret Thatcher's victory in the general election removed
devolution from the political agenda. But the federal idea did not

die. In the run-up to the 1997 general election, some Welsh Conservatives, conceding the inevitability of change, argued that a federal constitution for the whole of the UK was the appropriate way forward (Melding, 1996: 15).

Conservatives and Devolution

Dicey's conservative orthodoxy on constitutional matters presumed the preservation of and respect for established constitutional conventions and parliamentary procedures. At a deeper level there was a significant but implicit assumption that Britain possessed an integrated, heterogeneous society. Only in such a context could a sovereign parliament be politically legitimate, because Members of Parliament would be elected to represent the *national* interest. Dicey did not address the problem of competing national interests, although one presumes that logically each national interest would require its own national parliament. However, that road leads not to devolution but to independence, a conclusion which those Irish nationalists who read *Law of the Constitution* would doubtless have reached. Dicey's perception of the British political system in the last quarter of the nineteenth century is open to criticism, but it certainly does not accord to the pattern of politics in the last quarter of the twentieth century. He presumed a series of continuities: a two-party system producing a distinct confrontation between government and opposition; the regular swing of the electoral pendulum to ensure fairness in practice as well as in theory; and the development of consensual politics and policies. None of these applied to Britain (Harvie, 1989: 47) in the 1980s and 1990s.

Not all Conservatives are fully persuaded by Dicey's constitutional critique; some accept the idea of limited political devolution to Scotland and, while Wales is not specifically excluded, it does not register on the political significance scale. For Conservatives the issue of political devolution has been pre-eminently about Scotland.

The first Conservative leader to make an unambiguous commitment to Scottish devolution was Edward Heath. At the Perth conference of the Scottish Conservatives in 1968 he declared in favour of a Scottish Parliament. There was good reason to do so. The Scottish National Party (SNP) was riding high in the opinion polls and threatening Conservative seats in Scotland. However, Heath's Perth Declaration was not the product of electorally determined pragmatism. He had negotiated British entry to the European Community in 1972, in clear recognition of the changed nature of British sovereignty in the modern world of global economies. In his Perth speech he acknowledged the need for Scottish devolution to act as a counterweight to the European Community.

Heath also took the initiative in developing a Conservative policy for Scottish devolution. A committee was set up in 1968 under the chairmanship of Lord Home with terms of reference to preserve parliamentary sovereignty while giving the Scots a greater say in the conduct of their own affairs. An ingenious but probably unworkable legislative process was recommended. The First Reading and Third Reading of Scottish legislation would continue to be considered in the Westminster parliament with the proposed Scottish Assembly responsible for the Second Reading and the Committee and Report stages (Russel, 1978). In an attempt to square the constitutional circle it revealed the difficulties confronting a Conservative party seeking to develop a devolution policy. It foundered on the parliamentary sovereignty issue. The plain fact was that Heath could not carry his party. After 1970 the devolution commitment waned and Mrs Thatcher's election as party leader in 1975 confirmed Mr Heath's lack of support in the parliamentary party. By 1977 the Conservatives were again the party of the Union and parliamentary sovereignty.

THE THATCHER LEGACY

When John Major became prime minister in 1990, it was already apparent that the SNP was not going to disappear from the Scottish political scene, for the party had tapped a deep well of political discontent in Scotland. The question of the future governance of Scotland needed to be addressed. We have already seen that there were precedents in the Conservative tradition which could have been utilised. Federalism would have provided a clear workable arrangement for the government of Scotland (and Wales and the English regions) within the United Kingdom. But that would have been a very radical policy to solve a distinctly Scottish problem and had the added disadvantage of constitutionally constraining the Westminster parliament. The other option, devolution, was already Labour party 'property' and posed real operational difficulties. Furthermore, Major with the precedents of Heath and

Thatcher, was acutely aware of the dangers of a Conservative leader adopting a policy which the parliamentary party would be reluctant to follow.

To a degree, Major's policy options in respect of Scottish and Welsh devolution were curtailed by the impact of Thatcherite policies on the economies of Scotland and Wales. In many ways, Margaret Thatcher was more a radical than a traditional Conservative. She argued that she was a devolutionist but believed in devolution to the individual citizen not to Scotland or Wales. She questioned the notion of society. She was a supporter of the Union but her unionism was stout and unyielding (Mount, 1992: 251), not flexible and innovative in the mould of traditional Conservative leaders.

James Mitchell (1995) argues that Mrs Thatcher was not a traditional Tory Unionist but an assimilationist. The distinction is valid, particularly after the 1987 general election when Mrs Thatcher decided that the 'Thatcherite revolution' had not made sufficient progress in Scotland because of the lack of enthusiasm by two successive Conservative Scottish Secretaries of State; George Younger and Malcolm Rifkind. The only Thatcherite in the Scottish Office was Michael Forsyth, and Margaret Thatcher's attempts to promote him (and her policy agency) within the Scottish party ultimately failed and alienated the traditional Scottish Conservative elite (Bradbury, 1997: 80). The events resulted in a weakened Scottish party and a deterioration of relations between Central Office and Edinburgh. The situation in Wales was not so dire. Wales was less significant in Conservative party politics and posed less of a threat to the Union. However, Thatcherite policies had a similar impact on the traditional industries in Wales as in Scotland, and in both countries, unemployment levels remained significantly above the UK figure.

In common with the rest of the UK, the authority of local government in Scotland and Wales was undermined and all the subnational institutions were in a mess (Mount, 1992: 252). The transfer of functions to quangos further marginalised elected local authorities, and alienated Scottish and Welsh electorates, who regarded them as alien instruments for the implementation of Thatcherite policies.

Margaret Thatcher was not entirely to blame for the parlous condition of the Conservative party in Scotland and Wales. The Conservatives had never been a significant force in Wales but Scotland was a different matter. As recently as 1955, the Conservatives had won a majority of the Scottish seats and had prided themselves on being a 'Scottish' party. This identification with the Scottish interest was so close that Churchill, when campaigning in the 1950 general election in Glasgow, had hinted at an electoral pact between Conservatives and Scottish nationalists against state socialism, and actually raised doubts about the legitimacy of the Westminster parliament by declaring that: 'I would never adopt the view that Scotland should be forced into the serfdom of socialism as the result of a vote in the House of Commons' (quoted in Bogdanor, 1979: 79).

But this proved to be a Churchillian idiosyncracy. Throughout the 1960s and 1970s, industrial decline weakened the attachment of the Protestant working class to the 'Conservative and Unionist Party', and the declining number of Scottish Conservative MPs in Westminster progressively reduced Scotland's influence in the party's policy-making structures. Margaret Thatcher's 'English and assimilationist' approach was merely a logical extension of a long-term process. The fact that her approach failed (Thatcher, 1993: 623) and that the Sottish Conservative elite would not impose a Thatcherite agenda on Scotland, left a policy vacuum for John Major to exploit when he became prime minister.

MAJOR'S FIRST GOVERNMENT (1990–92)

John Major's first administration was understandably limited in the range of policy options it could introduce. The new prime minister's first priority was to heal the wounds in the parliamentary party opened up by the Heseltine challenge to Margaret Thatcher. It so happened that reversing one policy – the community charge, or the poll tax as it was more generally known – had a double advantage; that of easing the crisis in the parliamentary party and placating Scotland. However, this did not fully mollify the Scots who felt that they had been 'guinea pigs' for an ill-considered new tax. Elsewhere Major continued Mrs Thatcher's programme; privatisation, closure of Ravenscraig steelworks and creation of new quangos all went ahead.

A similar continuity was evident in Wales, although Wales had received a different treatment from Scotland under Mrs Thatcher. Welsh Secretary of State Nicholas Edwards and his successor Peter Walker had been granted considerable freedom of action to modify the application of the Thatcherite agenda. Walker, a 'one-nation' Heathite, concentrated on developing the Welsh economic infrastructure, industrial renewal and increasing inward investment. In effect, Walker presided over a social democratic programme, reminiscent of government priorities of the 1960s and 1970s. As in Scotland, Major did not intervene nor seek to change Walker's approach. His appointment of Hunt as Walker's replacement was confirmation that, in Wales, at least, he was prepared to follow Margaret Thatcher's 'hands off' strategy.

Scotland

In Scotland it soon became clear that Major's perception was quite different from Margaret Thatcher's:

> For her, Scotland was a land full of moaning minnies, strangely resistant to the Thatcherite revolution. They were an ungrateful lot who never even said thank you for the subsidy they received from the (English) taxpayer. (quoted Hogg & Hill, 1995: 247)

Whereas Margaret Thatcher was a staunch unionist, her primary concern was the modernisation and integration of Britain. John Major was genuinely supportive of the Union and understood why the Scots were proud and why they wanted to be different. This was a strong personal belief (Hogg and Hill, 1995: 248; Junor, 1993: 249), as strong, in its own way, as Margaret Thatcher's assimilationist objective.

Yet John Major's personal belief in the Union of England and Scotland was both his strength and Achilles' Heel. Its strength derived from the fact that this was one area where there was no necessity for him to compromise and equivocate with his parliamentary party, as was the case on so many other policies. However, his very certainty in the Union rendered him less open to other ideas and less amenable to alternative arguments. His beliefs were such that he was both intellectually and emotionally unable to contemplate what other Conservative leaders did in a crisis; adopt pragmatic policies. These weaknesses were to become increasingly apparent during the 1992 general election campaign.

In his first Cabinet reshuffle (November 1990), John Major promoted Malcolm Rifkind to the Foreign Office and appointed Ian Lang to the Scottish Office. This replaced one Scottish Secretary of State who was 'suspect' on devolution (Rifkind had been pro-devolution in the 1979 Scottish Referendum) with another who was an intransigent Unionist and a much better collaborator (Bradbury, 1997: 81). On the question of the Union, Lang and the Prime Minister were of one mind; the Union was not negotiable, nor was any constitutional change that might endanger the historic relationship between Scotland and England (Hogg and Hill, 1995: 248).

John Major's speech-writer, Nick True, was, if anything, even more unequivocal in his support of the Union and had been instrumental in hardening the prime minister's position against any constitutional change (Seldon, 1997: 262). With such close confidants, Major's personal belief in the Union was confirmed and certainty in the rectitude of his own views strengthened.

By the late autumn of 1991 some Conservative activists, in Scotland and Central Office, voiced fears of an impending constitutional crisis and that the only way to head it off was for the government to offer some move towards devolution. These fears were reinforced by the Lib–Dem victory in the Kincardine by-election. Meanwhile virtually all the advice Ian Lang was receiving from Scottish Conservative activists 'was that some kind of devolution was inevitable (and that) it would, therefore, surely be better to make the concession now rather than be forced into it after the expected trouncing at the general election' (Hogg and Hill, 1995: 247).

These views represented the classic Conservative reaction to a crisis; minimise its impact by a policy change, regroup and prepare for the next battle. At this stage John Major's stubborn streak came to the fore. He was not interested in any pragmatic policy-shift. For him the Union was a matter of personal belief, not of political expediency. Speaking to Scottish Conservative candidates in February 1992, he declared his article of faith:

> And yet it is our party that supports the Union. Not because it's always been good to us, but because it has always seemed right to us. Not always in our political interest, but always in that of our kingdom and the countries within it. (quoted Hogg & Hill, 1995, 248)

The sentiments he expressed were not shared by many party officials in Smith Square, and when he insisted on returning to the issue in the last days of the campaign, most of his advisers were against the idea (Junor, 1993: 249).

The Conservatives' victory in the 1992 general election, largely the product of a late swing, appeared to vindicate John Major's

'Unionist' strategy. In Scotland the SNP tide had not swept all before it, and to the consternation of some Scots, and the surprise of all, Ian Lang retained his seat. Cooler recollections suggest that the 'Union card' was not decisive. The triumphalism of Labour's Sheffield rally, doubts about Neil Kinnock's personality and the intervention of the tabloids, particularly the *Sun*, in the last week of the campaign, were probably more salient factors.

Yet one could not disprove the impact of John Major's 'defence of the Union' strategy. The electoral outcome appeared to prove that a pragmatic approach on this issue had been unnecessary. For Major the issue of the Union was above party politics and when he spoke about it, he did so with a clarity and conviction not evident in other speeches. In a late stage in the general election he issued an apocalyptic warning, almost Churchillian in tone and style:

> The United Kingdom is in danger.
> Wake up, my fellow countrymen!
> Wake up now before it is too late!
> (quoted Butler and Kavanagh, 1992: 130)

MAJOR'S SECOND GOVERNMENT (1992–97)

During the last week of the general election campaign, John Major had indicated that he would listen to what the Scots had to say and 'take stock'. The impression was given that he might be more flexible on the devolution issue. Rumours had also surfaced during the campaign in Wales that a forum representing Welsh business interests might be set up to advise the Welsh Secretary. (*Western Mail*, March–April 1992, passim). It never materialised. However, significant, though limited, steps were taken to confront the devolution issue by the new Major government.

In 1993 a Welsh Language Act was passed, extending the legitimate use of the Welsh language by public and private bodies. The Welsh Language Board (another quango) was set up to supervise the application of the Act and encourage the private sector to adopt bilingualism wherever sensible and appropriate. This was precisely the form of territorial management of the United Kingdom which Major could apply without qualms. It coincided with the Conservative party's constitutional principles and its political interests. Special provision could be made for Wales without threatening the sovereignty of the

Westminster parliament. There was an added political bonus. Enhancing the status of the Welsh language might reduce its potency as a political issue to Plaid Cymru's disadvantage. Consistent with this interpretation was the appointment of Lord Elis Thomas (a past president of Plaid Cymru) as the Board's first Chairman.

A similar exercise in territorial management was attempted in Scotland where John Major sought to demonstrate the economic benefits of the Union. In March 1993 Ian Lang published a government White paper, *Scotland in the Union – a Partnership for Good*. This rehearsed the well-worn arguments of the benefits Scotland gained from the Union and the government's commitment to its maintenance. However, the White Paper also acknowledged certain limitations in the handling of Scottish parliamentary business in Westminster; specifically time-constraints and a lack of transparency which, it was argued, could be resolved by widening the powers of the Scottish Grand Committee. It was proposed that the Committee would meet more frequently (up to twelve times a session) with regular question-times, more ministerial statements and more meetings in Scotland to include Standing Committees on Scottish bills. It was claimed that the enhanced Grand Committee would be 'a mini House of Commons for Scotland within the orbit of the U.K. parliament' (Bradbury, 1997: 83).

This claim was at best debatable. It totally ignored the party-composition of the Scottish Grand Committee, which was dominated by Labour members hostile to the Conservative government and eager to dismantle its legislative programme. However, if that power were to be denied to the Scottish Grand Committee, it would be little more than a talking shop.

Despite the obvious limitations of the 'Grand Committee strategy' a similar plan was announced for Wales by David Hunt, the Welsh Secretary of State. It leaned heavily on the Scottish proposals but, lacking specifically Welsh legislation, its perceived role was even more dubious than that of its Scottish counterpart. These proposals were effectively deposited in the 'pending tray' following David Hunt's promotion to the Department of Employment in the May 1993 Cabinet reshuffle, and remained there until November 1995, when William Hague produced a modified plan, according to which the Welsh Grand Committee would meet more frequently and in various parts of Wales (not just Cardiff). It would debate government business as it affected Wales, receive ministerial statements and be able to question ministers.

But to what effect? The role envisaged for the Committee hardly merited the government's intention that it should meet up to seven times a year and its composition (only four Conservative MPs out of 38) and the requirement that it circulate throughout Wales led the political correspondent of the *Western Mail* to call it a 'mobile talking shop' (Settle, 1995: 1).

As well as evincing flexibility in the reforms of the Scottish and Welsh Grand Committees, Major was also prepared to adopt a pragmatic response to demands from the Celtic periphery. The Maastricht Treaty was seen by political observers, and by Major himself, as a measure of his negotiating skills. However, the special arrangements and opt-outs that he had won were as much to do with placating elements in the parliamentary Conservative party as with safeguarding key British interests. The passage of the Maastricht Treaty Bill through the Commons was, to say the least, problematic. A reduced parliamentary majority, an increasingly assertive group of Conservative Eurosceptics and an Opposition sensing an opportunity to bring the government down, all conspired to bring Major to the verge of parliamentary defeat.

One of the clauses in the Maastricht Treaty of particular significance to Scottish and Welsh nationalists related to the establishment of a Committee of the Regions. The SNP and Plaid Cymru had adopted parallel strategies of 'Independence within Europe' and both parties recognised the Committee's importance for future devolved governments in Edinburgh and Cardiff. Despite its title, the Committee of the Regions was intended to represent regional and local authorities. The local authority associations in England took the view that of the 24 seats allocated to the United Kingdom, 18 should go the English shire and metropolitan authorities with six to Scotland, Wales and Northern Ireland. However, a deal was struck prior to a crucial vote on the Maastricht Bill between the Government and the Welsh nationalists. Committee representation for Wales was increased from two to three, thus ensuring a Plaid Cymru representative on the Committee of the Regions. Major's sensitivity to these and other Celtic demands eventually resulted in a over-allocation of ten seats; five for Scotland, three for Wales, and two for Northern Ireland (Roberts, 1997, 262). English local authorities were understandably aggrieved but they lacked the nationalists' clout in the Commons.

Redwood in Wales

After winning the 1992 general election against the odds, it could be said that John Major was now his own man. No longer could it be argued that Margaret Thatcher was the back-seat driver. Indeed relations between Thatcher and Major were already deteriorating, largely because of his flexible line on Europe. A similar flexibility was also apparent in his dealings with Scotland and Wales. However, at this stage 'events', so feared by Macmillan, began to take a hand. On 16 September 1993 there was a catastrophic run on the pound which resulted in Britain leaving the European Exchange Rate mechanism. This became known as Black Wednesday. It was a personal disaster for Major, appearing to vindicate the arguments of the Eurosceptics within his own party and calling into question his whole European strategy. It also opened up a divide between Major and Norman Lamont, his Chancellor, which led to Lamont's resignation from Major's government in May 1993.

At this stage one can only conclude that Major took his eye off the 'devolution ball'. Clearly Major's overriding concern was to keep his government in office, while awaiting the political benefits of the hoped-for economic revival. Meanwhile, a symbolic concession was made to the Eurosceptic wing of the Conservative Party; John Redwood was brought into the Cabinet.

In retrospect, one suspects that John Major made Redwood Welsh Secretary of State for much the same reason that Margaret Thatcher had sent Peter Walker to the Welsh Office; to keep him occupied while sidelining him from the mainstream of British political activity. If this was the intention, it failed on two counts. Redwood did not allow himself to be sidelined but exploited his position in the cabinet to promote the Eurosceptic cause. He became what Major was to describe as 'one of the bastards' (Seldon, 1997: 390). Nor was Redwood prepared to be mired in Welsh politics. Instead of seeking to protect and promote the Welsh interest in the Cabinet (the traditional role of Welsh Secretaries of State since the establishment of the Welsh Office in 1965), he used the Welsh Office to promote a right-wing, Thatcherite agenda in Wales. He reduced staffing levels in the Welsh Office, hived off a series of functions to executive agencies (so adding to the quangocracy in Wales) and cut back administrative costs in the NHS by denying managerial appointments.

John Redwood also highlighted the issue of unmarried mothers and their alleged costs to society, both moral and financial. Originally focused on a Cardiff housing estate, it became a national British issue and illustrated Redwood's intention of using the Welsh Office as a launch-pad for the promotion of right-wing Thatcherite policies as an alternative to John Major's programme.

Redwood's impact on Wales cannot be over-estimated. His Conservative predecessors – Nicholas Edwards, Peter Walker and David Hunt – had worked to modify the impact of Thatcherite policies in Wales with some success. Their role was recognised, even respected, by Welsh local government politicians. For such hard-edged Thatcherite policies now to be applied, when Major's government appeared to be returning to more consensual policies, caused dismay and anger across Wales. The reform of Welsh local government added to the rising tide of Welsh discontent. In England, an independent Commission was appointed to consult with local authorities, but the Welsh Office decided to run its own consultation exercise. A Conservative-run Welsh Office dealing with largely Labour-controlled local authorities was bound to encounter difficulties, and the Welsh Office's proposed model of relatively small distinct councils was interpreted by the eight large Welsh counties as an attack upon themselves.

There was also a perception that the Welsh Office was intent upon constructing a weaker, more compliant local government system in Wales. Widespread opposition to the scheme both in Wales and among Welsh MPs (34 out of 38 were opposed to the government's plans) turned to real anger when the government suspended Standing Order 86, replacing the Welsh Parliamentary Committee with an ordinary Standing Committee composed of a majority of English Conservative MPs, and pushed the proposals through. Redwood's Thatcherite policies, the Major government's disregard of Welsh concerns on local government reform and its cavalier actions in overruling established parliamentary procedures persuaded many doubters in Wales that political devolution was now a necessity.

Forsyth in Scotland

The replacement of Ian Lang by Michael Forsyth as Scottish Secretary would appear, at the first sight, to have been a serious error. As a junior minister in the Scottish Office, Forsyth had been a vigorous Thatcherite 'assimilationist' and had alienated moderate Scottish Tories. Margaret Thatcher's attempt to appoint him

Chairman of the Scottish Conservative Party in 1989, and so change the culture of Scottish Conservatism, had precipitated a mini-civil war in the Scottish party such that Mrs Thatcher had reluctantly to concede defeat. Forsyth's appointment could thus be interpreted as a return to the Thatcherite assimilationist agenda, paralleling that which was taking place in Wales under John Redwood.

By 1995, however, Forsyth had himself changed, possibly because of the continuing strength of the Labour party and the SNP and the realisation that devolution was now a more immediate prospect. Forsyth's views on Scotland and the Union now coincided with those of Major; that Scotland could get more accountable government within the Union. He adopted Major's strategy, first stated during the last week of the 1992 general election; *viz.* recognising and supporting the special and beneficial arrangements for Scotland (the bloc grant based on the Barnett Formula* and Scottish representation in the House of Commons) while vigorously supporting the Union. At the time of Forsyth's appointment it was quite possible that the general election would take place in little more than twelve months. Aware that time was running out for the Government, Forsyth initiated what was, in effect, a 'pre-campaign campaign'. He had always been an energetic and effective campaigner and now set himself the task of winning the battle of ideas with the pro-devolutionists.

Part of Forsyth's strategy was to develop an intellectual argument for the Unionist cause. This he did in a succession of speeches, in which he described and explained those individual themes which under-pinned his central thesis. The first of these speeches was at a fringe meeting at the Annual Conservative Party Conference in October 1995 when he outlined *A Blueprint for British Devolution* (Forsyth, 1996). In November of that year he gave the Richard Stewart Memorial Lecture at the University of Strathclyde, in which he gave details of his plans to upgrade the Scottish Grand Committee. In January 1996 he addressed Scottish Conservative Party Delegates on 'Our Nation's Future' and two months later in March, speaking to the Central Council of the National Union in Harrogate, he argued elegantly in support of 'The Constitution'. In April,

---

* The Barnett Formula based on population and need was devised by the Labour Government in 1976–77 to allocate public expenditure between the four parts of the United Kingdom: England, Scotland, Wales and Northern Ireland. It increasingly worked to the advantage of Scotland.

giving the Williamson Memorial Lecture at Stirling University, he spoke emotionally about 'The Scottish Identity'. This was a bravura performance by a conviction politician, and represented a genuine attempt to win the hearts and minds of opinion-formers in Scotland. It was evocative of the campaigning style of a bygone age, eschewing the television sound-bite for face-to-face meetings, but there were serious doubts whether Forsyth could effect a significant change in Scottish opinion in such a limited period of time.

There were four elements to Forsyth's strategy. The first addressed the assertion, frequently made by John Major, that the government of Scotland could be brought closer to the Scottish people while preserving the Union. Part of this argument stemmed from the Thatcherite view that the only 'real' devolution was to the individual and the family. This had made little impact in Scotland and was now reinforced by further reforms to the Scottish Grand Committee so that 'subjects relevant to Scotland (would) be debated on Scottish soil with the participation of the Scottish people'; the Grand Committee would take Second and Third Readings of Scottish Bills, and UK Ministers (including the Prime Minister) would participate in Grand Committee debates (Forsyth, 1996: 21).

These proposals built on Alec Douglas-Home's recommendations of 1970 but they suffered from the same defect. Only non-contentious bills could be amended by the Grand Committee. The Major government of the Union would not be denied its political programme. Forsyth also attempted to extend the pro-unionist views beyond the ranks of Scottish Conservatism. His proposals to enhance the powers of the Scottish Economic Council (stimulated by the Scottish TUC) was an attempt to involve Scottish trade unionists and businessmen in Scottish institutions which reinforced the Union. Once again, however, the viability of the proposals foundered on the sovereignty of the Westminster parliament.

The second element of the strategy invoked the sense of a Scottish identity. Forsyth repudiated the sense of identity which was the 'product of the political proletarianism that dominates West Central Scotland – and peddle the mythology of class warfare' (Forsyth, 1996: 43). Instead, he argued that Scots should 'distinguish between the genuine quest for a national identity – more cultural than political – which has always engaged Scots'. (Forsyth, 1996: 47). A cultural national identity might not have a political resonance and thus not threaten the Union of Scotland and England. But Forsyth went further, claiming a duality to the Scottish identity; a division between the Highland and the Lowland cultures. If this were to be the case, the sense of a Scottish political identity would be seriously compromised.

Thirdly, Forsyth promoted the idea of an all-encompassing British identity, recalling the experiences of the Second World War in a highly emotive fashion, and presenting the Union, not as an arid constitutional mechanism, but a Union of peoples.

> Unity is our instinct and our strength. Unity forged and tested in peace and war. When survival was the issue, there were no doubts about our British identity then. When the bombs rained indiscriminately on Coventry and on Clydesbank, we knew we were one nation. We are one nation still. (Forsyth, 1996: 39)

This was a ringing declaration but the Second World War is history for most people. Some Scots, in their sixties and seventies, might have reacted positively to the Forsyth's message but not the majority. This part of the strategy would seem to have been seriously flawed.

Finally, Forsyth took the offensive, savaging Labour's devolution plans, highlighting their constitutional weaknesses, and focusing on the dangers to Scotland if devolution were to be enacted. The proposed tax-varying powers of a Scottish Parliament were dubbed by Forsyth as a 'Tartan Tax' which would stop the flow of inward investment to Scotland; the Scottish Secretary of State would be sidelined or abolished; the number of Scottish MPs in the House of Commons would be reduced, and all this plus the £45 million costs of a Scottish parliament (Forsyth, 1996: 49). Forsyth's attack on Labour's proposals touched a raw nerve, forced the Labour Party onto the defensive and obliged Blair to intervene and insist on a second referendum question to cover the tax option.

Hague in Wales

Michael Forsyth's Scottish strategy, with appropriate modifications, was also applied in Wales. John Redwood had resigned from the government in June 1995 to contest the leadership election. In the resulting reshuffle William Hague, regarded as a crypto-Thatcherite, became Welsh Secretary and, doubtless aware of the negative impact Redwood had on Wales, adopted a more emollient image. He introduced reforms to the Welsh Grand Committee (noted above) took steps to learn the words to the Welsh national anthem (something which Redwood had conspicuously failed to do, as was revealed in an embarrassing television recording rebroadcast during the leadership campaign) and rehearsed the arguments against devolution: that the proposed Welsh Assembly, lacking legislative powers, would be an even more pointless and costly exercise; and that devolution would marginalise Wales and weaken the Union. (Hague, 1996: 22).

The Conservative anti-devolution campaign in Wales never generated the political heat it had in Scotland, Plaid Cymru did not threaten the Union as could the SNP, and the Welsh devolution debate was less advanced than in Scotland. Perhaps this explains why Wales appeared more receptive to the Conservative warnings on devolution and why Welsh public support for it fell away during the general election and referendum campaigns. Nevertheless, Wales like Scotland became a 'Tory-free zone'. John Major's strategy of extolling the benefits of preserving the Union and warning of the dangers of devolution failed to sway sufficient voters in Scotland and Wales to support the Conservatives.

CONCLUSION

The Major premiership was crucial for Britain in many ways. Replacing Margaret Thatcher after a bitter leadership election, John Major had the difficult task of trying to bring the competing factions within the Conservative party together. Having negotiated the Maastricht Treaty, he was obliged to take Britain further into the European Union, to the dismay of many traditional supporters of the party. Finally, the emergence of devolution at the centre of the political agenda required him to re-evaluate a fundamental constitutional principle at the heart of the traditional Conservative thinking. It is no indictment of Major that he failed in all three areas. Each individual problem would have been difficult for a Conservative prime minister to resolve, because each related to the essential nature (and future) of the Conservative party. Taken together the task was immense. However, rather like a juggler who believes he can stave off disaster so long as he keeps all the balls in the air, Major was persuaded that the problems could be resolved and the general election won.

On the constitutional issue, John Major believed he was succeeding and that his evolutionary approach would prove the right one. In an interview with *The Independent* he indicated that he wished to be considered a constitutional reform prime minister (Marr, 1995). There is some evidence to support this claim. The Welsh Language Act did enhance the status of the language. The Scottish and Welsh Grand Committees were given more functions and parliamentary procedures were reformed. But all of Major's initiatives were consistent with the preservation of parliamentary sovereignty. So far as John Major was concerned that was the keystone of the Union, and as such, was non-negotiable. Consequently, those constitutional reforms he enacted were too little and too late for the developing situation in Scotland. Nor did the Language Act overcome the alienation that John Redwood's tenure at the Welsh Office had engendered.

In the final analysis, John Major's view of the Union and the Constitution, like that of many other Conservatives, was an English view. When he spoke of British values and traditions and linked them with references to warm beer and cricket matches on the village green, he was reflecting on life in southern England.

Major's inability to fully comprehend the strength of opinion in Scotland was illustrated by his initiative in Northern Ireland, the Joint Downing Street Declaration with Albert Reynolds, the Irish Prime Minister (see Chapter 6). Reynolds noted that Major was a Unionist but 'not in any narrow sense', and was aware that what he was proposing for Northern Ireland would create difficulties in Scotland; specifically that while an elected Assembly was necessary to solve the Northern Ireland problem it was quite unacceptable as a solution to the Scottish problem. Reynolds surmised that Major saw Britain as a unit that could not be broken up, but that Northern Ireland was 'over there' (quoted Seldon, 1997: 267).

This brings us to the nub of the matter. Although John Major's view of the Union might have been more geographically limited than Dicey's, in all other respects he subscribed to the classical Dicean view of the Constitution. The themes which emerged in Conservative campaign literature in the 1997 general election confirm this view. On the Constitution, the campaign literature referred to its 'evolution over many centuries'; that 'it embodied the wisdom of the ages'; that 'it is a seamless webb providing a flexible basis upon which our nation has prospered'; that to tamper with the constitution 'would threaten instability'; that 'the left-wing agenda' (shared by Labour, Liberal Democrats, Welsh and Scottish Nationalists) threatened the whole constitutional structure. The implication of these statements is that the constitution is best left alone, but that if it is to be reformed, it is best done in an 'evolutionary' manner by the Conservatives, because they alone appreciate that the 'only genuine reform is that which helps strengthen the Union' (Cooke, 1997; Conservative Research Department, 1996).

John Major has frequently been contrasted with Mrs Thatcher; she being a conviction politician and he not. This is far too facile a comparison. On constitutional matters, he was very much a conviction politician, believing in traditional Conservative constitutional values, pre-eminent among them the supremacy of Parliament. But whereas Edward Heath had seen the implications of Britain's membership of the European Community in 1972 for British domestic constitutional arrangements, John Major did not. Major shared responsibility for the creation of the single market, British membership of the Exchange Rate Mechanism and the Maastricht Treaty, all of which had profound implications for the British constitution, the concept of British sovereignty, and the supremacy of Parliament.

Yet he appeared unable or unwilling to recognise the parallels between subsidiarity for the UK within the European Union and devolution for Scotland and Wales. Thus in his approach to devolution, the British constitution remained inviolate and inviolable. Despite the electoral advance of the SNP, the new Labour party's constitutional proposals and, from time to time, cautionary voices within the Conservative party, Major was convinced that his view was right. He could argue that his decision, to use the British patriotic Union card in the last week of the 1992 general election had helped the late swing. In the last week of the 1997 general election he forsook London to fly around the four constituent parts of the United Kingdom – England, Scotland, Northern Ireland and Wales – where he issued the same warning: 'The Union is in danger'. In 1997, however, there was to be no late swing.

8 The 3 Rs – Reform, Reproach and Rancour: Education Policies under John Major
Peter Dorey

The education policies pursued by the Major governments constituted a clear example of inheritance in public policy, entailing as they did the continuation and consolidation of initiatives originally introduced while Margaret Thatcher was Conservative party leader and Prime Minister.

Crucial in this respect was the 1988 Education Reform Act, which laid the foundations for the reforms which subsequently characterised the Major premiership *vis-à-vis* education policies. The 1988 Act also enshrined various contradictions which only became fully apparent during the period that John Major was prime minister, and which in turn prompted certain additional initiatives under Major's premiership in order to ameliorate these tensions.

The 1988 Education Act had entailed seven main features, namely:

(1) Transferring responsibility for management of schools from Local Education Authorities (LEAs) to schools' own governing bodies.
(2) Permitting schools to 'opt-out' of LEA control, and, instead, become 'grant-maintained'. This meant that they would be funded directly from central government.
(3) Facilitating 'open enrolment', whereby parents would be empowered to choose which school in their locale they wished their children to attend.
(4) Introduction of a National Curriculum, whereupon all pupils would study certain 'core' subjects up until the age of 14 (when they pursued their GCSE options).
(5) Establishment of City Technology Colleges, in an attempt to provide a greater emphasis on vocational education.

(6) Abolition of the Inner London Education Authority (ILEA).
(7) Freeing polytechnics from LEA control and finance.

These provisions reflected a number of specific principles and objectives derived from Conservative philosophy during (and after) the Thatcher era. Firstly, permitting parents to decide which school they wished to send their children to was explicitly linked to the Conservative emphasis on freedom of choice. Yet as many Conservatives – particularly Thatcher herself – have been quick to point out, choice also entails responsibility, and in the context of education policy, bestowing upon parents the right to choose their children's school was simultaneously envisaged as a means by which parents would assume greater responsibility, by considering which school would provide the best education (in terms of quality of teaching, exam passes, qualifications and discipline).

Secondly, Conservatives envisaged that once parents were empowered to choose which school they wanted their children to attend, a significant degree of competition would be fostered, as schools vied with each other to convince parents that they would provide the best education. This in turn would effectively compel schools to improve standards, in order to attract more pupils, for funding was to be linked in large part to pupil intake and recruitment. 'Good' schools, it was envisaged, would prosper, while schools with lower levels of educational attainment would suffer financially, by being unable to convince a sufficient number of parents to enrol their children.

In this respect, the Conservative governments from 1988 onwards sought to instil key elements of market criteria into the realm of education, with the intention that a school's reputation and resources would become increasingly dependent on its ability to attract 'customers' (i.e. pupils), which was in turn dependent upon the provision of a good-quality product (education, largely measured in terms of tests passed and qualifications achieved by pupils).

Thirdly, Conservatives envisaged that permitting schools to opt out of LEA control, coupled with the legal and financial autonomy bestowed upon polytechnics, would further weaken and marginalise local government, against which the Thatcher and Major governments evinced unyielding hostility. With the funding and administration of schools, polytechnics and FE colleges being assumed by central government, various education quangos and agencies, and local management (via governing bodies), local government was to be deprived of one of its most important responsibilities, thereby enabling Conservatives to argue even more vehemently that local government – at least in its traditional form – was largely superfluous.

Fourthly, and finally, the National Curriculum, by ensuring that all pupils were taught the same core subjects, was intended to facilitate the measurement of standards throughout the country, for comparisons could now be made concerning the performance of pupils at different schools. In effect, it was anticipated that like could now be compared with like, which, in turn, corresponded to the issue of parental choice, for parents would apparently have 'performance indicators' upon which to base their decision about which school to send their children to.

Furthermore, once the principle of 'comparative performance evaluation' between schools was invoked, then the practice of national tests logically followed. Furthermore, the desire to make such information available to parents, while compelling schools to improve their performance, also led inexorably to the publication of 'league tables' for schools.

Thus it was that the reforms enshrined in the 1988 Education Act reflected and reinforced the discourse of contemporary Conservatism, with its buzz-words of choice, competition, (parental) responsibility and standards.

MAINTAINING THE MOMENTUM: THE 1993 EDUCATION ACT

Under John Major's premiership, these reforms have been consolidated, and the discourse sustained, via the further legislation and ministerial initiatives. In July 1992, just a few months after Major's government had been re-elected, a White Paper entitled *Choice and Diversity: a New Framework for Schools* was published, much of it written by the new Education Secretary, John Patten, himself. Patten explicitly drew attention to the words 'choice' and 'diversity', deeming them to be two of the most important objectives of the Major government's reform of education (although among officials in the Department of Education, the White Paper apparently became known as 'Chaos and Perversity').

A few months later, the proposals outlined in the White Paper were enshrined in what became the 1993 Education Act. This legislation:

(1) Streamlined the 'opting-out' process, in order to make it quicker and simpler. It was clearly felt by ministers that an insufficient number of schools had opted out since the 1988 Education Act, and hence it was deemed necessary to simplify the process.

(2) Established a new body, the Funding Agency for Schools, which would be responsible for allocating and administering finance to those schools which had chosen grant-maintained status by virtue of having 'opted out'. This was intended further to reduce the role of LEAs.

(3) Limited still further the role of LEAs by confining their responsibilities to the provision of special needs, transport, monitoring of pupil attendance, and competing to provide various services to grant-maintained schools. Here, too, therefore, the Conservative notion of a division between purchasers and providers was evident, as was the concept of local authorities being transformed into 'enablers', rather than providers.

(4) Permitted secondary schools (irrespective of whether grant-maintained or LEA-controlled) to specialise in one or more subjects alongside teaching the 'core subjects' enshrined in the National Curriculum.

(5) Established 'Education Associations' which would act as 'hit squads' investigating schools deemed to be 'failing'. These 'Education Associations' would be empowered to take over the management of a school deemed to be 'at risk', or even recommend its closure. There was a clear implication that when and where a school's poor performance warranted a visit from an 'Education Association', taking it out of LEA control and designating it 'grant-maintained' might be desirable, this possibly being presented to staff as the only alternative to complete closure.

(6) Merged the National Curriculum Council and the School Examinations and Assessment Council, to form a new School Curriculum and Assessment Authority.

Although the 1993 Education Act was deemed by the Major government to complete the process begun back in 1979, namely that of increasing parental choice, improving quality, facilitating diversity, giving schools greater autonomy and enhancing accountability, it is perhaps significant that the legislation introduced by John Patten was actually twice the length of Kenneth Baker's 1988 Education Act, indicating, perhaps, that the latter had somewhat underachieved.

Furthermore, the provision for streamlining the 'opting-out' process reflected the Major governments' disappointment that relatively few schools (and parents) had hitherto taken advantage of the right to become 'grant-maintained'. Indeed, Major himself remained disappointed throughout his premiership at the pace at which schools were 'opting out' of local education authority control, to the extent that he found himself in conflict over the issue with one of his Secretaries of State for Education, Gillian Shephard (Seldon, 1997: 598).

Much of the blame for the apparently slow pace at which schools were choosing to 'opt out' was, predictably, levelled against local education authorities and Left-wing Labour councils themselves, who were accused of deliberately obstructing the programme and its procedures in order to retain their monopoly and power over education provision (Major, 1992: 10).

John Major's impatience at the 'insufficient' numbers of schools (and parents) exercising their right to 'opt out' of LEA control was such that, in the final two years of his premiership, he made public his desire to see *all* schools eventually become 'grant-maintained', although he also acknowledged that while he was 'impatient for change ... we must move forward at measured pace' (Major, 1995: 7).

In conjunction with the legislative reforms delineated above, the Major premiership evinced three further initiatives in the sphere of education, namely: a concerted attempt at reforming the character of teacher-training, and teaching methods in the classroom; a drive to instil a greater emphasis on 'moral education' in schools; and a high-profile attack on bad schools and teachers, with a view to 'weeding out' the latter.

SCAPEGOATING THE 1960s AND 'PROGRESSIVE' METHODS

With regard to teacher-training and teaching methods in the classroom, it was consistently alleged that since the 1960s, there had been far too much emphasis on 'progressive' methods, leading to 'trendy' teachers who focused too much on 'pupil-centred' and 'creative' learning.

This premise had been readily accepted and articulated by many Conservative Education Secretaries, and also reflected the prejudices of Margaret Thatcher (who had herself been an Education

Minister in the 1970–74 Heath administration). In Thatcher's view, for example, 'too many teachers were less competent and more ideological than their predecessors'. She distrusted 'the new "child-centred" teaching techniques [and] the emphasis on imaginative engagement rather than learning facts' (Thatcher 1993: 590).

This perspective also entailed a strong hostility towards the so-called 'education establishment' which many Conservatives believed was dominated by left-wingers and 'progressives' pushing their own subversive agenda. One of the leading Thatcherites in the Conservative Cabinets of the 1980s, Norman Tebbit (who was actually offered the post of Education Secretary towards the end of the decade, but declined it) was convinced that:

> The disdain for industry and commerce which has long been a feature of our educational establishment within schools and universities is now partnered and supported by an outright hostility towards business, stemming from the modern left-wing public-sector education establishment. . . . The poor condition of our state education has as its roots the socialist-inspired egalitarian reforms of the 1960s . . . [when] achievement became devalued, discipline despised. . . . Literacy and numeracy began to take second place to 'self-fulfilment', 'creativity', and 'participation' . . . . teachers of quality could find little job-satisfaction in such a system and were steadily replaced by ill-disciplined, intellectually lazy if not lacking, third-raters. (Tebbit 1991: 99–101)

One is sorely tempted to suggest that the adjectives in the final sentence might equally be applied to many in John Major's Conservative party, for whom populist, saloon-bar prejudice prevailed over intellectual analysis and rational argument.

Kenneth Baker, the Education Secretary who was formally responsible for the 1988 Education Act, certainly seemed to share Thatcher's and Tebbit's prejudices, claiming that:

> Of all the Whitehall Departments, the Department of Education & Science was among those with the strongest in-house ideology. There was a clear 1960s ethos and a very clear agenda which . . . was rooted in 'progressive' orthodoxies, in egalitarianism, and in the comprehensive school system. It was devoutly anti-excellence, anti-selection, and anti-market. The DES represented perfectly the theory of 'producer capture', whereby the interests of the producer prevail over the interests of the

consumer ... the Department [was] in league with the teacher
unions, University Departments of Education, teacher training
theories, and local authorities. ... (Baker 1993: 168)

These prejudices were later aired by John Patten, after he had been
appointed Education Secretary in April 1992, the former Oxford
don claiming that:

> The reform of the way in which teachers are educated is the
> task with which we should have started precisely because it was
> in many of our Teacher Training Colleges that some dreadful
> and damaging practices began. ... Even after recent legisla-
> tion ... trying to improve teacher education, the problems of theory
> dominating practice remain. ... Too many people have recently
> left teacher education establishments conversant in the rituals of
> progressive orthodoxy [and] jargon-riddled claptrap ... teacher
> education is at present the source of too many of the problems
> in state education, and also the home of a culture which is
> endemically anti-elitist, anti-testing and at times apparently op-
> posed to academic rigour or structure in teaching and therefore
> learning. (Patten 1995: 196–7)

Patten's prejudices were echoed by one of his junior ministers at
the Department of Education, Baroness Blatch, when she alleged
that progressive teaching methods developed since the 1960s had
belittled the 3Rs, to the extent that Britain now had four million
adults who were illiterate (*The Times*, 13 February 1993). Meanwhile, John Major himself railed against 'the giant left-wing ex-
periment in levelling down' (Major, 1992: 9), 'the failed nostrums
of the 1960s and 1970s' (Major, 1993: 31), and 'the fads and fashions
that short-changed a generation of children ... called ... progressive
education' (Major, 1997: 20).

Consequently, the Major governments periodically published proposals whereby teacher-training would no longer be primarily provided by university education departments, but would be learnt *in
situ* in the classroom. This was deemed to have the added advantage of shifting the emphasis of teacher-training to the acquisition
of practical skills in front of pupils, as opposed to theoretical knowledge derived from university lectures and seminars.

'MORAL EDUCATION' IN SCHOOLS

The second key education initiative pursued while John Major was prime minister – and one which followed directly on from the concern over teacher-training and teaching methods – was the desire to instil a greater emphasis on 'moral education' into the classroom. This aspect actually emanated from two discrete sources.

Firstly, it emerged as part of Major's ill-fated 'back to basics' campaign, launched at the Conservative party's 1993 annual conference. Although it was widely perceived (and portrayed in the press) as an exercise intended to revive traditional sexual morality and promote the nuclear family, Major himself was emphatic that 'back to basics' was not primarily concerned with condemning single parents or preaching about how people should conduct their private lives. Instead, he claimed that it was an initiative intended first and foremost to restore the principle of individual responsibility, as well as fostering respect for other people (courtesy, deference and good manners).

With specific reference to education, 'back to basics' sought to facilitate a renewed emphasis on the so-called '3 Rs' (reading, writing and arithmetic), and as such, represented another manifestation of the Conservative attack on 'trendy' or 'progressive' teaching. Furthermore, by fostering a renewed emphasis on the '3 Rs', it was envisaged that the tide would be turned against 'interpretive' learning and subjectivity in the classroom. Instead, the '3 Rs' were deemed to be objective and factual, and thus more readily quantifiable in the form of assessments and tests.

This desire to go 'back to basics' in the form of the '3 Rs' also reflected the Conservatives' antipathy towards the what they saw as 'cultural relativism', in which all viewpoints and ideas were treated as equally valid, with no one answer or perspective being considered right or wrong. Cultural relativism was also viewed by Conservatives as another 'trendy' left-wing phenomenon serving to undermine standards, and as such, was compared extremely unfavourably to the 'moral absolutism' which many Conservatives hankered after. Furthermore, it was also deemed to make it extremely difficult for pupils' academic performances to be assessed; how could an individual's record be considered 'good' or 'bad' if there was no 'right' or 'wrong'?

The second discrete source from which the drive to instil a degree of 'moral education' in the classroom emanated was John Patten himself. Patten sustained the attack on 'progressive' teacher-training and 'trendy' teaching methods, believing that the British education system was 'not competitive enough – that 'C' word is still a very dirty one in educationally correct circles' (Patten 1995: 193).

A few months after John Major had launched his 'back to basics' initiative, Patten explained what this meant with regard to education in particular. He called upon schools to give greater priority to the teaching of certain basic values, most notably: self-reliance, self-restraint and self-discipline; individual responsibility; respect for authority; courtesy and respect towards others; honesty and trustworthiness; loyalty and fidelity.

However laudable these values might be, many teachers felt that they were being patronised, and exhorted to do what they were already doing anyway. As such, distrust between the Major government and the teaching profession widened and deepened yet further. In any case, the advocacy of such values as self-restraint, honesty and fidelity was undermined somewhat by the various sexual scandals in which some of Major's ministers subsequently became embroiled. Indeed, 'back to basics' eventually proved such an embarrassment to the government in the light of media revelations about the private lives of certain ministers that before too long, the initiative was quietly laid to rest.

However, several months before the launch of 'back to basics', Patten had himself sought to introduce morality into the classroom by issuing guidelines for sex education. Patten wanted sex education in the classroom to transcend mere reproductive biology, with sexual relationships being placed in a moral framework. This meant, in effect, that pupils were to be taught 'the benefits of stable married and family life' and 'the importance of loving relationships', while also being warned of 'the physical, emotional and moral risks of promiscuity' (*The Times*, 23 April 1993). Pupils were also expected to be taught the importance of 'self-restraint' in sexual matters. Furthermore, teachers were warned that if they gave advice about contraception to girls under 16 years of age, without the parents' knowledge or consent, they might be subject to criminal charges.

Patten's strictures not only irked the teaching profession further still, but also resulted in conflict between the Department of Education and Science and the Department of Health, for the latter was keen to halve the number of teenage pregnancies in Britain by the end of the decade (in accordance with a Health of the Nation programme launched in 1991). Health ministers and their officials believed that sex education was being undermined by the 'crusading moralist' wing of the Conservative Party's right wing, who were themselves being encouraged by 'religious fundamentalists' (*The Times*, 20 February 1994). Education policies under Major were not only causing further conflict between the government and the teaching profession, therefore, but also creating tensions within the government itself.

The vexatious issue of morality in the classroom re-emerged in the autumn of 1996, when a National Forum for Values in Education and the Community (set up under the auspices of the Schools Curriculum and Assessment Authority) suggested a number of ways in which the teaching of morality could be enhanced within schools. In particular, the National Forum, comprising 150 members drawn from business, the clergy, teachers, school governors, and parents and business, recommended that school pupils should be taught about their responsibilities as citizens, and about the importance of the family in child-rearing and caring for relatives. It also urged that children should be taught about the importance of such values as truth and integrity, coupled with respect for the law.

Yet while the broad thrust of the National Forum's recommendations were welcomed by the government, there was disappointment – both among some of the National Forum's own members as well as within the Cabinet – that the recommendations on moral teaching within schools did not place a greater and more explicit emphasis on the importance of marriage itself (*The Observer*, 27 October 1996; *The Guardian*, 28 October 1996).

CONTINUED HOSTILITY TOWARDS TEACHERS AND EDUCATIONALISTS

A further aspect of education policy during the Major premiership which represented a continuation of the Thatcher years was the unrelenting hostility evinced towards the teaching profession and the 'education establishment'. Reflecting the anti-intellectualism endemic in Conservatism – and the Thatcherite reliance on populism – Major's premiership evinced no abatement in the deep distrust between Conservative ministers and those working in education.

The original Education Act of 1988 had reflected a widespread view in the Conservative party (particularly on the right) that the teaching profession, in terms of teacher-training as well as classroom teachers, was overwhelmingly left-wing in philosophy and political orientation. The opposition to the measures enshrined in the Act which emanated from the profession was then viewed by many Conservatives as further evidence of the left-wing bias of teachers and educationalists, their concerns over the impact and consequences of the government's education reforms largely considered to be 'politically motivated'.

The teaching profession, however, insisted that many of the Government's measures had placed an intolerable administrative burden on teachers and school Heads, to the extent that increasing amounts of time and energy were being expended on paper work and bureaucratic exercises, rather than on teaching in the classroom. The irony that this was taking place under Conservative governments which talked repeatedly about slashing bureaucracy, cutting red tape, and generally 'getting government off people's backs', was certainly not lost on the teaching profession.

THE IMPORTANCE OF PERSONALITIES

The animosity between the teaching profession and the Major governments was compounded by the personalities and styles of his first two Education Secretaries. The first, Kenneth Clarke, revelled in his tough, plain-speaking style, and although he was on the left/one-nation wing of the Conservative Party (from where conciliation and a desire for consensus would normally be expected), his combative approach, and apparent enjoyment in attacking and insulting 'vested interests' and 'producer groups' endeared him to many on the right of the Conservative party (his pro-European views notwithstanding). With Clarke having relished his battles with the medical profession over NHS reforms while Secretary of State for Health prior to November 1990, his appointment as Education Secretary clearly indicated that the replacement of Margaret Thatcher by John Major would not herald a rapprochement with the education establishment. The reform of education would continue apace.

There were hopes in the teaching profession that Clarke's replacement by John Patten, in April 1992, would finally herald a more conciliatory phase, for not only was Patten believed to be on the left of the Conservative Party, he was also a former lecturer at Oxford University, and as such, was expected to have a much more sympathetic, insider's view of the problems facing those working in education. Yet it was not to be, for instead of articulating the views of the education profession, Patten effectively acted as poacher turned gamekeeper, displaying the same arrogant disregard and cavalier contempt for the teaching profession as most of his predecessors.

Indeed, within three months of Patten's appointment, the recently retired Senior Chief Inspector, Eric Bolton, was publicly complaining about the Major government's propensity to ignore the views and advice of those who actually worked in education, while readily listening to the recommendations of organisations such as the Adam Smith Institute and Centre for Policy Studies, or individuals articulating similarly ideological perspectives (quoted in Chitty & Simon 1993: 15).

REFORM OF THE NATIONAL CURRICULUM

One of the key measures enshrined in the 1988 Education Act, namely the National Curriculum, also proved to be one of the most controversial, to the extent that it was subject to a number of reforms during the period of John Major's premiership. In its original guise, the National Curriculum had comprised three 'core' subjects – English, maths, and science – and six 'foundation subjects: geography, history, arts, music, PE, and a foreign language (the last of these was not applicable to primary school pupils). Each of these was then arranged into ten levels, with every level possessing a specified 'attainment target'.

Attainment in the ten levels of these core and foundation subjects was then to be measured via assessments at the ages of 7, 11, 14 and 16, which were known as the four Key Stages (so that a pupil at 7 years of age would be at Key Stage One). These assessments comprised a combination of teacher evaluation of pupils' progress in the classroom and national tests. These tests were to be introduced on a rolling basis, with the tests for 7-year-olds commencing in 1991, and those for 14-year-olds scheduled for 1993. Tests for 11-year-olds were to commence the following year.

Both dimensions of the National Curriculum (the nature of the compulsory subjects, and the programme of tests) were strongly criticised by many within the education profession, as well as by a number of commentators or experts on educational affairs. The Conservative governments' selection of compulsory subjects was criticised by some for being too narrow or traditional (omitting other subjects such as sociology or computing, for example), while others actually thought that it was overly ambitious, and sought to include too much.

John Patten made clear his desire to see 'a counter-revolution against the pseudo-religions of radical sociology, the flabbier social sciences, and the apocalyptic diatribes of extreme environmentalism'. Such a 'counter-revolution', Patten envisaged, would herald a return to 'academic disciplines with serious intellectual rigour' (Patten, 1993: 14).

Meanwhile, some critics on the right of the Conservative party questioned the very efficacy of a National Curriculum, fearing that it constituted the 'nationalisation' of education in Britain, while imposing a rigid, bureaucratic and top-down framework on schools which was at variance with the renewed Conservative emphasis on choice, diversity and market criteria in the provision of services. From the opposite political perspective, it was noted with considerable suspicion that it was only state schools which were to have the National Curriculum imposed on them, while independent or private schools were to be exempt.

Other critics were concerned that some of the subjects within the National Curriculum were themselves too narrowly or traditionally defined, most notably English and history, with the latter being particularly criticised for its emphasis on British (English) history taught from a highly ethnocentric or parochial perspective, as well as the strong emphasis on factual materials, such as key dates and chronological developments, as opposed to social history and the interpretation of events.

However, the aspect of the National Curriculum which proved most problematic for the Major governments was the Key Stage tests, particularly those for 14-year-olds, which were due to have been introduced in 1993. By this time, however, the Major government had succeeded in uniting the various teaching unions in opposition to the tests to such an extent that teachers effectively boycotted them (John Patten's decision to write to the chairpersons of school governing bodies reminding them of their statutory obligation to conduct the tests merely serving to harden the resolve of teachers to boycott them). One calculation indicated that if a teacher in charge of a class of 35 pupils carried out all of the tests and assessment exercises officially required, he or she would be making 8000 assessments per annum.

The success of the teachers' boycott was such that Patten deemed it necessary to ask Ron Dearing – chairman-designate of the School Curriculum and Assessment Authority, which replaced both the National Curriculum Council and the School Examinations and Assessment Council – to conduct an urgent review of the National Curriculum, with a clear expectation that he would recommend 'thinning it out', while also simplifying the tests involved. Sir Ron's appointment to head such a review was a clear acknowledgement by the Major government that compulsion and coercion in the implementation of Conservative education reforms had failed.

This review therefore entailed a remarkable (for the Thatcher–Major governments) degree of consultation with the teaching profession, their consent and cooperation now acknowledged to be essential to the future of the National Curriculum and the Key Stage tests.

When the 'Dearing Report' was published in December 1993 – an Interim Report having been published in August – it did indeed recommend that the National Curriculum be slimmed down, in order that 20 per cent of teaching-time would be freed up for use at each school's discretion. The Report also recommended simplifying not only the tests, but also the administration of them. Furthermore, Sir Ron suggested that the attainment targets should be similarly rationalised. Finally, he recommended that once these modifications had been implemented, there should be an interregnum of five years before any further changes were pursued.

Although the government readily accepted Sir Ron's recommendations, an official report published almost three years later claimed that while the revised (post-Dearing) National Curriculum was an improvement on the original, it was still too 'crowded', with many teachers continuing to struggle in their attempts at covering all the requisite subjects. Furthermore, the report pointed out that many schools and teachers were experiencing difficulties in meeting all the requirements stipulated in the National Curriculum, owing to insufficient resources, caused by lack of funding (*The Independent*, 11 November 1996).

REFORM AND EXPANSION OF HIGHER EDUCATION

Although the main thrust of the education reforms pursued during Major's premiership concerned schools, and to a lesser extent, further education for 16–18 year olds, higher education did not remain unscathed by the government's ideological obsessions and political incompetence. Higher education was the focus of four main developments while John Major was prime minister.

Firstly, there was the abolition of the binary divide between universities and polytechnics, with the latter being granted university status by virtue of the 1992 Further and Higher Education Act (thereby enabling Conservative Ministers to claim that they had massively increased the number of young people receiving a university education).

The second development concerning higher education during John Major's premiership was the programme of expansion, with the government seeking virtually to double the number of young people attending university by the year 2000, meaning, in effect, that by the end of the decade, one in three 18-year-olds would study for a degree. However, ministers were emphatic that this expansion would not be financed by increased government expenditure on higher education. Instead, the rhetoric was of encouraging universities 'to look for increased levels of funding from private sources', while simultaneously securing greater efficiency and cost-effectiveness with existing resources and funding (Department of Education and Science, 1991).

The third main development, and one which followed on from the above, was the reform of financial support for students. It became clear that the reference to 'private sources' not only meant that universities should look to private-sector support and sponsorship in order to increase their revenues, but also that students themselves would be required to take out loans in order to support themselves while at university. The Major governments wanted virtually to double the number of people attending university, but baulked at concomitantly doubling the number of student maintenance grants paid via local education authorities.

In some respects, the introduction of student loans, in 1990, could be portrayed by Conservatives as a further means of encouraging individual responsibility and self-reliance, while simultaneously eradicating the dependency culture that 'handouts' from the taxpayer or government, in the form of student grants, apparently symbolised. Ministers also doubtless anticipated that once students had to finance their university education via a loan (to be paid back after graduation), they would be more discerning about which courses and degrees they enrolled for, increasingly opting for 'relevant' subjects which would maximise their employment opportunities (as opposed to 'less serious' or 'relevant' degrees which were not deemed 'appropriate' to the needs of the British economy). In this respect, ministerial rhetoric about greater choice for consumers (in this case, students) belied the hope that certain degree subjects would fare less well than those deemed 'relevant' to the economy and labour market.

Furthermore, while higher education in Britain has long been viewed instrumentally – certain qualifications being equated with career prospects, as opposed to a degree being studied primarily because of its intrinsic intellectual interest – the Major governments' approach to higher education ensured that this purely instrumental or economistic attitude towards studying for a degree would become even more pronounced.

Implicit also in this perspective was the expectation that once students had to take out loans in order to finance their studies, they would become more discerning consumers, seeking 'value for money', which would in turn compel universities to raise standards in order to attract 'customers'. Universities were not to be exempt from the process of 'marketisation' being imposed on the rest of the public sector.

The fourth and final development concerning higher education under John Major's premiership was the burgeoning bureaucracy which was engendered by the professed objectives of gauging academic standards and measuring output. The former of these two objectives served to ensure that universities (just like other public services subjected to 'marketisation' and 'quality assurance' initiatives) and their staff increasingly became preoccupied with paperwork and form-filling, while countless hours which could actually have been spent teaching were spent in meetings or on committees which merely talked about teaching, and 'quality assurance'.

Furthermore, just as schools were subject to periodic inspections by members of appropriate quangos to ensure that standards were being maintained (or improved), so too were universities subjected to Teaching Quality Assessments (TQAs), the lengthy and elaborate preparation for which often detracted from teaching in the first place. Yet some of these TQAs seemed less concerned with actual teaching in the lecture theatre or seminar room than with ensuring that appropriate administrative and bureaucratic procedures were adhered to by university staff.

Meanwhile, in order to gauge academic output and productivity, the Major governments, via their higher education quangos (such as HEFCE, the Higher Education Funding Council for England), decided to measure research and publications, rather than numbers of students taught or the proportion of students getting upper seconds and firsts. A Stalinist culture subsequently became established in higher education, whereby academics were (and remain) expected to produce ever more books and articles in readiness for the periodic Research Assessment Exercise (RAE), to which funding is partly linked.

For too many academics, meeting the targets and deadlines of the RAE has become an obsession, with serious repercussions for students (and the quality of teaching), and also for those academics who are old-fashioned enough to believe that the primary function of a university is to teach and impart knowledge to undergraduates. Indeed, some academic staff now try to avoid teaching students altogether, insisting instead that they are 'actively engaged in research'. One marvellous irony of this 'publish or perish' culture is that while the Major premiership witnessed a proliferation of academic books and articles (and a plethora of new journals to accommodate these articles), cutbacks in education funding meant that university libraries could not afford to stock more than a proportion of these publications.

END OF TERM REPORT: 'A DISAPPOINTING PERFORMANCE; COULD HAVE DONE MUCH BETTER'

Right from the outset of his premiership, John Major decreed that education was one of his top priorities. A number of sympathetic commentators have suggested that Major's professed concern about education in Britain was derived in large part from 'his own experience of leaving school with no qualifications and finding himself on the wrong side of the education tracks' (Hogg and Hill 1995: 89). Consequently, Major's apparent prioritisation of education was 'spurred by his own experience of leaving school with few O-levels and having to struggle through several years of arduous work ... earning his banking qualifications' (Seldon, 1997: 185).

Yet as in so many other areas, Major's warm words were belied by actions, coupled with constant ministerial attacks on the teaching profession. Major once claimed that he wanted to see the professional status of teaching increased, and good teachers rewarded, yet his governments constantly denigrated teachers (and the so-called 'education establishment'), and consistently focused on the need to 'weed out' and sack 'bad' teachers, rather than praising and rewarding 'good' teachers (although to be fair to Major, the professed desire to reward 'good' teachers encountered opposition from a most unlikely alliance, namely the teaching unions – who saw such a move as divisive – and the Treasury, which was primarily concerned to constrain public expenditure, and thus hostile to making additional funds available to boost the salaries of 'good' teachers).

At the same time, the constant denigration of teachers, coupled with both curbs on salaries (deriving from the Major governments' determination to hold down public sector pay in order to control public expenditure generally) and ever-increasing administrative work-loads, yielded a 'double whammy' for the Major governments, namely a record number of older, experienced teachers seeking earlier retirement, coupled with shortages of graduates entering the profession.

One manifestation of the twin problems of teacher 'exit' and 'entry' *vis-à-vis* the profession was that the Major governments presided over an increase in class-sizes, with the average size of secondary-school classes increasing from 20 pupils in 1990–91 to 22 in 1995–96. During the same period, the proportion of secondary-school classes with more than 30 pupils rose from 6.3 per cent to 8.5 per cent, while the corresponding figures in secondary schools were 25.5 per cent in 1990–91 and 31.7 per cent in 1995–96. Meanwhile, the proportion of secondary schools with class sizes of 21–30 pupils increased from 62.0 per cent to 67.7 per cent between 1990–91 and 1995–96 (*Social Trends 27,* 1997: 58). Furthermore, according to OECD statistics, Britain's class-sizes were the highest in Europe, with the exception of Ireland, and were increasing precisely as European class-sizes were being reduced (*The Guardian*, 8 May 1996).

Meanwhile, although the Major premiership did yield an increase in expenditure (in real terms) on education, from 4.8 per cent of GDP in 1990–91 to 5.2 per cent in 1994–95, this was less than it had been back in 1980–81, when education expenditure represented 5.5 per cent of GDP. Furthermore, the 1994–95 figure for education expenditure (5.2 per cent of GDP) was exactly what it had been back in 1970–71! (*Social Trends 27,* 1997: 69).

These figures are imbued with even greater resonance when placed in an international context, for OECD figures reveal that, in 1992,

France spent 5.9 per cent of GDP on education, whilst Finland spent 7.9 per cent (*The Guardian*, 8 May 1996).

Britain's universities, meanwhile, were also beset by funding crises during John Major's premiership. Although the expansion of higher education which was pursued during the first half of the 1990s was accompanied by some increase in government funding, the additional sums did not match the increased number of students attending university. In other words, the government's headline figures belied the fact that less money was subsequently being spent per undergraduate . Furthermore, the annual funding for higher education assumed yearly 'efficiency savings', however unrealistic or unfeasible these might prove to be in practice.

However, the Major government was eventually compelled to halt the expansion of higher education, pending an inquiry chaired by Sir Ron Dearing, into the future funding and functions of higher education. In the meantime, from 1995 onwards, universities were subjected to actual cuts in funding, it being envisaged that the higher education budget of £3438 million in 1996–97 would be reduced to £3336 million in 1997–98 (*The Guardian*, 29 November 1995).

A further damning indictment of education policies during the Major premiership was provided by a report published in October 1996, by the Swiss-based international Institute for Management Development. This report revealed that in a world league table (league tables being an innovation that Major and his ministers were usually so keen on), Britain had slipped from 35th to 42nd overall (out of 48 countries). With regard to government expenditure on education, Britain ranked 17th, while the country was placed 23rd for teacher–pupil ratios (Institute for Management Development, 1996).

By the end of his premiership, John Major wanted to see opted-out schools given more power to select their pupils on the basis of ability or aptitude. The Major governments' education policy seemed to have gone virtually full circle, from the advocacy of parental choice, whereby parents chose a school for their children, to a system in which 'opt-out' schools would increasingly be permitted to choose their pupils. It was deeply ironic that John Major seemed so determined to recreate and return to the type of pre-comprehensive education system which had apparently 'failed' him during his adolescence.

9 Rolling Back the (Welfare) State: the Major Governments and Social Security Reform

Michael Hill

INTRODUCTION

There are two alternative ways of interpreting the Major governments' social security policies. One is to see them as very much a continuation of the Thatcher governments' struggle merely to contain social security expenditure, the growth of which had derailed Margaret Thatcher's attempts at cutting public expenditure. As Peter Lilley, Major's Secretary of State for Social Security from April 1992 until the government fell, put it:

> the DSS budget is huge, has grown rapidly and is set to continue outstripping national income in future. . . . It means that to finance social security, every working person now pays, on average, over thirteen pounds every working day. (Lilley, 1993)

By the time Major came to power, social security expenditure amounted to £70.3 bn per annum (1990–1 figures at 1996 prices from Public Expenditure Statistics, March 1997). When he left power it was £95.1 bn (ibid. 1996–7 estimate, using the same price base).

The other way of interpreting the social security policy of the Major governments is to note the speeches of the Secretary of State for Social Security, Peter Lilley, one of the most outspoken right-wingers in the Cabinet, and conclude that the Major governments were engaged in an ideological crusade to cut social security expenditure. For example, Peter Lilley told the Social Market Foundation:

> We have seized the initiative in social security. It used to be a no go area to Conservative reformers. Now Labour are on the defensive. Since we opened up the debate on social security reform

commentators across the political spectrum have come to recognise that the key issue is affordability. (Lilley, 1995)

Any realistic interpretation of the policies adopted needs to take
account of both explanations. The struggle to contain expenditure
on social security continued throughout the period of John Major's premiership (and continues with the Labour government led
by Tony Blair). On this issue there would not seem to be much
separating ideologically Major and his last Chancellor, Kenneth
Clarke from Blair and his Chancellor, Gordon Brown.

Yet this clearly renders it convenient to place in charge of social
security strategy someone who is prepared to transform necessity
into a crusade. As Lilley's comment suggests, all too often in the
past, the 'expenditure constraint' strategy has been derailed by
Secretaries of State from spending departments who wanted to make
their mark politically by spending more. Interestingly, however, even
Lilley was not as 'hawkish' as some of his Treasury colleagues wanted
(according to a leaked memo he told the Chief Secretary to the
Treasury that 'your proposed settlement on running costs fills me
with despair' (*The Guardian*, 8 February 1996).

RESTRAINING SOCIAL SECURITY EXPENDITURE

Major and Lilley inherited a social security system which Margaret
Thatcher had made extensive efforts to transform. Targeting had
been the dominant motif for her policies. The Thatcher governments took some crucial steps away from social insurance. In 1983
earnings-related short-term benefits were abolished and the main
onus for support during sickness for the employed was shifted on
to employers. Under legislation passed in 1986 the earnings-related
part of the pension system (SERPS) was weakened and the means-
testing system was restructured to enable it to function as a more
universal support scheme. In addition, changes to the arrangements
for benefit-uprating during the 1980s had the effect of reducing
the value of insurance benefits. Yet, as has been shown, social security expenditure had grown rapidly. That growth may be attributed to a combination of:

(1) Factors outside government influence – above all the growth
    in the numbers of the elderly.
(2) Factors which (depending upon the way one wishes to inter-

pret the economic policies of the 1980s) might be said to be a combination of consequences of inevitable economic changes coupled with deliberately chosen outcomes, namely the growth of unemployment, part-time employment and low-paid work (manifestations of the much-vaunted 'labour market flexibility').

(3) Factors which were very definitely a product of deliberate policy choice – housing policies which sharply increased the burdens on those aspects of social security concerned with support for rents and mortgages, and local-government taxation increases which increased the demand for rebates.

The policies of the Major governments can then be seen in terms of their reactions to these three factors. As far as the demographic trend was concerned, by the time Major came to power, the recent steep rise in the numbers of the elderly had levelled off, the percentage of the United Kingdom population aged over 65 having stabilised at about 16 per cent, after a rise from about 13 per cent in 1971 and 15 per cent in 1981. However, the size of the pension bill was still increasing relentlessly. The newest pensioners – whose working lives had been mostly after the social security reforms of the 1940s, who had enjoyed high levels of labour market participation and many of whom had entitlements under the SERPS scheme introduced in 1976 – tended to have superior rights to those who were at the end of their lives. The Thatcher government had curbed pension increases by linking them to increases in prices, rather than earnings (an approach inherited from the previous Labour government).

Hence Major was in a position whereby he and his Cabinet colleagues could do little more to curb the growth of the pension bill, unless his government was prepared to countenance a radical attack upon a group whose claims find widespread popular support. It is interesting to note that during the 1997 election campaign, Major seemed to be visibly wounded by a Labour allegation that he was planning to pursue significant cuts if re-elected.

If, however, further cuts in existing pension provision was 'no go' territory for the Major governments up until 1997, then his ideological 'hawk' Peter Lilley was left with two options. One was to try to prepare the ground for privatization of pensions in the future. The other was to try to pick up the pieces from an aspect of privatisation which had run into trouble, the efforts under the 1986 Social Security Act to encourage the selling of private pensions. We will return to these themes shortly.

The impact upon public expenditure of persistent high unemployment, and other forms of economic disadvantage, had an important effect upon the social security policies of the Major governments. There are three integrated themes here. The most straightforward, and politically least problematic of these, was the exploration of new ways to reduce public support for the unemployed, both by cutting benefits to claimants and by reducing the numbers of claimants. The latter theme was particularly beneficial politically, since Thatcher had redefined the British unemployment rate as not the percentage of the potential workforce out of work but as the percentage out of work *and claiming benefit*. Hence one of the key measures of Major's premiership – to be described below – was the replacement of unemployment benefit by the job-seekers' allowance.

A little more difficult for the Major governments was the fact that one of the consequences of high unemployment is rising numbers of people on sickness and disability benefits. The connection between rising unemployment and rising claims for benefits for people in poor health has been observed both in Britain in earlier eras and in many other countries (Kohli *et al.*, 1991). Any explanation of the connection needs to take into account both the consequences of unemployment for ill-health and the difficulties people with disabilities have in getting work at a time of high unemployment.

Furthermore, questions need to be asked about the extent to which the way benefit systems work encourage the connection. In Britain during the early 1990s, many of those who were both unemployed and in poor health were encouraged to move on to other benefits, most notably sickness or disability benefits. The harsher rules and lower rates of benefit which applied to the unemployed by comparison with the sick therefore meant that advisers would always encourage sickness or disability claims wherever there seemed to be a choice. For the government, this helped to curb the official statistics for those registered as unemployed and seeking work.

Furthermore, an interesting comparative study of the rise of early retirement has suggested that where other countries (France, for example) had developed early pension schemes, the British had used invalidity benefit as a kind of surrogate early retirement benefit (Kohli op. cit., 1991). When, therefore, Peter Lilley's speeches began referring to the need to attack rights to invalidity benefits, this author was inclined to think that Lilley would get into political difficulties. The discussion of the introduction of incapacity benefit below will show that I was wrong.

The third issue was the growth of low-paid and part-time employment. The problem about this growth was that Britain has a number of benefits designed to subsidise low wages – notably family credit and housing benefit. The government could not readily attack these benefits without at the same time acknowledging that there were problems about an economic strategy which encouraged these more casual forms of work, offering neither adequate legal protection against exploitation nor a statutory minimum wage. Furthermore, the Major governments' efforts to shift people out of unemployment often entailed shifting them into very poorly remunerated work, whereupon they would still be 'reliant' upon various social security benefits, such as Family Credit and/or Housing Benefit.

Meanwhile, back in the early 1980s, the Thatcher governments thought they spied another good target for social security expenditure cuts, namely the universal Child Benefit scheme. Later, however, they had come to see Child Benefit as another source of support for their efforts to get family members into low-paid employment. Regular upratings of Child Benefit occurred. The idea of developing a means-tested alternative – along antipodean lines – clearly got some consideration, but this would have exacerbated the problems associated with the 'poverty trap', whereby the withdrawal of means-tested benefits as incomes rise operates as a severe disincentive to work harder or find better-paid employment.

There was, however, one target which particularly appealed to Thatcherite Conservatives and seemed to offer prospects of benefit cuts, namely welfare support for single-parent families. This strategy had two dimensions to it. One, developed modestly by the Major governments, involved increasing incentives for single parents to seek paid employment. The other – enshrined in a policy initiative advanced so radically and rapidly that it almost became Major's equivalent of the 'poll tax' fiasco – was to seek increased contributions from the 'absent fathers' of children in single-parent families. This was the Child Support Act, on which there will be much more to say later.

Lastly, in this general account of the quest for social security savings, something more needs to be said about the most evident of the Thatcherite 'own-goals', namely housing policy. This had three aspects. One was the shift of public housing subsidy from 'bricks and mortar subsidy' to individual subsidy, which meant that many of the savings on the public housing expenditure account turned up as new elements in the social security housing benefit account

(Hills and Mullings, 1990). The second was the general strategy to push rents for houses – both public and private – up to market levels. This was largely sustained, initially at least, by the capacity of the Housing Benefit scheme to 'cover' increased rents for tenants on low incomes. The third was the encouragement of owner occupation – as manifested both in the sale of local authority houses, and in the dramatic mortgage-lending boom of the late 1980s. These two measures had the effect of increasing the numbers of owner-occupiers in insecure jobs. If they then became unemployed, a large proportion of their housing costs (mortgage interest) was underwritten by the social security Income Support scheme.

The Major governments dealt with these phenomena by a complex battery of measures which sought to push housing costs more heavily upon benefit recipients. The measures adopted were complex, and were often only manifest in their implementation. Hence the government was able to exploit complexity to avoid political attack.

This section has thus suggested that the social security policies of the Major governments were characterised by an elaborate quest for ways to control expenditure, rather than by either a shift away from the main thrust of Thatcher's policies or a dramatic leap in a new and much more explicitly right-wing direction. The next sections look at the key interventions in more detail. This will be done, not in the order in which they have been introduced above, but in order of their salience to the Major governments' social security policies.

BENEFITS FOR THE UNEMPLOYED

The Thatcher governments had substantially weakened the system of benefits designed to protect the unemployed, via such measures as making welfare provision for under-18s conditional upon undergoing training, and sharply reducing the help available to other young unemployed people. Penalties for refusing to undergo training and for leaving jobs (becoming 'voluntarily unemployed') were made much more severe.

In 1995, unemployment benefit was renamed the 'job-seekers' allowance', to emphasise the expectations which the government had of the unemployed. At the same time, this new 'benefit' was to be means-tested for all recipients after the first six months. As the name suggests, in order to qualify for this benefit, a person has to make a clear undertaking, signing a 'job-seekers' agreement', with regard to the steps s/he will take to find work. Contributory benefits for unemployed people had always been limited by strict conditions pertaining to previous contributions and current eligibility (for example, entitlement to benefit is denied if there is evidence that unemployment is somehow 'self-inflicted', such as having been sacked for misconduct or poor time-keeping).

With the introduction of the job-seekers' allowance, entitlement was reduced to six months (whereas Unemployment Benefit had been payable for twelve months). After six months, or if the previous contributions and other tests do not bestow eligibility, job-seekers' allowance is means-tested (its rules being broadly those applying to Income Support).

INCAPACITY BENEFIT

In 1995, under the Social Security (Incapacity for Work) Act 1994, the Major government replaced long-termed invalidity benefit with incapacity benefit. The implication of this was that whereas previously claimants had to prove that they were unfit for any work which was available and which they would be capable of performing, they now had to prove that they were unfit to do any work. There was established what the government described as an 'objective' test carried out by a doctor, employed by the Benefits Agency, which individuals had to pass to obtain incapacity benefit.

In justifying this change Peter Lilley claimed that:

> The number of people receiving Invalidity Benefit has doubled in the last ten years although the nation's health has been improving. Our Incapacity for Work Act will introduce a more objective medical test of incapacity for work. (Lilley, in a lecture to the Social Market Foundation, London, 1995)

Lilley's use of the word 'objective' is questionable, since it is not self-evident that there is an objective medical test of incapacity for work which is independent of any real work context. The actual consequence of the message was to force a group of people off a relatively generous insurance-based benefit on to the lower and means-tested job-seekers' allowance. A group of ageing workers were subjected to demands that they should seek work, regardless of whether or not they had any realistic prospects of getting any. But at least the Exchequer made a saving!

SINGLE-PARENT FAMILIES AND CHILD SUPPORT

The British treatment of single parents has been relatively generous, at least by comparison with other countries (Bradshaw *et al.*, 1993). The main means-tested benefit, Income Support, has been available to single parents, while unmarried/separated/divorced mothers have not been required to become labour-market participants until their youngest child reaches 16 years of age. Absent fathers have been expected to make contributions, but these have often proved difficult to secure because of the extent to which the fathers themselves are often on low incomes, and/or have commitments to new families.

Charles Murray's tirade against single-person households in the United States (1984) was taken up in Britain during the late 1980s and into the 1990s. Conservative politicians especially began to attribute the growth in single-parenthood to the availability of benefits and local authority housing (Dorey, 1998). This stimulated a political debate about (a) work opportunities for single parents and (b) contributions from absent parents.

Attention to the first issue is difficult at a time of high unemployment, but some efforts were made to increase work-incentives for single parents who were eligible for Family Credit, with a 'disregard' of £40 per week for child care costs being introduced in 1994 (and later increased to £60).

At the same time, the Major government decided to tackle the issue of contributions from absent parents by means of a comprehensive, formula-driven, scheme to replace both the assessments made as part of the administration of the existing means-tested benefits (via what used to be the 'Liable Relatives' section located in many Department of Social Security Offices), and the assessments made by the courts in determining maintenance following the breakdown of a relationship. To this end, the Major government enacted the Child Support Act in 1991, setting up the Child Support Agency (CSA) – which actually commenced its operations in 1993 – to administer it. However, the CSA ran into considerable difficulties, primarily because of the haste with which the government expected it to introduce the scheme and then deliver results (namely obtaining maintenance payments from 'absent fathers' which would thereby reduce the amount of Income Support having to be paid to single parents). Yet there were also problems about some of the rules embodied in the Act.

In fact, there were four main objections to the new legislation. Firstly, it was retrospective, so that existing maintenance agreements, including court settlements made in the past, were overturned (a particular problem here is the overturning of agreements in which the absent parent has relinquished an interest in a house in return for a lower maintenance expectation).

Secondly, where the absent parent has obligations to a second family these are given relatively low weight in the calculations.

Thirdly, the parent 'with care' has nothing to gain from collaborating with the CSA if she (over 90 per cent of single parents are women) is on Income Support, because all maintenance payments obtained from the 'absent father' are automatically deducted from their social security payments, in order to reimburse the Treasury.

Fourthly, the operation of a rigid formula is unfair when the absent parent has regular contact with their child(ren), but thereby incurs extra costs (such as travelling expenses) which might not be acknowledged in the rigid formula deployed by the CSA to assess child-support payments.

The enforcement of the Child Support Act was not helped by the income targets imposed on the Agency, which effectively meant that it either started with the easier cases first, such as families on Income Support, or that it targeted those 'absent fathers' with stable and accessible incomes, and from whom more money could be demanded (hence the subsequent 'white-collar' backlash which the government experienced).

Consequently, in 1995, the Major government amended its Child Support legislation, thereby bowing to a vociferous middle-class, male lobby which had coalesced in response to the iniquities of the Child Support Act. Major and his ministers did not change the basic principles of the Act, but did give the Agency some limited discretion and scope to modify its assessments, so that, for example, account could be taken of instances where the 'absent father' had signed over his share of the matrimonial home to his former wife as part of the divorce settlement.

HOUSING BENEFIT AND SUPPORT FOR OWNER-OCCUPIERS ON INCOME SUPPORT

There has long been an anomaly in the British system of means-tested benefits to the extent that while housing benefit may meet all or part of the housing costs of low-income rent-payers whether or not they are in work, the housing costs of owner-occupiers may only be met if they are out of work and in receipt of the main means-tested benefits – means-tested job seekers' allowance or income support. Under these circumstances, at least part of the 'mortgage interest' may be paid via Income Support.

Since the main thrust of Conservative housing policy had been to encourage owner-occupation – both through the sale of council houses and through measures to deregulate the mortgage market and encourage lending even to relatively 'high-risk' borrowers – the continuing incidence of high unemployment engendered a situation in which there were likely to be many owner-occupiers on these means-tested benefits. For such individuals a shift out of unemployment into work could involve considerable financial sacrifices since all housing cost support would be lost. There was a kind of 'trap' here, tending to operate as a disincentive to acceptance of work, particularly if it was relatively poorly paid. The combination of the slump in the housing market in the early 1990s – creating a situation of negative equity for many low-income recent house-buyers – with high unemployment helped to put this issue on the government's agenda.

Not surprisingly, perhaps, the Major government did not respond to this problem by extending housing benefit to owner-occupiers. Rather, it sought to limit the housing cost support available to owner-occupiers who became unemployed. After October 1995, owner-occupier recipients of job-seekers' allowance and Income Support (under 60 years of age) were not entitled to financial help with mortgage interest payments during the first eight weeks of their claim, and thereafter, were only eligible for half of those payments until they had been on benefit for six months. Even more stringent rules were applied for mortgages taken out after the enactment of this measure, the implication being that borrowers should take out 'mortgage protection insurance' to cover the risk of unemployment.

Fiscal austerity thus led the Major government to adopt a hard line against what had been seen as a significant element among the Conservative electorate, namely low-income owner-occupiers. Meanwhile, low-income tenants did not escape the government's search for social security savings either. At the time John Major became prime minister, nearly all claimants of housing benefit without 'non-dependent adults' in their households could expect to have their full housing costs taken into account. However, during Major's premiership, a sequence of complicated and obscure adjustments to housing benefit radically changed the situation for private tenants. These have primarily involved shifts from the use of actual rent-payments in benefit calculations to general average rents as determined by Rent Officers. There is a particularly restrictive version of this rule which is applied to childless single persons under 25, basing their rent 'norm' on single-room rents in houses with shared kitchens and bathrooms. There were also changes to the rules relating to 'non-dependant adult contributions', these seeking to pass a greater proportion of the rent burden on to these 'non-dependent adults' (although there was no guarantee that they would actually contribute the amount deducted from the claimant's benefit).

REVIEW OF PENSIONS AND EXPANSION OF PRIVATE PENSION SCHEMES

When Margaret Thatcher's government enacted the 1986 Social Security Act, it would dearly have liked to have swept away all of the National Insurance pensions system. In particular, it would have liked to have replaced Barbara Castle's 'state earnings related pensions scheme' (SERPS), which offered employees the possibility of joining a state scheme to supplement their flat-rate state pension, rather than a private one. The Conservatives stepped back from that option because they realised that, in a situation in which pension finance depends upon the 'pay as you go' principle (that is that current pension payments are paid for out of current government social insurance income), any measure to shift contributors out of the state scheme would reduce the money available to enable the government to meet current pension obligations.

The government therefore opted instead for a more limited approach, one which reduced the benefits available under the 'Castle scheme', and gave further encouragement to the private pensions industry through tax relief and a National Insurance contribution rebate. The government also abolished the requirement that any approved private scheme should be (potentially) at least as good as SERPS. These measures unleashed a massive sales campaign by the private pensions industry, with salespeople exploiting long-run fears about the growth of the elderly population, coupled with suggestions that the state could not be trusted to deliver in the long run. Not only were individuals encouraged to leave SERPS for worse schemes, but in some – subsequently highly publicised cases – public employees, such as teachers and nurses, were lured out of their very generous government-protected occupational schemes into inferior private insurance schemes.

This particular Thatcherite 'balloon' was burst for the Major government in a rather dramatic way. When the publishing tycoon Robert Maxwell drowned, it was discovered that he had been sustaining his extravagant lifestyle by raiding the pension funds set aside for his employees. The government set up a committee, the Goode Committee, to investigate the regulation of the private pensions industry. That committee recommended strengthening the regulatory and appeal mechanisms for the private pensions industry, although it stopped short of arguing for a system of government guarantees for private pensions (Goode Committee, 1993).

The Goode Committee's recommendations were enacted in the Pension Act 1995. However, they neither satisfied those who wanted to see a return to the original SERPS principles, nor those who wanted to see the government grasp the privatisation nettle more firmly. Clearly the Secretary of State for Social Security was in the latter camp, and thus his search for ways to develop a combined public/private pensions pillar continued.

One other policy theme, relating to elderly people, which should perhaps be briefly mentioned here is that Major inherited legislation from the Thatcher governments designed to shift the subsidy of private institutional care off the social security budget on to the local authority social services budget. This was a complex matter, which – given the backwash from the poll-tax affair – required slow implementation during the period of Major's premiership. Social-security savings were achieved – partly at the expense of the local-government budget, and partly at the expense of old people themselves (and their carers). There remained, however, a range of complex boundary issues between social care and social security, although these are beyond the brief of this chapter.

MARKET TESTING AND NEW RULES FOR DECISION-MAKING

Other contributions to this volume have dealt with administrative changes, motivated both by 'New Public Management' (NPM) ideologies but also by the search for cost savings. With specific regard to social security, though, the emphasis has primarily been on efforts to achieve savings in benefit costs, and thereby curbing the hitherto relentless growth of the welfare budget. However, the related quest for savings in the relatively low administrative costs of British social security expenditure should not be disregarded. The crucial administrative changes to the benefit-delivery system – the shift of all services into Agencies (the Benefits Agency, Contributions Agency, Child Support Agency, etc.) – occurred before Major's succession to power.

However, the NPM movement did not then leave the Major administrations alone. They too were subjected to a 'market testing' process in which they have had to open services to private tenders. Although these had a marginal effect upon the mainstream services, they did pose a threat to the staff, while raising the possibility that the day would come when the banks and building societies collected contributions and administered benefit payments.

More serious for the operation of the benefits system has been the imposition upon the Agencies of draconian targets for reductions in staffing (often euphemistically termed 'efficency savings' in the New Right's discourse). These had a variety of consequences, not least of which is that the social security system has increasingly become one in which face-to-face contact between officials and 'customers' has diminished. One knock-on effect of this seems to have been a dramatic increase in error rates. Another may (though the author is reluctant to accept the Major governments' perspective on this) have been an increase in fraud. A paradoxical consequence of the government's obsession with the latter has been increased expenditure on specialist fraud-investigation staff at a time when levels of routine investigation are going down. People have also been urged – through an expensive advertising campaign – to report their neighbours if they suspect them of dishonestly obtaining welfare benefits. Certainly, it seemed that during Major's premiership, as much as during Thatcher's, a speech at the Conservatives' annual conference denouncing social security fraud and pledging a new drive to tackle the alleged problem was guaranteed to receive warm applause and plaudits from the delegates.

Among the last acts of Peter Lilley's regime at the Department of Social Security was an initiative to streamline benefit administration. A Green Paper was published drawing attention to inconsistencies in the way different administrative issues were handled for different benefits – the existence of very formal adjudication procedures for some issues but not for others, and a plethora of different appeal procedures. However, the Major government fell before any action could be taken – apart from some minor amendments to regulations limiting appeal rights somewhat.

CONCLUSION

This chapter has charted the various ways in which the Major governments continued to try to restrain the growth of social security costs – running hard against the movement of the cost-increase escalator. In so doing, Major and his ministers were consolidating and continuing the principles and policies which characterised the Thatcher governments *vis-à-vis* social security and the welfare state. Indeed, with the distinctly Thatcherite Peter Lilley at the Department of Social Security from 10 April 1992 (the day after Major was re-elected and the day he reshuffled his Cabinet) onwards, and another staunch Thatcherite, Michael Portillo, in the role of Chief Secretary to the Treasury during the middle years of Major's premiership, it is hardly surprising that social security remained a prime target for curbs and cutbacks while John Major was prime minister. In the sphere of social security policy, therefore, as in so many others, the Major premiership witnessed the continued pursuit of a broadly Thatcherite agenda and programme, even though Major himself tended to deploy slightly less strident language than his predecessor.

Acknowledgement
I am very grateful to Geoff Fimister for reading this chapter, for drawing my attention to press cuttings and for valued discussions over several years about the 'political functions of complexity'.

10 No Return to 'Beer and Sandwiches': Industrial Relations and Employment Policies under John Major

Peter Dorey

MAJOR'S INHERITANCE

When John Major became prime minister in November 1990, the industrial relations scene was markedly different to that which had existed a decade earlier, while the character of the labour market had also experienced profound changes during the 1980s.

With regard to industrial relations, the trade unions had been seriously weakened by the five substantive pieces of legislation passed by the Thatcher governments (Dorey 1993: 1995b), namely the Employment Acts of 1980, 1982, 1988 and 1990, along with the Trade Union Act of 1984. The combined effect of these Acts had been: to make secret ballots compulsory prior to strike action, and for the election of senior trade union officials and leaders; to require ballots of union members to confirm their support for the operation of a 'political fund'; to outlaw the closed shop; to narrow the definition of a 'trade dispute'; to place strict curbs on 'secondary' or 'sympathy' action by trade unions; to permit the 'selective dismissal' by employers of workers engaging in unofficial strikes; to provide legal protection for workers refusing to participate in strike action (even when the strike had been endorsed by a secret ballot); and to expose trade unions to liability for damages in cases of unofficial industrial action, unless the trade union had expressly disassociated itself from such action.

This legislation had been presented by the Thatcher governments as a means of 'handing the unions back to their members', by making trade union leaders accountable to those in the workplace, and thus of instilling democracy into Britain's trade unions. At the same time, legal protection was afforded to employees who did not wish to belong to a trade union, or who did not wish to take part in industrial action. These measures were presented via a discourse of workers' 'rights', although it was the 'rights' of employees *vis-à-vis* their trade unions and union leaders that the Thatcher governments were concerned about, not the 'rights' of these employees against employers. On the contrary, the ultimate purpose of the Thatcher governments' industrial relations reforms was not the empowerment of workers at all, but their subjugation and submissiveness *vis-à-vis* their employers, for while Conservative ministers waxed lyrical about restoring rights to ordinary trade union members, they also invoked, throughout the 1980s, the mantra of 'management's right to manage'. Managerial authority in the workplace was to be inviolate, and against this, the proclaimed 'rights' of ordinary trade union members and employees counted for nought. The Thatcher governments had also presided over the marked decline of Britain's manufacturing industry, to the extent that while this sector of the economy had employed over 7 million people in 1979, its employment had fallen to less than 5 million by 1990.

This change in the structure of the economy and the concomitant character of the labour market also yielded a marked decline in trade union membership during the 1980s. For example, whereas the Transport & General Workers Union had enjoyed a membership of almost 2.1 million in 1979, this had fallen to less than 1.3 million by 1989. Similarly, the same period witnessed a decline in the Amalgamated Engineering Union's membership from just over 1.2 million to less than 750 000. Meanwhile, membership of the National Union of Railwaymen fell from 180 000 to 103 000, while during the same period, the General, Municipal & Boilermakers' Union experienced a drop in its membership from 967 000 to 823 000.

This decline in trade union membership was not just a consequence of the high level of unemployment which the Thatcher governments presided over, but was also due to the fact that increasing numbers of those still in work declined to join (or remain a member of) a trade union, either because they did not believe the unions to be effective, or because a growing number of emboldened employers refused to 'recognise' or allow trade unions in their workplace or company (for example, the 1990 Workplace Industrial Relations Survey discovered that whereas in 1980, 64 per cent of all workplace establishments in Britain 'recognised' trade unions, 'only' 53 per cent did so in 1990, with the private manufacturing sector witnessing the largest decline, from 65 per cent in 1980 to 44 per cent in 1990 (Millward *et al.*, 1992: 71).

This trend ensured that the decline in trade-union membership overall was accompanied by an even more significant reduction in trade union density (i.e. the proportion of the workforce which belonged to a trade union). For example, whereas in 1979, 13 289 000 employees, out of a total labour force of 23 206 000, belonged to a trade union, yielding a density of 56.9 per cent, by 1990 there were only 8 192 000 trade unionists out of a total labour force of 22 703 000 workers, constituting a union density of 36 per cent.

Meanwhile, the decline of Britain's manufacturing industry was accompanied by an expansion in service-sector employment, from nearly 13.3 million in 1979 to just under 15.2 million by 1990. Yet this sector of the economy was characterised by lower levels of trade union membership, particularly as many of the jobs in the service sector were filled by women and/or part-time workers, two 'categories' also traditionally less inclined to belong to a trade union.

Another notable trend pertaining to the character of employment, and *inter alia* trade-union membership, during the Thatcher years, was the increasing number of new enterprises, many of which were smaller than most more established firms. This, in turn, also had a negative impact on trade-union membership, for as Millward *et al.* (1992) discovered, union membership is invariably higher in larger and older, workplaces. For example, in 1990, trade-union density was only 19 per cent in private-sector workplaces employing less than 50 people, whereas in private-sector establishments with a workforce of 1000 or more, union density was 53 per cent. At the same time, trade-union density was 25 per cent in private-sector workplaces less than three years old, compared to 44 per cent in establishments which had existed for more than 20 years (ibid.: 64).

Finally, it should be recognised that these trends corresponded to one other significant trend in industrial relations during the 1980s, namely a contraction of collective bargaining, to the extent that whereas 71 per cent of all employees in Britain had been covered by collective bargaining in 1984, this figure had fallen to 54 per cent just six years later (ibid.: 94).

The cumulative effect of these changes ensured that when John Major became Conservative party leader and Prime Minister in 1990, Britain's trade unions had been greatly weakened by a lethal cocktail of government legislation, the decline of manufacturing industry and the rise of a much less unionised tertiary and service sector (often characterised by predominantly female and/or part-time employment), a decline in trade-union recognition by employers, and a contraction of collective bargaining and national pay agreements, the latter increasingly being replaced by individual or local-level (for example, 'cost centres', NHS Trusts, etc.) bargaining and pay awards.

In the context of such significant changes, John Major's elevation to the Conservative leadership immediately raised the question of whether his premiership would evince a more conciliatory and constructive approach to the trade unions and industrial relations, or whether the hostility of the Conservative governments towards the unions which had prevailed throughout the 1980s would be sustained during the 1990s.

EXPECTED RETURN TO ONE NATION

If John Major had genuinely desired the revival of the Conservative's 'one-nation' tradition after Margaret Thatcher's downfall, then it might have been expected that he and his ministerial colleagues would subsequently have pursued a rather more conciliatory and constructive approach towards the trade unions, coupled with a greater emphasis on the concept of partnership in industry. After all, these had been key objectives of previous 'one-nation' Tories, with many senior post-war Conservatives – Rab Butler, Ian Gilmour, Joseph Godber, Iain Macleod, Harold Macmillan, Walter Monckton, James Prior, Peter Walker, Harold Watkinson – passionately pursuing or urging such an approach.

Some commentators certainly anticipated that Major's election as Conservative party leader would herald a more consensual and incorporationist approach towards the trade unions, after eleven years of relentless governmental hostility and exclusion from economic policy-making. For example, Holliday was among those commentators who, in the early 1990s, speculated that 'some form of neo-corporatism might be reconstituted. . . . A gradual reconstitution of neo-corporatist arrangements remains a clear possibility' (Holliday 1993: 316), while during Major's first administration, this author also speculated that it is not inconceivable that the Conservative government under John Major might move in the direction of some aspects of corporatism, now that its arch foe, Mrs Thatcher, has departed.... The 1990s could yet prove to be a decade of revival for some form of corporatism in Britain. (Dorey, 1991: 27)

Yet such expectations proved unfounded, for Major's premiership was characterised by a continuation of the industrial relations policies and trade union reforms pursued during Margaret Thatcher's 11 years as Conservative prime minister, involving not only another tranche of 'employment' legislation, but also further initiatives intended to facilitate a 'more flexible' labour market. Major's period as prime minister also witnessed the final abandonment of the last vestige of British corporatism, namely the abolition of the National Economic Development Council in 1992.

In spite of his self-professed 'one-nation' inclinations, Major did nothing to foster a new, closer relationship with the trade unions, nor did he seek to provide workers with greater employment protection or job security (the latter having been a key objective of Conservatives such as Monckton and Macleod during the 1950s). On the contrary, Major's premiership was characterised by increasing ministerial insistence that employment protection and job security were impossible in the new global economic order, and incompatible with the Conservative objective of establishing 'flexible labour markets' which would enable Britain to compete with the so-called 'tiger economies' of south-east Asia, and thereby attract the inward investment upon which employment was increasingly deemed to depend.

Indeed, some Ministers quite openly peddled the view that 'low pay was better than no pay', so that Conservative 'choice' for many in the labour market meant having to choose between employment paying poverty wages or remaining unemployed (the latter 'option' itself likely to yield considerable coercion to find work, as part of the drive against the 'dependency culture'). Major's language and tone might not have been as abrasive or antagonistic as Thatcher's when speaking about trade unions and industrial relations, but his overall attitude was remarkably similar. Actions certainly spoke louder than words in this sphere of policy.

TRADE UNION REFORM

Although Major's premiership was characterised by only one significant piece of trade union legislation, this reflected not a more
conciliatory approach to organised labour, but the fact that the
five main 'employment' and trade union laws passed by the Thatcher
governments had left little more to be achieved. With ballots having been introduced for trade union leadership elections and political funds, as well as prior to strike action, and the closed shop
outlawed, it seemed that little remained for Major and his ministers
to do by way of legislating against the trade unions. Indeed, Major's
first Employment Secretary, Michael Howard, had himself declared,
in January 1990, that – with the introduction of the 1990 Employment Act – the 'long process of industrial relations reform' had
reached its conclusion (HC Debs, 6th series, V.166: c.38). Yet 18
months later, Howard himself published a Green Paper presaging
yet more 'employment' legislation, this time declaring that: 'Important as the achievements of the 1980s have been, it would be
wrong to assume that the process of reform is completed and that
the progress which has been made is sufficient or permanent.' On
the contrary, it was now argued that: 'The government believe it is
necessary to consolidate and build on what had has been achieved
over the past twelve years.'

The justification offered for this new tranche of trade union legislation was the need to underpin the competitiveness of the British economy in lieu of the completion of the European Union's
Single European Market, scheduled for the end of 1992. As ever,
the weakening of the trade unions was presented as a means of
protecting or promoting jobs. There was an insistence that 'If our
unit wage costs increase faster than those of our competitors in
the markets of the world, the inevitable consequence will be lost
jobs and a lower standard of living' (Department of Employment,
1991: 6).

What resulted from these declarations was the 1993 Trade Union
Reform and Employment Rights Act (which itself maintained the
Thatcher tradition of a piece of trade union or 'employment' legislation being introduced immediately following a general election
victory, at which time a mandate from the electorate could – however spuriously – be cited by way of justification). The main provisions of the 1993 Trade Union and Employment Rights Act were
that

- All trade union ballots were to be postal, and conducted under the auspices of an independent scrutineer.
- Employers were to be provided with seven days' notice in lieu of strike action.
- Employees were required to give their employers written approval every three years *vis-à-vis* the automatic deduction from their wages or salaries of trade union membership 'dues'.
- Employers were to be entitled to offer 'financial inducements' to relinquish trade union membership.
- Wage Councils were to be abolished.
- Terms of reference of ACAS were to be amended, so that it is no longer concerned to promote or encourage collective bargaining.
- Users of public services were entitled to seek injunctions to prevent unlawful industrial action.

Although a few positive measures were also enshrined in the Trade Union Reform and Employment Rights Act, namely the right of employees to choose which trade union – if any – they wished to belong to, along with the introduction or entrenchment of rights relating to maternity leave, and protection for those employees victimised as a consequence of lodging complaints concerning health and safety matters, these were not enough to muffle the sound of ministers desperately scraping a virtually empty barrel. By this time, even employers' organisations such as the CBI and the Institute of Directors were deeming such legislation to be unwarranted and unwanted. Meanwhile, Michael Howard's successor at the Department of Employment, Gillian Shephard, declared that the Trade Union Reform and Employment Rights Act heralded the end of the Conservative Party's 'war' with the trade unions, constituting little more than a 'tidying up' exercise to round off the Government's programme of industrial relations legislation.

Yet the end of this 'war' was not followed by any new peace initiatives. No olive branches were proffered. Instead, Major and his ministerial colleagues continued to treat the trade unions with undisguised contempt, viewing them as an irrelevance in the brave new post-Thatcher world. If no further legislation was invoked after the Trade Union Reform and Employment Rights Act, it was not because the Major government wished to foster a more conciliatory and constructive relationship with the trade unions, but simply because for most of the subsequent period of Major's premiership, none was deemed necessary.

However, the last six months of Major's premiership did see the government mooting another batch of trade union reforms in the event of the Conservative party winning a fifth successive election victory (which by this time seemed extremely unlikely in view of Labour's large and long-standing lead in the opinion polls). The main target of the government's nine proposals, outlined in a Green Paper published by the Employment Secretary, Ian Lang, was industrial action in the public sector, for which it was suggested that legal immunity should be removed for strikes which exerted a 'disproportionate or excessive' effect (disproportionate defined in terms of four criteria: risks to life, health or safety; threats to national security; serious damage to property or the economy; significant disruption to everyday life). However, like the Thatcher governments before it, the Major government shied away from pursuing a complete ban on strikes in the public sector.

As well as favouring further curbs on industrial action by public-sector workers, the government's proposals included a recommendation that any strike should be supported by all of those eligible to vote (rather than a simple majority of those who actually did vote). Furthermore, it was suggested that the period of notice which trade unions were required to give employers of imminent strike action should be doubled, from seven to 14 days, while strikes already under way ought to be reaffirmed through subsequent ballots every three months (*The Daily Telegraph*, 2 November 1996).

However, these proposals merely served to highlight the relative paucity of trade union legislation during Major's premiership (apart from the 1993 Act, of course), and the extent to which earlier Acts had largely achieved Conservative objectives concerning trade unionism and industrial relations. On the other hand, legislation is certainly not the only means by which governments pursue their objectives, and thus it was that the Major governments sought to effect the continued marginalisation of trade unionism via other policy mechanisms and initiatives, as delineated below.

PAY DETERMINATION

When the Conservative party entered office in 1979, its policy concerning pay-determination had shifted decisively towards the restoration of free collective bargaining, thereby rejecting the incomes policies pursued by successive governments during the 1960s and

1970s, although strict cash – and hence pay – limits were applied to the public sector. However, by the time that John Major became Conservative leader and prime minister, ministers had grown confident enough to urge that, as far as possible, collective bargaining should be replaced by individual negotiations over terms and conditions of employment (Dorey, forthcoming).

Given that *collective* bargaining has always been a key function of the trade unions – their very *raison d'être*, perhaps – the desire to replace collective bargaining by individual bargaining between employer and employee can be seen as a means of rendering trade unions redundant, while simultaneously enhancing the individualist, anti-collectivist strand of Conservatism which Thatcher had vigorously espoused.

The shift in this direction had already been signalled during the latter half of the 1980 when the third (and final) Thatcher government decreed that employees' remuneration should 'reflect their own skills, efforts, capacities and circumstances' rather than being 'solely the outcome of some distant negotiation between employers and trade unions'. To achieve this objective, it was suggested that:

> many existing approaches to pay bargaining, beloved of trade unions and employers alike, will need to change. . . . In particular, 'the going rate', 'comparability', and 'cost of living increases', are all outmoded concepts – they take no account of differences in performance, ability to pay or difficulties of recruitment, retention or motivation. . . . National agreements . . . all too often give scant regard to differences in individual circumstances or performance. (Department of Employment, 1988: 18–24)

The momentum was sustained under John Major's premiership, with a White Paper entitled *People, Jobs and Opportunity* being published just two months before the Conservatives' April 1992 general election victory, in which it was argued that

> There is a new recognition of the role and importance of the individual employee. Traditional patterns of industrial relations, based on collective bargaining and collective agreements, seem increasingly inappropriate and are in decline. Many employers are replacing outdated personnel practices with new policies for human resource management which put the emphasis on developing the talents and capacities of each individual employee. Many are also looking to communicate directly with their employees

rather than through the medium of a trade union or formal works council. There is a growing trend to individually negotiated reward packages which reflect the individuals personal skills, experience, efforts and performance. (Department of Employment, 1992: 6)

This undermining of collective bargaining – entailing as it did the further marginalisation of the trade unions – was aided and abetted by the growth of local-level pay bargaining, which increasingly replaced national pay agreements. Local-level pay bargaining was facilitated by privatisation and, in what remained of the public sector, marketisation, whereby 'cost centres' and a degree of financial devolution encouraged pay bargaining at local level. For example, the privatisation of British Rail yielded a number of regional companies, along with the further fragmentation of the industry whereby different companies undertook specific functions (track maintenance and signalling, for example), which thereby ensured that pay awards in the rail industry were increasingly determined according to the section of the industry employees worked in, and the regional company they worked for.

The Major governments clearly envisaged that this would herald the demise of national pay awards in the railway industry, as rail workers focused on local or regional-level negotiations with their own particular company. Not only was this intended to replace collective bargaining by individual or local-level bargaining over terms and conditions of employment, it was also envisaged that the power of the trade unions – in this case, ASLEF and the NUR – would be weakened further, for there would be far less scope for national-level industrial action.

Meanwhile, in the health service, the plethora of NHS Trusts served to ensure that here too, pay determination was invariably conducted at local level, as nurses negotiated with their own particular NHS Trust, rather than the RCN negotiating with the Secretary of State for Health for a national pay deal covering all nurses. However, the autonomy of NHS Trusts to determine pay at local level was severely circumscribed by the Major governments' determination to control public expenditure, which thus entailed that strict cash limits were applied to public sector services. Furthermore, even though ministers frequently promised improved pay in return for increased productivity by public sector workers, such workers invariably found that however much harder they worked, the corresponding increase in pay never materialised.

Not surprisingly, therefore, the Major era witnessed the continued growth of the earnings gap between the public and private sectors. Major and his ministers wanted public-sector employees to emulate the ethos and values of the private sector, and adopt private sector practices, but effectively debarred them from enjoying earnings similar to their private-sector counterparts. Indeed, some ministers seemed to believe that those who chose a career in the public services should view the job-satisfaction they apparently derived from serving the public as a reward in itself, rather than expect reasonable remuneration. Furthermore, the Major governments were inclined to argue that in careers such as nursing, improved salaries were unnecessary, either because there was no problem with recruitment (the implication being that existing salaries were not deterring new entrants to the profession), or because someone who was only willing to enter the nursing profession if higher salaries were offered was obviously not motivated by nursing *per se* (*ergo*, better salaries would attract the 'wrong sort of person' to the profession). Needless to say, such arguments were never applied by Conservative ministers to private sector professions.

ABOLITION OF THE NATIONAL ECONOMIC DEVELOPMENT COUNCIL

A further indication of John Major's lack of 'one-nation' inclinations towards the trade unions was provided by the government's abolition of the National Economic Development Council (NEDC) following his general election victory in 1992. Yet in many respects, it was remarkable that the NEDC had survived 13 years of Conservative government, symbolising as it did a bygone corporatist era of tripartite economic policy-making involving ministers, trade-union leaders, and employers' representatives.

The NEDC had been steadily downgraded during the latter years of Thatcher's premiership, with its meetings becoming more infrequent and increasingly attended by junior ministers or even civil servants rather than cabinet ministers themselves, while shortly after the Conservatives' 1987 election victory, meetings of the NEDC had been reduced from one per month to one every three months. Meanwhile, Nigel Lawson, the Chancellor of the Exchequer from 1983 to 1989, had alleged that 'no useful purpose was being served by the National Economic Development Council . . . it should therefore be abolished' (Lawson, 1992: 713). Yet, remarkably, it was not until a couple of months after the Conservatives' 1992 election victory that its abolition was finally announced.

Meanwhile, other tripartite forums on which trade unions had traditionally enjoyed representation were also restructured or marginalised during John Major's period as prime minister (again maintaining a policy approach initiated during Margaret Thatcher's leadership). All along the corridors of power, the trade unions found doors being closed to them, or fewer seats provided at the table in committee rooms. For example, in 1992, of the 1136 directors of the Training and Enterprise Councils (which were relatively recent descendants of the Manpower Services Commission, on which trade unions had enjoyed equal representation with employers), only 82 (5 per cent) were trade unionists (McIlroy, 1995: 207).

Meanwhile, in March 1994, John Major refused to reappoint Gavin Laird, leader of the AEEU, to a third consecutive four-year term of office as a trade union representative on the governing board of the Bank of England (even though the convention had been established since 1946 – when the Bank was nationalised – that the trade unions would be entitled to representation on the Bank's governing body). Major insisted that Laird's place be filled by someone whose 'individual expertise' would be more useful to the Bank, a clear intimation of Major's preference for a businessman. Indeed, on a whole range of public bodies – including the plethora of quangos established during Major's premiership – businessmen (and occasionally, businesswomen) were readily awarded extensive membership, while trade unions were increasingly excluded, or granted only token representation.

ABOLITION OF WAGES COUNCILS

In accordance with the Thatcherite objective of ensuring that wage-determination took place in the context of market forces, and in accordance with such criteria as commercial viability, competitiveness, productivity, profitability, individual bargaining, etc., Major's premiership also witnessed the abolition of Wages Councils, via the aforementioned 1993 Trade Union Reform and Employment Rights Act.

Although Margaret Thatcher's government had instigated the attack on these wage-fixing bodies by introducing the 1986 Wages Act, this merely excluded employees under 21 years of age from entitlement to pay levels determined by wages councils; younger workers were explicitly expected to work for lower rates of pay, but presumably be grateful for the 'work experience' which their employers kindly provided them with instead.

It was not until the third year of Major's premiership, however, that ministers felt bold enough to abolish Britain's 26 Wages Councils altogether, linking such a move to the wider objective of creating a more deregulated and flexible labour market, one in which wages were determined solely by economic – as opposed to political or social – criteria.

The abolition of the Wages Councils, which had covered 2.5 million workers, also afforded Major and his ministers another opportunity to argue that by reducing such 'burdens' on employers, and removing such obstacles to market forces, new employment opportunities would present themselves to employees who would otherwise be 'priced out of work'. Again, too, ministers liked to argue that 'low pay was better than no pay'.

REJECTION OF THE EUROPEAN UNION'S 'SOCIAL CHAPTER'

Once it became clear that John Major intended to sustain the Thatcherite revolution *vis-à-vis* industrial relations, then opposition to the European Union's 'social chapter' became inevitable. The 'social chapter' had been part of the Maastricht Treaty, which formally established the European Union (as opposed to the European Community), and paved the way for closer European integration. Whereas previous initiatives had primarily been economic, most notably the 1986 Single European Act, seeking to achieve the Treaty of Rome's ultimate goal of establishing free trade between member states, the 'social chapter' sought to imbue the European 'project' with a social dimension, whereby some of the negative effects or consequences of 'the market' were tempered by measures intended to afford some protection for European workers, coupled with certain statutory rights in the workplace. Hence the incorporation into the Maastricht Treaty of a 'social chapter' which comprised no less than 47 items pertaining to the rights of employees.

For most of the European Union's member states, the 'social chapter' was perfectly in accordance with their notions of a 'social market economy', along with 'social partnership' between Capital and Labour, something which European Christian Democratic parties had consistently supported. Yet for many within John Major's Conservative party, the 'social chapter' was incompatible with the pursuit of a freer economy and deregulated labour market, either in Britain or in Europe. Whereas Britain's European partners viewed the 'social chapter' as a vital adjunct to the establishment of a single market and economic and monetary union, Major's governments (just like Thatcher administrations previously) saw it as an impediment to the economic objectives embodied in the Treaty of Rome and the Single European Act.

Thus it was that when European leaders met at Maastricht in December 1991 to determine the details of the new Treaty on European Union, Major insisted that Britain would only be a signatory to the Treaty if the provisions pertaining to the 'social chapter' were removed. When the other 11 member states agreed to Major's demands, he was able to present this 'opt-out' as a great victory for Britain, while also hoping that his own leadership credentials and authority would be enhanced.

Right until the end of his premiership, Major and his ministerial colleagues insisted that British acceptance of the 'social chapter' would impose unacceptable costs and burdens on employers, undermine the competitiveness of Britain's economy, and – as a consequence of these two effects – result in higher unemployment. The Major governments consistently argued that the people who would ultimately be most harmed by measures such as the 'social chapter' were the very people that such measures purported to protect.

Furthermore, refusal to accept the 'social chapter' also became an important symbol of the increasing Europhobia which characterised Major's premiership. Rejection of the 'social chapter' could be portrayed as a valiant stance by John Major against attempts by 'Brussels bureaucrats' to impose unacceptable costs on British industry and thereby undermine the competitiveness of Britain's economy (to the advantage of other EU states).

Not surprisingly, therefore, the same arguments and criteria were invoked in December 1994, when the then Secretary of State for Employment, Michael Portillo, exercised Britain's veto to block a European Union directive (issued under the auspices of the 'social chapter') which would have provided part-time employees with the same employment rights and protection as full-time workers. With its usual perversity and penchant for Orwellian double-speak, the

Major government presented this opposition to the extension of employment rights as an important and impressive victory on behalf of millions of part-time workers, whose continued employment would apparently have been jeopardised by the additional costs which their employers would have incurred had Michael Portillo not courageously and patriotically resisted this EU proposal.

However, a fortnight later, Portillo reluctantly abandoned his opposition, following a House of Lords decision which decreed that denying part-time workers the same employment rights as their full-time counterparts constituted discrimination, not least because the vast majority of part-time workers were women. Yet Portillo declared that: 'It is not a set-back for me at all, but it may be for part-time workers and women. It may mean men replace part-timers who are women and I would regret that very much' (*The Guardian*, 21 December 1994).

Just under two years later, the Major government was embroiled in yet another conflict with the European Union concerning employment rights, this time over the '48-hour directive', which decreed that employees could not be compelled to work more than 48 hours per week; they could only work in excess of 48 hours in a week if they had voluntarily agreed to do so.

This directive had originally been challenged via the European Court of Justice back in June 1994, by the then Employment Secretary, David Hunt, with much of the Government's case deriving from the argument that the '48 hour directive' was wrongly being issued under the auspices of EU health and safety – rather than employment – policy (although back in Britain, Conservative ministers once again distorted the truth by deliberately giving the impression that the Directive prohibited anyone from working more than 48 hours per week, thereby depicting it as a flagrant denial of people's rights in the workplace, rather than a means of enhancing them). However, the European Court's decision, in November 1996, rejected the government's case, whereupon Major – in the manner of a spoilt child not getting its own way – declared that he would embark upon a policy of obstruction and non-cooperation *vis-à-vis* forthcoming EU business, until or unless Britain was exempted from the '48 hour directive'.

One other aspect of the Major government's opposition to the 48-hour Directive which seemed somewhat bizarre was ministerial claims that restricting the hours that employees could be compelled to work would increase unemployment; common sense would suggest

Table 10.1   Average hours worked per week by full-time employees in
EU member states, 1996

United Kingdom	43.2	France	39.7
Portugal	41.0	Luxembourg	39.5
Spain	40.3	Holland	39.3
Greece	40.2	Finland	38.7
Ireland	40.0	Denmark	38.5
Austria	40.0	Italy	38.1
Sweden	40.0	Belgium	37.8
Germany	39.9	EU average	41.1

Source: Calculated from *Social Trends 28* (1998: 83).

that if those in employment can be made to work a limitless number
of hours, then many employers will choose precisely this option,
lengthening the working week for their existing staff, rather than
recruiting new staff from the dole queues. Put another way, the
Major governments would presumably have preferred it if five
employees worked 55 hours per week rather than having six employees working 46 hours.

CONCLUDING OBSERVATIONS

In the realm of industrial relations and labour-market policies,
therefore, it is clear that Major's premiership represented a continuation of the Thatcherite approach pursued during the 1980s.
Major's 'one-nation' pretensions and slightly less abrasive rhetoric
counted for naught when it came to his governments' actions and
policies towards the trade unions and employment matters.

While between two and three million people languished on the
dole, being told that in the brave new global order and technologi-
cal age, there were no longer enough jobs for everyone who wanted
to work, many of those still in full-time employment were compelled to work ever-longer hours, and cope with ever-increasing
workloads. Indeed, by the end of Major's premiership, British employees overall worked several hours more each week than their
European counterparts, as Table 10.1 indicates.

Full-time employees in Britain worked, on average, 43.2 hours
per week, compared to an average of 41.1 hours per week for the
European Union as a whole. In Belgium the average working week
for full-time employees was 37.8 hours.

It was an irony lost on Major and his Cabinet colleagues that while they were preaching the virtues of family life, and urging parents to spend more time with their children (partly in order to curb the rise in youth crime and juvenile delinquency, some of which was attributed to 'latch-key kids'), the same ministers were extolling the alleged virtues of longer working hours.

Nor did these ministers appreciate how other principles and policy objectives promoted by the Conservative party, such as home-ownership or private pension provision for the future, were largely dependent on the availability of secure, long-term employment. How workers employed on short-term contracts – another manifestation of the labour market flexibility which the Major government proudly promoted – were supposed to obtain mortgages (usually repaid over a 25-year period) was not an issue which Major and his Cabinet colleagues ever seemed concerned about.

Furthermore, many of those in full-time employment not only experienced greater stress due to their long hours and relentless pressure to reach targets or meet deadlines set by management, they were also experiencing increasing 'job insecurity', as companies relentlessly sought to cut costs by cutting jobs, and ministers repeatedly warned that 'jobs-for-life' were a thing of the past. Conservative ministers repeatedly told Britain's employees to expect periodic redundancies and changes of employment during their working lives, but simultaneously claimed that job losses should be viewed as opportunities to pursue new employment and career paths.

On the other hand, some ministers dismissed 'job insecurity' as being 'all in the mind', implying that employees were worrying unnecessarily, and even suggesting that the average tenure of employment was barely less than it had been twenty or thirty years ago.

Such cavalier dismissal of the anxieties experienced by increasing numbers of ordinary working people during the 1990s was just one more example of the arrogance and aloofness which afflicted so many of Major's ministers – victory in the 1992 general election having convinced them of the Conservative party's apparent invincibility. Yet had Major and his ministers been willing to pause for reflection, and evince even a modicum of humility, they might have acknowledged that 'job insecurity' (even if it was 'all in the mind') was hardly conducive to Major's professed objective of creating a nation at ease with itself.

One small indicator of the extent to which 'job insecurity' increased during the Major premiership is provided in Table 10.2,

Table 10.2   Employees' views about what ought to be the primary
objective of trade unions (percentages), 1989 and 1996

Trade union objective	1989	1996
Protect existing jobs	28	33
Improve working conditions	21	22
Improve pay	28	21
More say over long-term plans	6	7
Reduce pay differentials	6	4
More say over day-to-day affairs	3	2
Pursue equal opportunities for women	3	2

Source: *Social Trends 28* (1998, 86).

which shows the results of attitude surveys into employees' views
about the objectives which trade unions should pursue. It is clear
that by 1996, the single most important objective which employees
ascribed to trade unions was 'protecting existing jobs', with a third
of employees subscribing to this view. During the same period, the
proportion of employees who believed that a trade unions' primary
objective should be to seek improvements in pay declined from
well over one-quarter to barely a fifth.

Meanwhile, Major and his ministers often cited the relatively small
number of strikes during the 1990s as evidence of a new era of
industrial relations in Britain, one characterised by harmony and
cooperation in the workplace between employers and employees
(compared to the conflict and confrontation of the 1970s). Yet such
a claim was somewhat disingenuous, for while a high incidence of
strikes is undoubtedly a sign of poor industrial relations, it does
not follow that a relative absence of strikes is indicative of good
industrial relations (as Major's ministers liked to claim). Instead,
lack of strike activity and industrial disruption can just as readily
reflect fear, fatalism or a sense of futility among employees, and it
seems highly likely that these were the most common sentiments
among many employees during the 1990s, rather than happiness
and harmony in the workplace. It is hard to believe that an era of
'down-sizing', 'delayering', longer working hours, pay cuts, job insecurity, and 'macho management', was simultaneously an era of
good industrial relations, however small the number of strikes.

Certainly, the electorate appeared less and less enamoured with
the Major government's policies towards the trade unions and the
labour market as the 1990s progressed. For example, an NOP poll

conducted during the summer of 1996 discovered that 56 per cent of respondents believed that the Conservative governments' restrictions on the trade unions had 'gone too far', while a further 18 per cent thought that the legislative curbs placed on the unions during the 1980s and 1990s should be repealed. Even among Conservative voters, 48 per cent believed that their government's attacks on the trade unions had 'gone too far', compared to the 42 per cent of Conservatives who thought that the right balance had been struck. Meanwhile, 75 per cent of the public felt that if more than half of the workforce wished to be represented by a trade union, then the employer should be required by law to negotiate with the union(s).

The same poll also revealed that the Major government was out of touch with public opinion in opposing European Union measures concerning employment rights and protection. For example, over three-quarters of the public believed that part-time employees should enjoy the same legal rights as full-time workers, while 78 per cent of voters agreed that it should be 'illegal for employers to force their staff to work more than 48 hours a week, if the staff don't want to' (*The Observer*, 4 August 1996).

Meanwhile, other opinion polls revealed widespread and consistent support among the electorate for a national minimum wage, with about three-quarters of voters in favour of such a measure (see, for example, the MORI poll in *The Times*, 31 August 1995).

By the time of the 1997 general election, the Major government was unable to extract any more mileage out of attacking the trade unions. Although Conservative ministers sought to raise the spectre of revived trade-union power and industrial disruption under a Labour government during the election campaign – particularly in the context of Labour's commitment to adopting the 'social chapter', and its manifesto commitment to require employers to 'recognise' trade unions for bargaining purposes when over 50 per cent of their employees wished to belong to a union – the vast majority of voters were immune to such propaganda. Indeed, a MORI poll conducted shortly after the start of the election campaign revealed that in terms of issue-salience, voters ranked 'trade unions' fourteenth out of the 15 issues cited (*Independent on Sunday*, 6 April 1997).

The industrial relations and labour-market policies which accompanied the Major premiership represented a continuation of the Thatcherite agenda and programme in this sphere. Indeed, in certain respects, the Major governments went even further than Thatcher's administrations, as evinced by the abolition of both the NEDC and the Wages Councils. While Major's rhetoric might have been less strident or acerbic than Thatcher's, his attitude towards the trade unions was just as contemptuous and hardly less confrontational. Yet the period of Major's premiership also indicated the extent to which (free-market) economic dogma, applied to industrial relations and the labour market, was totally at odds with the pre-Thatcher Conservative emphasis on social stability and industrial partnership.

11 The Limitations of Likeability: the Major Premiership and Public Opinion
David Broughton

INTRODUCTION

With hindsight, one of the biggest surprises of the May 1997 general election was that so many people were surprised at the outcome. The Labour party won its biggest-ever number of seats in the House of Commons (419) and its overall majority of 179 represented the largest for any government since 1935. In stark contrast, the Conservative party's share of the vote fell to just over 30 per cent, their worst result since the beginning of modern party politics in 1832. With just 165 seats, the Conservative party's representation in the House of Commons was the lowest since 1906, and the party was reduced to an English rump, with no MPs in either Scotland or Wales, emphasising the decline of the Conservatives as a national political force (Norris, 1997).

The above statistics provide a clear picture of the calamitous state of the Conservative party in the wake of Major's premiership. It is important to stress in particular that such a disaster did not come about as the result of sudden and overwhelming changes in public opinion in the immediate run-up to the 1997 election. Instead, many analyses of the 1997 election result emphasise the long-term significance of 'Black Wednesday' on 16 September 1992 when sterling was forced out of the European exchange rate mechanism (ERM). This débâcle, with interest rates rising from 10 per cent to 12 per cent to 15 per cent and then down again to 12 per cent by the end of the day, and the consequent shattering of notions of Conservative economic competence, resonated throughout the 1992–97 parliament. The failure to restore its reputation as a party which could be trusted to run the economy robbed the

199

Conservatives of a traditionally powerful electoral card. Whiteley sums this point up neatly by stating that, 'in a real sense, the Conservatives won an election (in 1992) and then lost another election in the same year' (1997: 542).

In addition, the Labour party was finally rebuilding its credibility with the voters by engaging in a serious and far-reaching process of internal reform in terms of its image and policies. A clear sign of this was the Labour party's poll-lead over the Conservatives which was often substantial throughout the five years from 1992. The upward trend in Labour support became particularly marked from late 1993, with the party scoring an average of between 46 and 48 per cent support between October and December 1993. The Conservatives, in contrast, received an average support of between 27 and 30 per cent during the same period (Broughton *et al.*, 1995: 245).

The position of the Labour party, and its poll-lead over the Conservatives, was consolidated throughout the first half of 1994, before increasing further still in the latter half of the year, when Labour reached the dizzying heights of nearly 60 per cent support from the British voters, based on the party's average monthly poll-rating between October 1994 and June 1995. The comparable average for the Conservatives was 24 per cent (Rallings *et al.*, 1996: 197; Farrell *et al.*, 1996: 255). The second half of 1995 saw Labour's average poll-rating level out at 56 per cent, while, on average, the Conservatives scored 26 per cent (Farrell *et al.*, 1996: 255). Throughout 1996, Labour's rating on average never dropped below 50 per cent support, while the average support achieved by the Conservatives was 28 per cent (Pattie *et al.*, 1997: 251).

The apparent certainty of a Labour victory at the next election, whenever it was called, was reinforced with the election of Tony Blair as Labour leader in July 1994 and his subsequent moves to redefine and project 'New Labour' to a generally receptive audience. Indeed, throughout 1995, the incumbent Conservative administration under John Major's premiership could be categorised as being the most unpopular government since 1945 on the basis of monthly polling data collected by Gallup, with average monthly support ranging between 23 and 27 per cent support (Farrell *et al.*, 1996: 255; Gallup Political and Economic Index, July 1995: 10). One ICM poll and one Gallup poll in June 1995 both gave the Conservatives only 20 per cent support (Farrell *et al.*, 1996: 255).

Over and above opinion-poll ratings, the parlous state of the Major government could also be seen in 'real' votes at by-elections, even after substantial allowance is made for the often high degree of 'protest voting' and low turnouts. As usual, the smaller parties such as the Liberal Democrats and the Scottish National Party benefited from the unpopularity of the government but the Labour party was also winning seats – such as Dudley West in 1994 and Staffordshire South-East in 1996 – from the Conservatives, exactly the type of English seats which Labour had to retain at the general election to win an overall majority. In Dudley, the Conservative vote declined by 30 per cent at the by-election, compared to the 1992 general election, and in Staffordshire South-East, it declined by 22 per cent (Rallings *et al.*, 1996: 194–5; Pattie *et al.*, 1997: 246). It was back in February 1989 when the Conservatives last retained a seat (Richmond in Yorkshire) at a by-election, a seat won by John Major's successor as Conservative party leader, William Hague.

On the basis of past experience, the loss of a string of by-elections was certainly not a main source of alarm on its own, given the expectation that such seats would be duly won back at the next general election. This is precisely what had happened at the 1992 general election, when the Conservative recaptured all the seven seats they had lost in by-elections during the 1987–92 Parliament. However, at the 1997 general election, this 'rule' did not operate, with the Conservatives only recapturing one seat (Christchurch) of the eight seats they had lost during the 1992–97 Parliament.

In local government, the Conservatives had become the third force behind both Labour and the Liberal Democrats, with only 4400 councillors compared to 11 000 for the Labour party and 5100 for the Liberal Democrats after the 1996 local elections. The Conservatives controlled only 13 local authorities in England, Scotland and Wales, while Labour controlled 212 and the Liberal Democrats controlled 55 (Norris, 1997: 511; Pattie *et al.*, 1997: 256–9; for a consideration of the 1997 local elections, held on the same day as the general election, see Rallings and Thrasher, 1997b). At the last election to the European Parliament in 1994, the Conservatives held only 18 seats out of 89 (none in Scotland and Wales), having won 32 seats in 1989 (Rallings *et al.*, 1996: 204–11).

However, there were a few straws for John Major to clutch at amid the extended carnage set out above, such as hopes of an economic recovery producing a renewed 'feel good' factor in time for the 1997 general election.

In addition, there were continuing suspicions that the opinion polls were not accurately measuring the depth of commitment of those people claiming that they would vote Labour. This was based on the problems which the pollsters faced at the 1992 general election when 'silent Conservatives' apparently caused the polls' failure to prophesy a narrow Conservative victory, as opposed to a narrow Labour win or a hung Parliament (Crewe, 1992; Broughton, 1995; Curtice, 1996). Certainly, when the potential impact of these 'silent Conservatives' on party support was taken into account, often on the basis of past voting habits, support for the Conservatives increased to nearer 30 per cent than 20 per cent, and sometimes, in individual polls, to nearly 35 per cent. Such 'adjusted' figures were a reaction by the polling firms to the severe criticism of their methods in 1992 but the basis for making those adjustments remained a matter of dispute, even among the pollsters themselves (Crewe, 1997; Curtice *et al.*, 1997).

Finally, it was also possible that the Conservative government was suffering a very bad case of mid-term blues but that the 'reality' of the choice to be made by voters would become clearer as the approaching general election concentrated minds. Certainly, John Major had acquired a reputation as a forceful campaigner at the 1992 general election, and an aggressive campaign stressing his personal qualities of likeability and patent humanity, along with a strong emphasis on the strength of the economy, appeared a reasonable basis for going to the country, particularly when allied with the alleged prospects for Britain of 'risking' an untried and inexperienced Labour government.

These grounds for some optimism at least were, of course, to prove ultimately illusory. Given the 1997 election outcome, the obvious question to ask is whether there was anything that John Major could have done to pull his Conservative government out of the electoral mire. Once again, with hindsight, some assert that there was nothing he could do, while others allege that his downfall can be clearly traced both to the hand he was dealt and the way in which he chose to play it (see, for example, Seldon, 1997).

One freely available source for analysing these differing interpretations is public opinion poll data. This chapter will consider such data, collected during John Major's time in office between late 1990 and the 1997 general election, to examine his impact on the fortunes of his party and whether he ultimately made much difference to the 1997 election outcome.

THE IMPACT OF PARTY LEADERS

For many people, it would seem instinctively counter-intuitive to argue that political leaders, whoever they are, make little difference to the popularity of their parties. After all, many election campaigns now concentrate heavily, if not exclusively, on the party leaders and the party's image is moulded by the party leader and his or her immediate entourage in ways which ensure that the leader retains overall control. This development is often imprecisely described as the 'presidentialisation' of British politics, a process underpinned by the ever-increasing need to project tightly controlled, coherent and standardised views through the mass media.

Despite this development, it remains perfectly possible still to argue that leaders do not make very much *direct* difference to an overall election outcome. On a banal level, this is obviously and inevitably true, given the fact that few voters ever get to actually meet a party leader in the flesh. In this sense, the perceptions of the voters must be *indirect*, mediated and shaped by the images they read in the newspapers and see on television.

Essentially, this debate over 'leader effects' is a question of 'the direction of the causal arrow' or more simply, 'which came first?' – did voters like John Major because they support the Conservative party or did they support the Conservative party because they like John Major? Untangling this web of politically relevant attitudes and opinions is very complex, particularly over time.

The principal difficulty in confronting such a task is to separate out the different strands that together comprise the political views of a voter. For most voters, this will encompass a range of judgements and evaluations relating to their social background, general partisan views based on party identification, retrospective evaluations of the incumbent government's performance, prospective evaluations of the different parties (both government and opposition), evaluations of specific leadership traits, and, finally, overall evaluations of the various parties and their leaders. Together, these influences ultimately crystallise in making the final vote choice on polling day (Johnston and Pattie, 1997b: 42–3).

These various influences inevitably interact and overlap with one another in a continuous and dynamic process of evaluation to such an extent that it is especially problematic to ascribe to any one influence the predominant role in voter decision-making. Some argue that 'leader effects' in this context have increased in importance over time (Lanoue and Headrick, 1994; Stewart and Clarke, 1992). Others argue, additionally, that voters' assessments of party leaders are comparative and prospective rather than individual and retrospective (Nadeau *et al.*, 1996).

The main underlying reason for this trend towards a greater impact for leaders is the breakdown of instinctive party loyalty which used to characterise the voting habits of most of the British electorate. However, after about 1970, 'voter dealignment' meant that party loyalty became increasingly contingent on government performance and leader perceptions relating to competence and responsiveness in particular, as a more 'functional' and sceptical electorate emerged.

THE IMAGE OF JOHN MAJOR

When John Major entered the race to replace Margaret Thatcher in November 1990, he was little known by the British public. By the end of the leadership contest, his name was known by the vast majority of the voters but his strengths and weaknesses could inevitably only be surmised. However, by mid-1991, a clearer picture had emerged. Based on Gallup polls taken in January, February, May and July 1991, Major was widely regarded by the British voters as being caring, trustworthy, competent, likeable and as someone who listened to reason (Gallup Political and Economic Index, July 1991: 10).

However, in terms of assessing his performance as prime minister, other characteristics and traits are more important and on the questions as to whether Major was a strong or weak personality, whether he was a winner or a loser, whether he was firmly in charge or not, whether he was decisive or not, and whether he was able to unite the nation or not, the Gallup data show much more variability, with the sample often being split roughly down the middle. These potential weaknesses were to prove impossible for Major to overcome throughout his time in office, and on the key perceptions relating to performance and achievements, they became more negative during his premiership. For example, in a Gallup poll taken in March 1996, Major was regarded as 'not being tough' by 73 per cent of the sample, 'ineffective' by 71 per cent, 'a loser' by 63 per cent, 'not really in charge' by 78 per cent, 'indecisive' by 66 per cent, and 'not able to unite the nation' by 81 per cent (Gallup Political and Economic Index, March 1996: 7). Jones and Hudson (1996)

Table 11.1   John Major's public image (per cent)

	July 1993	May 1994	July 1995
Caring	52	55	59
Tough	18	15	25
Effective	18	17	26
Competent	34	33	44
A loser	64	69	58
Not really in charge	85	84	76
Indecisive	77	75	64
Likeable as a person	66	64	67
Listens to reason	51	52	55
Able to unite the nation	15	13	20

Note: The question was 'Which, if any, of these phrases more applies to Mr Major?'

Source: Gallup Political and Economic Index, August 1995: 6

conclude that the most important personality attributes for a leader are those which contribute to the belief that he or she can govern in a 'business-like fashion', especially in terms of 'effectiveness'.

In this particular context, it is important to remember that Major was not only confronted by the leaders of the other parties, principally the Labour party, initially under Neil Kinnock, then the late John Smith and, finally, Tony Blair, but he was also forced to live in the shadow of Mrs Thatcher. It was unfortunate for Major that his perceived weaknesses were Mrs Thatcher's main strengths, and that those strengths were the traits that form the basis of most people's assessment of a prime minister. A considerable number of voters had disliked Margaret Thatcher, but she had also been respected by many, and admired by some. For Major, however, the reverse applied throughout his premiership (see Tables 11.1 and 11.2). Despite the lack of precise comparability between the questions asked, the overall picture is one of sharp and sustained contrast between Major and Thatcher in terms of their perceived images and their respective strengths and weaknesses.

THE PROBLEMS OF THE MAJOR GOVERNMENTS

Despite these apparent personality weaknesses, Major made a good start as prime minister. In the last two months of 1990, throughout

Table 11.2   Margaret Thatcher's public image (per cent)

	April 1978	July 1984	April 1989
Strong personality	80	95	93
Speaks her mind	82	89	90
Thinks a lot of herself	62	72	75
Has good/new ideas	53	40	47
Doesn't come over well	45	44	36
Is a snob, talks down to people	43	58	54
Divides the country	40	67	72
Her ideas are destructive	30	47	41
Knows what she is talking about	67	63	63

Note: Precise question wording not given but based on agreement by respondents with a range of statements about Mrs. Thatcher

Source: Gallup Political Index, April 1989: 7

1991 and up until September 1992, Major achieved a 'positive' balance of approval drawn from responses to the Gallup question as to whether the respondents were satisfied or dissatisfied with his performance as prime minister. Indeed, in February 1991, this 'balance' was +39 per cent. It is, however, important to point out that the 'balance' started to diminish towards the end of 1991, shot up again to +19 per cent in May 1992 in the aftermath of Major's general election triumph, then declined again rapidly to reach a 'negative' balance of −46 per cent by November 1992, in the aftermath of the ERM débâcle (Crewe *et al.*, 1992: 236; Norris *et al.*, 1992: 189; Denver *et al.*, 1993: 15).

Major's ratings on this question of satisfaction were negative for the whole period between 1993 and 1996, reaching a low point of −58 per cent in June 1993 and December 1994 (Broughton *et al.*, 1995: 245; Rallings *et al.*, 1996: 198; Farrell *et al.*, 1996: 256; Pattie *et al.*, 1997: 252). There was only a slight recovery in the ratings of satisfaction with his performance as prime minister after he resigned as the leader of the Conservative party in June 1995, telling his colleagues in the party 'to put up or shut up'. If this move was intended to re-establish his authority as prime minister and/or to quell the seemingly constant bickering on the Conservative backbenches over the question of further European integration, it clearly failed, producing neither greater, and lasting, popular approval, nor the means to create genuine party unity.

One obvious way in which Major might have been able to mitigate his perceived weaknesses among the electorate was to lead a successful administration able to point to a series of achievements for which he could duly claim the credit. Yet, despite the election victory of April 1992 against the odds, the lasting impression of the Major premiership for many is one of drift and indecision, a government 'in office but not in power' to use the damning phrase of the former Chancellor, Norman Lamont.

Arguably, it was not Major's fault that much of the radicalism of the Thatcherite agenda had been implemented or set in irreversible motion by the time he came to office. In addition, he did continue with its basic thrust in some respects, by privatising the railways and developing plans for pension reform in particular, and re-assessing welfare-state provision in general.

Nevertheless, other attempts at stamping a distinctive mark on his governments, such as the Citizen's Charters, attracted wide-spread derision rather than applause. The 'strangling' of inflation was undoubtedly a substantial economic achievement but it was hard to demonstrate its value and impact to an ungrateful electorate which was, however, acutely aware of a range of tax increases since 1992.

The overall performance of the Major governments must, however, be seen in the context of a small parliamentary majority of 21 which was eventually whittled away to nothing through by-election losses, thus increasing the potential for backbench revolts, particularly on the issue of European integration. This issue engendered repeated and severe problems of internal party management, initially over the ratification of the Maastricht Treaty in 1992–93 and the multi-faceted questions of the United Kingdom's relations with the European Union from then on (see Chapters 1 and 5).

The claim that, by May 1997, it was 'time for a change' after 18 years of Conservative government was difficult to refute in the absence of 'big' new ideas. The evidence of the alleged need for a change was regularly reinforced by a range of allegations of sleaze and the apparent arrogance of a Conservative party and government more focused on its own internal divisions and clinging desperately to power, than any wider concerns. The term 'sleaze' was an umbrella-term which effectively condensed a number of different ideas such as financial gain and self-interest with a variety of sexual practices into a single, powerfully reverberating, overarching image, which became strongly associated in the public mind with the Conservative party during the 1990s.

In response to the statement as to whether the Conservatives gave the impression of being very sleazy and disreputable, more than 60 per cent of various Gallup samples agreed with that statement between September 1994 and November 1996. Agreement with the statement reached a peak of 75 per cent in June 1995 and it never fell below 61 per cent in the 11 polls in which the question was asked between the above dates (Gallup Political and Economic Index, June 1996: 5 and November 1996: 6).

In addition, the changes brought about by Tony Blair in terms of modernising the Labour party, restoring its electoral credibility and extending its appeal into social groups never before reached represented another nail in the Conservative party's coffin.

For John Major, the 1992 election victory had one unfortunate consequence in that Neil Kinnock resigned as Labour leader and was replaced by John Smith. Throughout 1991, Kinnock had consistently negative ratings on the question as to whether he was proving to be a good leader of the Opposition, while Major often had strongly positive ratings as prime minister (Norris *et al.*, 1992: 189). This all changed with the election of Smith as Labour leader in July 1992 (Denver *et al.*, 1993: 15). Smith immediately received a positive 'balance' in response to this question and this continued right through until his death in May 1994 (Rallings *et al.*, 1996: 198). Blair's election in July 1994 made things even worse for Major, with the former racking up even bigger positive 'balances' than Smith, reaching a maximum of +51 per cent in June 1995, when Major's equivalent rating was −49 per cent (Farrell *et al.*, 1996: 256).

However, even if we accept that these contextual influences set tight and constraining parameters which reduced John Major's room for manoeuvre, it remains the case that for many analysts, it was the loss of his government's long-standing reputation for economic competence arising from the ERM débâcle mentioned earlier that lay at the heart of the Conservative election defeat in 1997.

In terms of the reaction of public opinion, we can consider the question of economic competence overall by examining data drawn from general questions as well as questions on specific aspects of economic policy.

THE MAJOR GOVERNMENTS AND 'ECONOMIC COMPETENCE'

Gallup has long asked a general question about which party would best handle economic difficulties. We can trace responses to this question right back to the 1992 general election. For April, May and early September 1992 (immediately before the ERM crisis), the Conservative party held a lead over Labour of 18, 12 and 5 per cent respectively. The ERM crisis transformed this perception as to which party would best handle economic difficulties into a Labour lead of 18 per cent in October 1992 (Farrell *et al.*, 1996: 259), a lead the party never lost again in the 54 months up until the 1997 general election.

On some occasions, Labour's lead over the Conservatives on this question was enormous (30 per cent in May and June 1995, for example) with the whole period evincing remarkable stability in the responses given. Support for the Conservatives as the best party to handle economic difficulties ranged between 20 and 30 per cent for almost the whole period, while for Labour, it varied between 40 and 50 per cent, with the rest being made up of either those who felt there was no difference between the parties or those who didn't know.

A second measure which Gallup regularly employ is their set of economic indicators comprising four questions designed to gauge whether (a) respondents feel that the economic situation of the country has improved or deteriorated during the last 12 months, (b) whether it will improve or deteriorate during the next 12 months, (c) whether the financial situation in their household has improved or deteriorated during the last 12 months and (d) whether they think that the financial situation in their household will improve or deteriorate during the next twelve months.

The answers to these four questions can then be used to produce an index showing the 'balance of opinion' in terms of both the past and the future for both the country as a whole and for the households of the individual voters. These data are often used to measure the extent of the 'feel good' factor, in particular whether voters are hopeful about the immediate future economically.

Once again, the Gallup data collected during the period of Major's premiership strongly suggest that the Conservatives were blamed for what many voters perceived to be a poor national economic situation with little sign of improvement in the future, along with a sense that the voters' households had also not fared well in the last 12 months. The 'balance of opinion' about the retrospective national economic situation hit rock-bottom in late 1992 with negative index scores of -83, -88, -85 and -78 per cent between September and December 1992 (the balance of pessimists over optimists) (Farrell *et al.*, 1996: 258) and although this negative balance did improve considerably for the rest of the 1992–97 parliament, it was still negative throughout 1996, ranging between -11 per cent and -36 per cent (Pattie *et al.*, 1997: 254).

Intriguingly, the figure for perceptions of the respondents' own household financial situation 'in the forthcoming 12 months' was much more variable, with that particular index even recording a positive balance of optimists over pessimists in early 1992, before following the other indexes by becoming negative for most of the period up until 1997 (Farrell *et al.*, 1996: 258; Pattie *et al.*, 1997: 254).

For the Conservatives, the 'feel good' factor did show some signs of reappearing towards the end of 1996, with a small positive balance of $+3$, $+4$ and $+2$ per cent between September and November 1996 (Pattie *et al.*, 1997: 254). Indeed, by April 1997, the positive balance was even better for the government, at $+11$ per cent (exactly the same figure as in April 1992) (Clarke *et al.*, 1997: 163) but it was certainly too late to save the party from electoral disaster at that stage – the serious damage had been done years before, and it would have required an almost unimaginable political shock to swing the votes of enough electors to produce the required figures for a Conservative victory. One prediction, in early 1996, had suggested that the Conservatives should achieve a popularity rating of around 36 per cent by the spring of 1997 on the basis of various economic models (Sanders, 1996). In fact, the Conservatives only achieved just over 30 per cent at the actual election.

The 'objective' figures for the economy were in fact promising in late 1996 but, crucially, perceptions did not alter sufficiently to give the Conservatives any real chance. In one important sense, though, the initial signs of economic recovery may nevertheless still have been important in staving off an even heavier defeat than the one that actually occurred.

We can examine another aspect of the weakness of the Major government in its 1997 campaign when we analyse the data more specifically by moving from general perceptions of overall economic competence to particular aspects of economic policy.

Table 11.3   The best party to handle economic problems (percentages)

	March 1996		September 1996		December 1996	
	Lab.	Con.	Lab.	Con.	Lab.	Con.
Inflation and prices	39	37	36	40	40	37
Unemployment	63	13	65	17	63	15
Taxation	45	27	39	33	45	28
Pensions	54	17	53	21	59	16

Note: The question was, 'I am going to read out a list of problems facing the country. Could you tell me for each of them which political party you personally think would handle the problem best?'

Sources: Gallup Political and Economic Index, March 1996: 7 and December 1996: 5

It is often worthwhile to separate out the different aspects of economic policy to ascertain whether the voters are thinking of specific aspects, or whether their judgements are focused more on broad ideas relating to the economy as a whole. One way of doing this is to ask the voters whether, in their opinion, one party or another would handle various problems and policy issues the best. Gallup conduct such research regularly and we can see from Table 11.3 that the Labour party was clearly viewed as the best party to handle problems on four key aspects of the economy (inflation and prices, unemployment, taxation and pensions), aspects widely assumed to be influential in terms of voting decisions.

The Conservatives and Labour are regarded as being close competitors in terms of being the best party to handle the issue of inflation and prices, but the Labour party's lead on taxation was arguably more significant since the party explicitly linked its stance on taxation with the party's emphasis on the question of trusting the party in general and trusting Tony Blair in particular. The poll data also reflect the dissatisfaction with the Conservatives' tax rises since the 1992 election. Labour's lead as the best party to tackle unemployment is long-standing, but being regarded as the best party to handle the problem of pensions was also useful in that it helped to sustain the credibility of the party among social groups usually unsympathetic to the Labour Party cause.

Even given the general acceptance that economic issues deserve to be at the forefront of analyses of the 1997 election outcome, it is interesting to consider other potentially important political issues that played their own part in the 1997 election campaign.

Table 11.4   The best party to handle problems (percentages)

	March 1996 Lab.	Con.	September 1996 Lab.	Con.	December 1996 Lab.	Con.
Strikes and industrial disputes	45	30	42	35	45	31
The National Health Service	63	11	66	10	65	13
Education and schools	54	17	55	19	59	18
Law and order	41	27	39	30	43	29
Homelessness	62	8	63	8	63	9
Europe	37	29	35	32	41	24
Public transport	59	11	59	13	60	13
The status of women	48	10	47	14	55	11

Note: The question was the same as for Table 11.3.

Sources: As for Table 11.3.

THE MAJOR GOVERNMENTS AND NON-ECONOMIC ISSUES

The Labour party has long been associated with a positive profile on the 'caring' issues such as health and education but, at previous elections, this has not been enough to make up for the widespread perception of weaknesses on crucial aspects of economic competence. Drawn from the same data as the economic problems set out in Table 11.3, we can now consider the data regarding the best party to address the 'caring' issues.

We can see from Table 11.4 that Labour was strongly favoured by the voters in the run-up to the 1997 general election on issues such as the National Health Service and education, which appeared to create further problems for the Conservatives in government. Radical changes introduced by John Major in both fields were not yet bearing positive fruit, and they were easy to attack as being both over-bureaucratic and expensive. The failure to provide an efficient health service was rated as the Major government's worse failing in a Gallup poll conducted in July 1995. Directly comparable data collected during the period of the Thatcher government in 1984 and 1986 show that the problems of the National Health Service were placed second behind the failure to prevent the rise in unemployment (Gallup Political and Economic Index, July 1995: 9).

Labour's lead as the best party to handle law and order was also useful for the party, reflecting the increasing credibility of the party's campaigning and propaganda in the context of rising crime figures and an ever-increasing prison population, while Labour's credibility as the best party to handle strikes and industrial relations was also arguably highly significant. The distancing of the party from the trade unions had begun under the leadership of Neil Kinnock, been continued by John Smith and strongly reinforced by Tony Blair, the latter emphasising 'fairness, not favours'. Such an attitude would have seemed highly unlikely only a decade before, but it represented an important practical as well as symbolic change which put the Labour party back as an electorally credible party in the minds of many voters whose support the party had to secure.

THE ALTERNATIVES

It is clear from the Gallup data cited above that John Major's task both in running his government on a day-to-day basis and simultaneously positioning the Conservative party to win the 1997 election appeared daunting at best and well-nigh impossible at worst. If the extent of the Conservative defeat in 1997 was under-estimated by most observers, it was mainly because they did not believe such a rout was possible and, in addition, the humbling experience of many pundits in 1992 in terms of the 'message of the polls' had taught them to exercise extreme caution.

Yet, even a cursory reading of the available data from 1992 onwards would have suggested that the writing was on the wall for the Conservative government for a very long time before the 1997 election. Using the alleged 'softness' of the Labour vote as a 'comfort blanket' was understandable in such a situation, but reliance on such hopes effectively ignored the new-found and widespread credibility of the Labour party under Tony Blair. Blair's modernisation of the party persuaded many that a vote for Labour was not really much of a risk at all, particularly when his grip on the internal organisation of the Labour party and his ability to lead from the front, contrasted so sharply with the persistent inability of the Conservatives to pull themselves together and to act as a unified entity. This, in turn, reinforced the image of John Major as a weak and vacillating leader.

Would any other leader than John Major have been able to prevent such a shattering defeat for the Conservatives at the polls? We can of course easily speculate about this question and such speculation would inevitably centre upon the main challenger to Margaret Thatcher in 1990, Michael Heseltine, as someone whose appeal went the widest of all the likeliest candidates when it came to assessing whether a particular leader would make voters more inclined or less inclined to vote Conservative.

Heseltine was widely seen as experienced, a strong, charismatic personality, willing to take risks and far-sighted and imaginative but he was also regarded as being cold and distant, ambitious for himself and not to be trusted. These results are drawn from Gallup polls conducted in November 1990 during the Conservative leadership contest (Gallup Political and Economic Index, November 1990: 5). These data inevitably fail to measure the internal state of the Conservative party in which Heseltine was seen to have struck the fatal blow against Thatcher, an action for which he will never be forgiven by some. In that sense, Heseltine's chances of turning the fortunes of the Conservative party around were certainly poorer than would be suggested by public opinion poll data alone, and his position within the party was further weakened by concern over his health after he suffered a heart attack in Venice in June 1993.

In addition, the internal divisions over Europe would almost certainly have been even worse under Heseltine's leadership, since his views on Europe were much more positive and pro-integrationist than many Conservative MPs'. Major's main instinct was to buy time on the European issue by obtaining negotiated opt-outs from the Maastricht Treaty, but Heseltine's reputation and record evinced a much more explicit willingness to support further integration between Britain and its European Union partners, including an acceptance of the need to join a single European currency.

On that basis, it seems very unlikely that the strongly embedded internal divisions within the Conservative party over the issue of European integration would have been any more soluble or any less entrenched under Heseltine's leadership. Indeed, they would have almost certainly become both deeper and more bitter and, thus, even less amenable to being papered over than the 'wait and see' policy on the single European currency instituted under Major's leadership.

CONCLUSION

On the basis of the above analysis of public opinion during the period of John Major's premiership, it is difficult to see what Major could have done to win the 1997 general election. While the economy was improving, with low inflation and falling unemployment, credit for such an improvement was not given to the incumbent government. Ferguson and O'Hara (*The Financial Times*, 28 April 1997: 12) argue that Major did the 'right thing' on the basis of the 'old rules' of political economy but that in a 'chaotic world', those rules relating to the creation of the 'feel good' factor ceased to apply. The links between economic change and political behaviour are unstable over time and therefore unpredictable. In addition, if a government succeeds in solving the problem it was elected to solve, it may find the achievement disregarded by the electorate. While the world may be 'chaotic', the presentation of policy certainly does not have to be so, but, as with other policies of John Major's governments, the overall impression in terms of the economy was that things were getting better more by accident than design.

Few people doubted Major's personal qualities of pragmatic competence and integrity, but internal Conservative Party divisions and regular bouts of sleaze muddied the waters to such an extent that his authority as Prime Minister was repeatedly undermined. His success in keeping the Conservative party in one piece through some exasperating and turbulent times was testimony to his ability to negotiate and to cut deals, but his lack of a clearly defined agenda means that his legacy comprises a few worthy individual policies, rather than anything that can reasonably be labelled 'Majorism'.

The inevitable test of time will focus upon how many of those policies survive, and there are grounds for some optimism in this regard in terms of the economy in particular, although the establishment of the National Lottery and the development of the Citizen's Charters seem likely to figure more highly in the minds of many. The criticism of Major in terms of his alleged vacillation and managerial, collegiate style seem more pointed in terms of any comparison with Thatcher, in whose shadow he was forced to live. This neglects the point that not being Thatcher was one of Major's clearest advantages and a key element in his appeal to the Conservative Party back in 1990.

The balance between advantage and disadvantage, however, still seems heavily weighted in favour of the latter. The ERM débâcle only five months after the April 1992 general election victory set the tone. For the next five years, the Conservative Party was playing 'catch up', limping along in the wake of New Labour, more focused on infighting, ritual disloyalty and self-interest than presenting a united front to an already sullen and sceptical electorate. Five years might seem more than enough time to turn such a disadvantageous situation around, but Major's authority was repeatedly questioned, and his instincts remained those of a whip, solid on tactics but with only underdeveloped ideas on overall strategy. Crucially, he failed to assemble a loyal block of supporters within the party to fall back upon, with many Conservative MPs more loyal to the party as a whole than to Major as an individual (Cowley, 1996b). The raucous, ill-disciplined nature of the Conservative party in the 1990s would have tested the mettle of any prime minister, and the real fear that the party might split over Europe was reason enough for Major to try riding at least two horses at once.

One particular disadvantage which Major suffered for most of his premiership, especially in the last three years, was an unusually hostile press who faithfully reproduced the image of a plodding underdog, someone devoid of consistent principle, incapable of setting any agenda and lacking the ability to mobilise support for what he wanted to do. The accusation that John Major could not 'run a bath' was typical of the insults thrown out by the tabloids (Seymour-Ure, 1997). John Campbell's view that Major was a 'caretaker for seven years' and Ben Pimlott's assessment that Major was a 'Harold Wilson without the intellect' clearly swam with the overwhelming tide of media opinion (*Independent on Sunday*, 11 May 1997: 17). In the end, Major had to fight the 1997 election campaign with six of the ten daily newspapers giving largely unqualified support to Blair's 'New' Labour party, including the *Sun* which came out in support of Blair at the start of the campaign.

The image created in the press was inevitably reflected in the contours of public opinion and Major appeared unable to turn around the nagging sense that he wasn't up to the job, particularly having had six-and-a-half years to do so. This is apparent in the qualitative research carried out at the 1997 election by Devine *et al.* (1997) in which lengthy, detailed interviews reveal a strong perception that Major was a weak and ineffective leader among loyal Conservative voters, particularly in comparison with both Thatcher and Blair. In this context, likeability, charm and transparent honesty were simply not enough.

A balanced appraisal of Major's premiership would nevertheless have to list in detail the persistently fractious nature of the Conservative party (see Chapter 1) and the seemingly intractable nature of the key issues that Major had to confront, in particular Europe (see Chapter 5).

A potent symbol of these problems was the BSE crisis which burst into the open in March 1996, when a report linking BSE (mad cow disease) with Creutzfeld-Jakob disease (CJD) in humans was published. This resulted in the European Commission imposing a total ban on the export of British cattle and beef products, both to other EU member states, and elsewhere in the world. From one perspective, this was simply yet more bad luck to descend on Major from an entirely unpredictable source. Kenneth Clarke, the former Chancellor of the Exchequer, for example, described Major as 'the unluckiest PM this century', asking, 'how could we have predicted cows suddenly getting this bizarre disease?' (*The Independent*, 4 August 1997: 11). From another perspective, to acknowledge Harold Macmillan's main fear in politics, 'events' might indeed produce bad luck, but a strong, decisive hand on the tiller would go a long way to mitigate their consequences.

Unfortunately for Major, politics at this level is not renowned for its innate sympathy for former prime ministers. Overall, public opinion seems likely to remember him as caring but weak; honest, but not really in charge and, likeable but, ultimately, unable to unite either the Conservative party or the nation.

12 Despair and Disillusion Abound: the Major Premiership in Perspective

Peter Dorey

CONSERVATIVE DISILLUSION WITH JOHN MAJOR'S PREMIERSHIP

When he was elected Conservative leader in November 1990, John Major raised the expectations of the left and the right of the party alike. Although, as Cowley has shown (Chapter 1), the party's remaining 'one-nation' Conservatives had not generally voted for Major – their vote being shared between Michael Heseltine and Douglas Hurd – they were nonetheless heartened by Major's self-proclaimed social liberalism, and his concomitant eulogy to Iain Macleod. The 'one-nation' Conservatives also anticipated that Major would herald a return to a more emollient and consensual style of leadership after the stridency of his predecessor. Such expectations were underpinned further by John Major's avowed desire to create 'a country at ease with itself', an apparent acknowledgement that the Thatcher years had been characterised by division and disunity. Yet Thatcher herself had begun her premiership with the words: 'Where there is discord, may we bring harmony . . .', a 'mission statement' which, as James Prior later remarked, proved to be 'the most awful humbug' (Prior, 1986: 113). And as Major himself was to claim when attacking Tony Blair during the 1997 election campaign, 'soundbites never buttered any parsnips'.

However, in spite of his self-professed social liberalism and emollient sentiments, Major was simultaneously viewed by the right of the Conservative party as 'our man', initially at least. After all, Thatcher herself had urged her acolytes in the Conservative party to vote for Major on the basis that he was her own choice of successor, and the candidate most likely to continue her 'revolution'. The Conservative right tended to focus on Major's apparent economic (as opposed to social) liberalism, which clearly endeared him to many of the economic determinists on the Thatcherite wing of the party.

Consequently, as one biographer of Major notes: 'Mrs Thatcher assumed, even Norman Tebbit, who led the praetorian guard in supporting him at that time, assumed, that John Major was going to carry on where she left off' (Junor, 1993: 201). Yet to describe Major as the 'choice' of those on the Thatcherite Right is to exaggerate the extent to which this section of the Conservative Party really had a 'choice', for the other two candidates in the second ballot were patently unacceptable to them. Heseltine was clearly an 'enemy within', having had the temerity to stand against Thatcher in the first place, and fatally damage her chances of remaining Conservative leader and prime minister. This was quite apart from the fact that Heseltine was viewed by the Thatcherites as an economic interventionist afflicted with pathological *dirigiste* tendencies. Furthermore, he was a leading pro-European in the Conservative Party, and this alone would have been sufficient to render him unacceptable to most of the right.

Yet the third leadership contender, Douglas Hurd, was equally unacceptable to the right, personifying the aristocratic, paternalist brand of 'one-nation' Conservatism which had consistently been derided by the Thatcherites. To the indictment of representing the tradition of *noblesse oblige* was added the charge that Hurd had been a close and loyal colleague of Edward Heath during the first half of the 1970s, thereby rendering him 'guilty by association'.

Thus it was that the right of the Conservative party actually had little effective choice when 'choosing' John Major to succeed Margaret Thatcher. Yet many of those voting for him did so in the belief that he broadly shared Margaret Thatcher's outlook and objectives, particularly with regard to curbing inflation and reducing public expenditure (Gorman, 1993: 18). The queen was dead; long live the king.

Yet having apparently given both the 'one-nation' and Thatcherite wings of the Conservative Party reason to believe that he was of their ilk, John Major's premiership subsequently proved a profound disappointment to the 'one-nation' Conservatives and Thatcherites alike.

The disappointment of 'one-nation' Conservatives has been articulated with characteristic clarity by Ian Gilmour, who laments that the Major governments 'did nothing to halt the trend towards growing inequality which had disfigured the 1980s, or to help the least well-off'. Citing a November 1995 opinion poll which suggested that two-thirds of voters thought that 'under Major's leadership,

Britain was becoming still further distanced from the One-Nation ideal', Gilmour adjudged this to be 'an accurate assessment'. As such, Major's public utterances in the 'one-nation' tradition, along with his invocation of Iain Macleod, are dismissed by Gilmour as mere 'rhetorical flourishes' (Gilmour and Garnett, 1997: 373).

Yet Gilmour does advance an interesting line of defence for Major, namely that by the 1990s, the Conservative party in Parliament had become so right-wing and fanatical – especially over Europe – that Major and other ministers did not realise how right-wing they themselves were. Consequently, because the Conservative party by now contained so many people who were even more besotted with Victorian economics than the Cabinet itself, some ministers considered themselves to be moderate and centrist (ibid.: 367). Meanwhile, one of Major's Cabinet colleagues, Ian Lang, suggested that John Major proved 'more Thatcherite than the lady herself... taking the Conservative agenda further than his predecessor did' (Lang, 1994: 3–4).

Major's subsequent failure to steer 1990s Conservatism in a more 'one-nation' direction resulted in defections by three Conservative MPs disillusioned and increasingly alarmed at the party's continued Thatcherite trajectory during the Major premiership. Alan Howarth, a junior Minister up until 1992, defected to the Labour party in October 1995, more in sorrow than in anger, complaining of 'an arrogance of power and a harshness within government which is damaging to our democracy and to the quality of relationships in our society' (*The Observer*, 8 October 1995).

Then, right at the very end of 1995, Emma Nicholson MP (and a former vice-chairperson of the Conservative party), defected to the Liberal Democrats, alleging that 'rather than my leaving the Conservative Party of Winston Churchill, Harold Macmillan and Edward Heath, the modern harsh and uncaring Conservative Party has left me' (*The Observer Review*, 31 January 1995), while also claiming that John Major was 'relying increasingly on the worst, hard-faced, populist instincts of the people' (*The Independent*, 1 January 1996).

Emma Nicholson's defection, coming just weeks after Alan Howarth's, prompted speculation about how many other 'one-nation' Conservatives would decide that John Major's Conservative party had moved too far to the right for them to remain within it. One un-named Conservative backbencher lambasted the Major government for increasingly 'appealing to base prejudice and the idiot, insolent and arrogant right', before warning John Major that while 'the right has nowhere else to go. The centre-left [does] have somewhere to go, and so too do the vast majority of the British electorate' (*Independent on Sunday*, 31 December 1995). Another similarly anonymous 'one-nation' Conservative backbencher admitted that 'it is only social reasons which are keeping me in the party really . . . I couldn't kick my constituency workers in the teeth after they have seen me through thick and thin. They're mild old-fashioned Conservatives just like me and I would not want to hurt them', although he made it clear that the loyalty of MPs like himself could not be taken for granted if John Major continued to 'pander to the right' (*Independent on Sunday*, 31 December 1995). Meanwhile, although he too refrained from defecting, Julian Critchley was another 'one-nation' Conservative who became increasingly disillusioned with John Major's 'weak and vacillating' leadership, although he acknowledges that the Conservative parliamentary party 'never gave him half a chance' (Critchley and Halcrow, 1997: 288).

Speculation about the likelihood of further 'one-nation' Conservative defections was increased by Alan Howarth's claim, immediately after Emma Nicholson had joined the Liberal Democrats, that six or seven other MPs were thought to be thinking about leaving the party. Howarth explained that when John Major had been elected to replace Margaret Thatcher, he had widely been expected 'to bring the party back to the centre ground. . . . It looked briefly as if he would do so. He spoke of a classless society. . . . It seemed that a humane Conservatism would be restored. But it wasn't.' Instead, Howarth lamented, Major subsequently bowed constantly to the right of the Conservative party and its cognate think-tanks, to the extent that by the last full year of Major's premiership, the government was only offering the electorate 'the last scrapings of decayed Thatcherism' and 'the politics of scapegoating'. As such, Howarth declared, it was time for other 'one-nation' Conservatives to follow him and Emma Nicholson in leaving the Conservative party, thereby making it clear that they 'will no longer put up with the harshness, injustice, dogmatism and stupidity of the dominant right' (Howarth, 1996: 13).

Yet, in spite of such discontent and disillusion among 'one-nation' Conservatives, the remainder of John Major's premiership witnessed only one further parliamentary defection, namely that of Peter Thurnham MP, who joined the Liberal Democrats in October 1996 – having already resigned the Conservative whip in February – claiming that John Major's Conservative party had lost touch with 'basic values of decency' (*The Sunday Times*, 13 October 1996).

Four main responses emanated from those 'one-nation' Conservatives who declined to follow the example of Alan Howarth and Emma Nicholson. Firstly, a number of them decided that they would stand down as candidates at the next general election, in which case defection was considered pointless during the final year or so of the Major premiership. Yet like Howarth and Nicholson, a number of these 'imminently retiring' Conservative MPs evidently felt that it was too late, that the battle against the right within the Conservative party had effectively been lost. Staying on to fight in a new parliament – assuming that they would retain their seats anyway in the context of a huge swing to 'New' Labour at the polls – was deemed by many 'one-nation' Conservatives to be futile.

A second response was to inaugurate or relaunch 'ginger groups' within the parliamentary Conservative party, to provide a focal point for 'one-nation' dissatisfaction with the Thatcherite orientation of the Major governments. Thus did the Macleod Group – which included Quentin Davies and Peter Temple-Morris among its members – publish a series of pamphlets during the course of 1996, which were intended 'to stop the party from fighting the next general election on an ultra-right wing platform' (McSmith, 1996: 3). Meanwhile, David Hunt, a Cabinet Minister for much of Major's premiership, launched 'Conservative Mainstream', which sought to bring together 'various Tory left ginger groups, to combat the "xenophobic hysteria" of the party's Eurosceptics' (Seldon, 1997: 650; *Independent on Sunday*, 26 May 1996; *The Times*, 27 May 1996).

The third response of 'one-nation' Conservatives who refrained from defecting was to advocate *ad hoc* alliances, joint ventures or 'trade-offs' with the Opposition parties over certain issues. For example, January 1996 heard Hugh Dykes call on John Major to do a deal with the Labour party and the Liberal Democrats whereby the imminent privatisation of British Rail would be abandoned in return for securing Opposition support for a single European currency, whereupon the Eurosceptics could be defeated by this cross-party alliance. At the same time, Edwina Currie, a leading pro-European Conservative, appeared on the same platform as two prominent Labour MPs in order to promote greater understanding of – and thus support for – a single European currency (*The Independent*, 6 January 1996).

The fourth and final response of some 'one-nation' Conservatives was to withdraw – or threaten to withdraw – their support from the Major government on specific issues, a tactic which acquired increasing resonance as defections and by-election defeats whittled away the government's parliamentary majority. For example, Hugh Dykes withdrew his 'support' from the Major government in protest over the threatened closure of the Edgware Hospital in his North London constituency, while Jim Lestor warned that the government could not rely upon his support for Michael Howard's hardline Asylum Bill during the winter of 1995–96.

Yet none of these episodes appeared to diminish the hegemony of the Thatcherite right in John Major's Conservative party. On the other hand, much to the anguish of the hitherto loyal and deferential 'one-nation' Conservatives, their responses merely served to compound the (accurate) public perceptions of a deeply divided Conservative party engaged in internecine warfare. Indeed, so deep and acrimonious were many of these divisions that the period of John Major's premiership was increasingly characterised by speculation – in the media, among academics, and even among some Conservative MPs themselves – that the Conservative party might even split completely, into a pro-European broadly 'Christian Democrat' party and a rabidly anti-European 'Little England' party.

Meanwhile, many on the Conservative right who had initially welcomed Major's election as leader became equally disillusioned and disappointed with his premiership, increasingly convinced (or convincing each other) that he was actually betraying Thatcherism, and pandering far too much to the 'one-nation' wing of the party. Indeed, one prominent Conservative observed that from the start of John Major's premiership, there were Conservatives who were 'getting ready to be "disillusioned" and who duly arrived at that state' (Clark, 1993: 377).

Certainly, many of those on the right of the Conservative party subsequently indicated that they had been mistaken in supporting John Major on the grounds that he was 'one of us'. Indeed, Thatcher herself let it be known on various occasions that she was disappointed with her chosen successor, claiming that she would not have signed the Maastricht Treaty, and that in her view, John Major had permitted public expenditure to rise too far. In short, Thatcher lamented that Major had presided over an erosion of her political legacy (see, for example, Thatcher, 1995: 474–5, 483; Thatcher, 1996: 8; *Newsweek*, 27 April 1992; *The Times*, 12 June 1995; *The Independent*, 12 January 1996).

Not surprisingly, others on the right of the party – particularly among the Eurosceptics – echoed these sentiments, with one of them declaring that 'at the time of the leadership contest we were lulled into thinking he was our man. We were completely self-deluded, partly because he was Margaret Thatcher's choice, and partly because we considered him the best bet to beat Heseltine' (Gorman, 1993: 21–2). Meanwhile, Norman Tebbit made public, on a number of occasions, his concerns and anxieties about the direction of policy under John Major, especially with regard to Europe (see, for example, Tebbit, 1991: 135; *Daily Mail*, 29 September 1992; *The Times*, 7 October 1992; *The Independent on Sunday*, 11 October 1992; *The Sunday Times*, 22 September 1996).

Other prominent Conservatives on the right of the parliamentary party who variously criticised Major's policies (deeming them to be insufficiently Thatcherite) and/or 'weak' leadership included his former Chancellor, Norman Lamont (*The Times*, 16 October 1994; *The Independent*, 20 September 1996), and another former Cabinet colleague, Nicholas Ridley, who lamented that with Major's elevation to the premiership: 'Normal, humdrum government has been resumed' (1992: 267). To this chorus of right-wing criticism was added Edward Leigh's allegation, following a Cabinet reshuffle in 1993, that: 'The left of the Tory party has now achieved its ambitions to control economic, foreign and industrial policy. The right sits beleaguered in isolated fortresses in the Home Office, Social security, and Wales' (Leigh, 1993).

Such attacks were buttressed by those routinely emanating from the plethora of right-wing groupings and tendencies within the Conservative party, most notably the Bruges Group, Conservative Way Forward, European Research Group, Fresh Start Group, 92 Group, and the No Turning Back Group.

Further condemnation of Major and his premiership – in the wake of the 1997 election defeat and his resignation – emanated from a number of Conservative academics, with John Campbell, for example, considering him to have been 'disastrous' as party leader, particularly because he failed to seize the opportunity offered by victory in the 1992 election to stamp his authority on the Conservative party, and establish a coherent alternative to Euroscepticism in the party's ranks. Consequently, Campbell laments, Europhobia spread through the party 'by default', undermining Major's authority and credibility as Conservative leader in the process. For Campbell, 'Major felt like a caretaker [leader] for seven years' (cited in Cockett, 1997: 17).

John Barnes also considers Major's premiership to have been 'pretty disastrous', with Major proving to be the party's worst leader since Balfour (who, in 1906, had also led a divided Conservative party to a calamitous electoral defeat). Indeed, Barnes alleges that Major 'never offered leadership', a failure which inevitably proved fatal (ibid.: 17).

Similarly, John Ramsden judges John Major to have been a 'catastrophically bad' Conservative leader, contributing, among other things, to the virtual collapse of Conservatism as a national force in Britain during the 1990s (ibid.: 17).

One of the few commentators to defend Major's premiership is Anthony Seldon, whose elegant biography of Major argues that many of the criticisms are vindictive and vacuous, not least because 'they have little regard for the circumstances under which Major served his premiership from 1990 to 1997'. According to Seldon, the circumstances which pertained during the 1990s were different – less propitious – than those which had existed during Margaret Thatcher's premiership in the 1980s. For example, Major faced a more united Labour party, one which also had more credible and effective leadership, while at the same time, he lacked 'a coterie of sympathetic interpreters of his policies and position in the media and intellectual life'.

Furthermore, by the time that Major became leader, 'the battle for ideas had been won', with old adversaries slain or lying in ruins (such as the former Soviet Empire), and the Labour party itself now embracing 'the market'. In such circumstances, Seldon argues, Major's opportunities and room for manoeuvre were extremely limited, and became even more constrained after 1992, due to a dwindling parliamentary majority which, in turn, seemed to strengthen the 'blackmail' potential of a hard core of Europhobes of the government's backbenches. Taking such circumstances into account enables Seldon to conclude that: 'Major was neither non-entity nor failure', but 'an important if unruly premier' (Seldon, 1997: 743).

Of the criticisms of Major delineated above, the most plausible are those of the 'one-nation' Conservatives, who lament that he merely drifted with a Thatcherite tide, thereby moving even further away from the 'one-nation' principles which he purported to believe in. In this respect, the allegations of the Conservative right that Major's premiership heralded a betrayal of Thatcherism seem bizarre, probably reflecting just how far from reality the Thatcherites had become.

Far from betraying Thatcherism, Major's premiership constituted a consolidation of it. 'Majorism' was merely Thatcherism without Thatcher, and with slightly less abrasive or strident rhetoric. Yet the overall objectives remained, along with the continued pursuit of a number of policy initiatives. As one commentator notes: 'It is difficult to construe the vote by Conservative MPs in 1990 as one for ideological change ... neither his election as party leader in 1990 nor his general-election victory in 1992 was a turning point. ... Differences between Major and Thatcher are largely of personality and rhetoric, and of style rather than substance' (Kavanagh, 1997: 202, 206). A similar conclusion is arrived at by Ludlam and Smith, who assert that '"Majorism" is more style than substance ... Major's direction has been one of implementing Thatcherism rather than challenging its key precepts. In policy area after policy area, Major has maintained the Thatcherite agenda' (Ludlam and Smith, 1996: 278–9; see also Dutton, 1997: 144–8).

THE MAJOR PREMIERSHIP'S CONTINUITY WITH THATCHERISM

As the chapters in this volume have indicated, the Major premiership represented a continuation of Thatcherism in a wide range of policy areas, even if Major's personal style of leadership and rhetoric was less rebarbative. John Major may have exuded a more conciliatory and collegial image, but as actions speak louder than words, Gilmour is among those who conclude that the Major governments were merely 'drifting with dogma' (Gilmour and Garnett, 1997: Chapter XV).

While there is considerable validity in Gilmour's claim, it would be somewhat misleading to claim that Major himself was merely 'drifting with dogma', which strongly implies that he lacked his own policy preferences and predilections. With regard to many objectives and policies, Major seemed more than willing to continue in a Thatcherite direction. While sympathetic commentators (such as Seldon) depict Major as constrained by circumstances, this overlooks the point originally made by Marx that men make their own history, even though it is not in circumstances of their own choosing. Within the constraints imposed by circumstances and a constellation of forces, there still exists at least some scope for choice and prioritisation. Thus, to characterise the Major premiership as one constrained by unfortunate or unfavourable circumstances is to veer perilously close to an unduly determinist, structuralist account of 'Majorism', whereby Major had little choice but to 'drift' with Thatcherite dogma.

Yet the Major premiership did evince a considerable degree of *choice* in the pursuit of a distinctly Thatcherite policy agenda. If John Major was a 'prisoner of circumstances', as some commentators intimate, then he gave ample indication of being a 'willing prisoner', declaring, for example, his determination to deliver a 'radical Tory agenda . . . a radical programme', based on 'four cardinal principles: choice, ownership, responsibility and opportunity for all'. In policy terms, this meant 'lower personal taxation . . . firm control of inflation . . . a rigorous approach to public expenditure . . . free up markets . . . we will carry forward the pursuit of economic liberalism' (Major, 1993; see also Major, 1992; 1997).

Major's premiership certainly evinced a continuation of the Thatcherite programme of reforming the institutions of the state and its public sector. Indeed, in a number of respects and areas, the Major governments went further and faster than those of Margaret Thatcher in the 1990s. As Theakston (Chapter 2) illustrated, in spite of the initial hopes among civil servants that John Major's elevation to the premiership would herald a calmer, more conciliatory approach, the scope and pace of civil service reform actually increased. The acceleration and extension of the Next Steps programme not only gave rise to growing concern about 'privatisation by stealth' in the civil service, but also about the decline of the public-service ethos. Furthermore, 'agencification' raised serious doubts about the continued efficacy of the traditional constitutional doctrine of individual ministerial responsibility. Major's determination to continue with the reform of the civil service, going further and faster than his predecessor had done, coupled with the rhetoric about 'rolling back the frontiers of the state' and introducing private-sector practices and management techniques into the public sector, certainly indicates remarkable continuity with Thatcherism.

Similarly, with regard to local government, Kingdom (Chapter 3) clearly illustrates the radical reforming zeal which characterised the Major premiership. As with the civil service, the early expectations were that Major would yield a more constructive relationship between central and local government, partly because of Major's apparently more consultative and collegial style generally, partly because

of his own background in local government, and partly because of
the haste with which a replacement for the poll tax was sought.
Yet it soon became apparent that the first two factors counted for
nought with regard to Major's approach to local government, while
the replacement of the poll tax was a policy reversal derived from
electoral expediency, not from any repudiation of Thatcherite objectives and policies generally.

Town halls thus found themselves subjected to the same type of
reforms as Whitehall itself. Indeed, the very *raison d'être* and rationale of local government were increasingly called into question,
as more and more services formerly provided by local authorities
were subjected to Compulsory Competitive Tendering and contracting-
out, both of which sought to introduce or incorporate market forces
and private-sector practices into local government, while also placing
a premium on the pursuit of efficiency and cost-effectiveness.

Yet while Major and his ministers waxed lyrical about greater
consumer sovereignty and the accountability of service-providers to
local users, Major's governments also presided over a proliferation
of unelected quangos – the new magistracy – whose members were
frequently subject to appointment or approval by government ministers. Furthermore, many such appointees were businessmen/women,
which in turn seemed to imply that they were probably Conservative
sympathisers or fellow-travellers. Why a successful background in
manufacturing biscuits or selling cars was deemed to render someone proficient in managing a hospital (via an NHS Trust), for example, remains one of the enduring mysteries of the Major premiership.

In education, meanwhile, Major and his ministers enthusiastically continued the reforms initiated under Thatcher, with the
National Curriculum, testing of pupils at 'key stages', and an emphasis on 'back to basics' in the form of a renewed emphasis on
the '3 Rs', all hailed as vital to the raising of standards (Chapter 8).
At the same time, the repeated attempts at encouraging more schools
to 'opt out' of the control of their local education authority were
depicted as crucial to the professed goal of increasing parental choice,
while simultaneously serving to reduce further the role of local
government, and virtually eliminating local education authorities
altogether. The Major premiership also invoked Thatcherite populism
in its repeated attacks on the teaching profession and the constant
denigration of the so-called 'education establishment', with 'incompetent teachers' and 'trendy teaching methods' subjected to particular scapegoating.

Meanwhile, when each August's A-level results indicated an improvement on the previous year's results, the immediate response of Major's ministers was not to praise either the pupils or the teachers involved, but to allege that standards had obviously been diluted, that examiners were obviously being 'soft' in their marking, and thereby awarding too many high grades. Such spiteful vindictiveness and mendacity were all too typical of the Major governments' attitude towards the public sector and those employed within it, whatever warm words Major himself might occasionally have uttered about wanting to see the provision of 'quality public services' or rewarding good teachers.

Similar hostility characterised the Major governments' attitude and approach towards the trade unions (Chapter 10). Again, there was some initial expectation that Major's election to the Conservative leadership might result in a more constructive and consensual stance *vis-à-vis* the trade unions and industrial relations after Thatcher's unrelenting hostility and attacks, but as with the civil service and local government, such anticipation proved groundless. Instead, Major's second government introduced further 'employment' legislation (presented as a means of enhancing the rights of trade union members *vis-à-vis* their unions while actually serving to weaken still further the trade unions *qua* institutions *vis-à-vis* employers), abolished both the NEDC and Wages Councils, encouraged the replacement of collective bargaining by individual or local-level bargaining, imposed a pay-freeze on public-sector workers, and fiercely resisted European Union initiatives – most notably the Social Chapter, and the 48-Hour Directive – to provide some rights and protection for employees. In all of these areas, Major and his Ministers invoked the rhetoric of 'labour market flexibility', being more 'competitive', keeping down labour costs, and upholding management's right to manage. In short, Major's approach to the trade unions and the labour market was entirely in accordance with the principles, prejudices and policies of Thatcherism.

At a wider level, the Major governments' refusal to welcome the trade unions back in from the cold was symptomatic of its attitude towards organised interests generally. As Baggott and McGregor-Riley explain (Chapter 4), while there were early expectations and indications that Major's premiership would herald a return to the 'philosophy of consultation', subsequent events indicated that in spite of his more conciliatory and collegial image, those organised interests which had been disregarded or excluded under Thatcher

– particularly at the formulation stage of the policy process – continued to be so under Major.

The Major governments thus found themselves embroiled in conflicts with a number of professions (and their representative institutions), most notably doctors, teachers and the police, all of whom sought to resist the imposition of reforms which they had not been consulted about. On the other hand, this also sustained a pattern which had been discernible under Thatcher, namely combative rhetoric and refusal to consult or compromise with organised interests at policy formulation stage, but then a subsequent tendency to seek a rapport and agreement on reforms at implementation stage. On the other hand, Major did appear ever-willing to listen to the views of the plethora of right-wing think tanks which had grown in number and/or influence while Margaret Thatcher had been Prime Minister. This, in turn, further indicates the extent to which Major *willingly* maintained a Thatcherite trajectory, as opposed to reluctantly doing so merely due to policy inheritance and extraneous circumstances constraining his room for manoeuvre.

One other area of policy which evinced continuity with Thatcherism during Major's premiership was that of social security. In this sphere too, as Hill explains (in Chapter 9), the emphasis was on curbing welfare expenditure, tightening up on eligibility for social security benefits, curbing housing benefit, emphasising the need for greater 'targeting' on those in greatest need, encouraging recourse to private pensions and other insurance schemes, and repeatedly attacking the 'dependency culture' which the social security system allegedly promoted.

Many of these concerns, in turn, prompted the most significant – and controversial – innovation concerning social security policy during John Major's premiership, namely the establishment of the Child Support Agency. Although this was portrayed by Conservative ministers as a means of ensuring that 'absent fathers' made an adequate financial contribution towards the raising of their children, it was widely seen as a Treasury-driven innovation, whose primary purpose was to yield savings in the social security budget. It also reflected the concern expressed by many Conservative ministers about the increasing numbers of single parents – particularly unmarried mothers – in contemporary Britain, with much of this increase being attributed to the 'generosity' and 'easy availability' of social security benefits.

However, some of the social security reforms pursued during John

Major's premiership alienated some of the Conservative party's own natural supporters, most notably older voters, among whom there was growing concern about the future safety and value of their pensions, and among those owner-occupiers who subsequently became redundant – as a consequence of the extensive 'delayering and downsizing' of the early 1990s – whereupon they discovered that the government – 'their' government – had placed significant new curbs on the payment of mortgage interest via Income Support. Thus did the Major governments discover the extent to which the politics of welfare reform clashed with the politics of electoral support. Railing against the 'workshy' and single parents was easy; reforming the 'middle-class welfare state' was rather less so.

One of John Major's boldest initiatives was undoubtedly his own contribution to the search for peace in Northern Ireland, for as Norton explains (Chapter 6), whereas previous initiatives had sought to incorporate the constitutional parties only in any dialogue and institutional innovations, Major's efforts actually included Sinn Fein and the IRA, reflecting, in large part, a belief that the Republicans genuinely yearned for an end to conflict in Northern Ireland. Meanwhile, the Downing Street Declaration sought simultaneously to assuage both Nationalist and Unionist aspirations in Northern Ireland, and in so doing, it went much further than previous peace initiatives.

Yet, ultimately, although the paramilitaries on both sides in Northern Ireland subsequently announced ceasefires in lieu of participating in talks about the future of Northern Ireland, expectations that John Major might actually secure an historic solution to the Troubles were not to be realised. Instead, his brave peace initiative foundered for similar reasons that previous peace initiatives in Northern Ireland had failed. The problems remained intractable.

Meanwhile, Major was faced with increasing nationalist aspirations in other parts of the United Kingdom, namely Scotland and Wales. Yet as Jones points out (Chapter 7), while John Major regularly invoked such principles as 'rolling back the state', devolving and delegating power away from central government, increased choice, diversity and flexibility, and the reform of government itself, he resolutely refused to countenance devolution for Scotland and Wales (in spite of also invoking the principle of subsidiarity when seeking to resist further European integration). Major maintained that 'the Union' (of England, Scotland and Wales) was inviolate and non-negotiable (a stance which seemed somewhat at variance with his stance towards Northern Ireland). Major was unable and unwilling to yield to Scottish and Welsh demands for devolution, insisting that acceding to such aspirations would herald the complete break-up of the United Kingdom. In this respect, Major apparently failed to appreciate the extent to which the future of the Union was threatened precisely by the intransigence of his government when faced with Scottish and Welsh demands for devolution. Yet having had their demands for devolution emphatically rejected by Major's government, the Scottish and Welsh electorates resoundingly rejected the Major government itself at the polls on 1 May, to the extent that the Conservatives were left without any MPs in Scotland or Wales.

Yet it was Europe which was undoubtedly the real *bête noire* of John Major's premiership, and which increasingly threatened to split the Conservative party in two. Yet as Wincott, Buller and Hay observed (Chapter 5), John Major initially seemed to enjoy considerable success in his dealings with Europe, having obtained 'opt-outs' for Britain when signing the Maastricht Treaty. However, his claim to have won 'game, set and match' in the wake of these opt-outs proved premature, for thereafter, Europe was to render the Conservative parliamentary party increasingly fractious and unmanageable, while also undermining John Major's own authority and credibility as party leader and prime minister. Major effectively permitted the vociferous Eurosceptics increasingly to set the terms of debate within the Conservative party – with much of the press enthusiastically encouraging them – over Europe, thereby ensuring that, in spite of Major's own claim about wishing to place Britain at the 'heart of Europe', his government's stance hardened against further integration.

Furthermore, it was Europe which was to yield probably the most calamitous event of the Major premiership, namely Britain's enforced withdrawal from the Exchange Rate Mechanism in September 1992. Not only was this humiliating exit seized upon by Conservative Eurosceptics as evidence of the futility of European economic and monetary union, it also fatally damaged the Conservative party's hitherto reputation as *the* party of economic competence. From this episode onwards, the party's Eurosceptics became ever more vocal and vicious in their attacks on Europe and John Major, while the Conservatives trailed the Labour Party by double-figures in the opinion polls for the next four-and-a-half years. If Europe was the issue which had, ultimately, heralded Margaret

Thatcher's own downfall, then it seems plausible to claim that it subsequently served to bring down John Major's government in its entirety.

What compounded John Major's problems *vis-à-vis* the Conservative party and Europe was the surprise 1992 election victory, for instead of providing him with a personal mandate to govern, it yielded him with a much reduced parliamentary majority which rendered him increasingly vulnerable to backbench rebellions. Furthermore, as Cowley points out (Chapter 1), the balance of the parliamentary party shifted after April 1992 in a Eurosceptic direction. Increasing Euroscepticism on the Conservative backbenches, aligned with a small – and diminishing – parliamentary majority, proved a lethal combination for Major. However, it was not just European issues which left him vulnerable to backbench dissent and rebellion; on a range of other policies and proposals also, the government was variously obliged to abandon or modify its plans due to the opposition of a number of Conservative MPs.

The much-publicised divisions and disagreements – mostly, but not solely, over Europe – which manifested themselves in the Conservative party during John Major's premiership also contributed towards the disappointing opinion-poll ratings which both Major himself, and his government, experienced from 1992 onwards. As Broughton's analysis reveals (Chapter 11), although Major initially enjoyed a positive image among voters, for most of his premiership – especially after the 1992 election victory – he fared badly in terms of public perceptions of his leadership, being seen increasingly as ineffective, indecisive, and 'not really in charge'. Furthermore, given that he had placed such emphasis on creating a nation 'at ease with itself', it is highly significant that by 1993, only 13 per cent of voters thought that he was 'able to unite the nation'.

Meanwhile, the 'popularity' of the Major governments was also seriously affected by a number of economic factors, including the débâcle of Britain's forced withdrawal from the Exchange Rate Mechanism in September 1992, white-collar redundancies, negative equity for home-owners, and various increases in indirect taxation. Indeed, having won a surprise victory in the 1992 general election largely, it seems, due to public perceptions of the Conservative party's economic competence, the ERM fiasco less than six months later destroyed this perception, and thereafter, the Conservative party trailed the Labour party in opinion polls concerning economic competence.

In short, Broughton illustrates that while John Major was widely liked as a person, this did not make him a popular premier. He was widely viewed by voters as affable, but ineffective. Yet with the Conservative party losing its reputation for economic competence in September 1992 (and never recovering it), and clearly divided over Europe, it is unlikely that the Conservative party would have fared much better under any other leader, particularly once the government also become mired in allegations about sleaze and corruption.

As well as evincing the continuation of Thatcherism *vis-à-vis* its policies and objectives, the Major premiership also witnessed a continued tendency for Ministers to seek scapegoats on whom the country's problems, or the government's own policy failures, could be blamed. The Soviet Union and Moscow were replaced by the European Union and Brussels as Britain's external enemies, while single parents and incompetent or 'trendy' teachers replaced the trade unions as the 'enemy within'. Being a minister under John Major – just like having been a minister in the Thatcher governments – meant never having to say sorry. The task of consolidating and extending Thatcherism precluded humility or the slightest degree of self-doubt. If policies appeared not to be working, then only one of three explanations was acknowledged: firstly, 'enemies', such as the European Commission, single parents or the 'education establishment', were obstructing or subverting the Government's objectives and policies.

Secondly, those charged with responsibility for implementing government policies were failing in their duties. For example, when prisoners escaped from top-security prisons, it was the Director-General of the Prison Service, along with prison governors generally, who were deemed responsible and blameworthy, rather than the Home Secretary. Similarly, the plethora of problems and blunders associated with the Child Support Agency were blamed on the officials running the CSA, rather than on the Secretary of State for Social Security. (It was one of the abiding ironies of the Major premiership that while ministers constantly preached the principle of individual responsibility – a cardinal tenet of 'back to basics' – they became less and less inclined to accept any such responsibility themselves.)

Thirdly, on those occasions when a policy was not working or not proving popular, the response of Major and his ministers was frequently that the policy itself was correct, but the message was not getting through; the policy needed to be explained more carefully or convincingly to the electorate. The certainties which Thatcherism inculcated in those subscribing to it meant that, with the exception of the poll tax, a policy could not publicly be acknowledged to be wrong; instead, problems signalled the need for better presentation, rather than any change to policy itself (an arrogant conceit which the Blair government also readily displayed during its first year in office).

Following on from these three responses to policy failure, one deeply disillusioned former Conservative MP – whose disillusionment was such that he decided to stand down at the 1997 election – observed that:

> the Tory right is closed to reason. Listening to them, I am reminded of nothing so much as my time in the Soviet Union and communist China. Question their stance towards Europe and you are an objective ally of Brussels. Sound warnings about the depredations of free markets and you are a protectionist. Draw attention to the persistent stratifications of British society and you are a class-warrior. (Walden, 1997: 17)

Furthermore, by virtue of being 'closed to reason', the Conservative right were – and remain – unable to comprehend the contradictions of the Thatcherite policies and principles which they myopically subscribed to, and which the Major premiership largely pursued. In abandoning the traditional Conservative scepticism of ideology and dogmatic schema derived from abstract principles, the Thatcherite right – oblivious to the irony – displayed the same mindset as many 'vulgar' or unreconstructed Marxists, entailing a fanatical and unshakeable belief in the theoretical and logical infallibility of its political doctrine, coupled with strong elements of economic determinism and faith in historical inevitability. As such, anything less than 100 per cent commitment to, and pursuit of, the ideology is deemed to constitute betrayal (by the leadership) and 'revisionism'. As George Watson observed: 'The New Right has hardly noticed how much of a mirror image of the Old Left it has become' (Watson, 1987: 71; see also Gray, 1997: 23).

CONTRADICTIONS OF MAJOR'S CONSOLIDATION OF THATCHERISM

Major claimed to believe in a classless society, and when elected leader of the Conservative party in November 1990, proclaimed his desire to create 'a nation at ease with itself'. Yet pleasant platitudes spoken to the press corps assembled in front of 10 Downing Street often bear no relation to the attitudes and actions which follow. After all, John Major's predecessor had stood in virtually the same spot in May 1979 and (mis)quoted St Francis of Assisi by suggesting that 'where there is discord, may we bring harmony', an apparent mission statement subsequently dismissed by James Prior as 'the most awful humbug' (Prior 1986: 113).

Major may well have been more genuine or sincere in his desire to achieve such an objective, but he was hardly more successful. On the contrary, his premiership left the country in deep despair and disillusion. Various reports and statistics confirmed that the gap between rich and poor had grown even wider than when Thatcher was prime minister, a direct consequence of the Thatcherite economic and social policies which John Major inherited, consolidated and, in some policy areas, extended. For example, whereas in 1991, the richest 1 per cent of the population owned 17 per cent of Britain's marketable wealth, but just three years later, their share had increased to 19 per cent, while the same period witnessed the top 10 per cent increase their share of marketable wealth from 47 per cent to 51 per cent. In stark contrast, by the time that John Major left office, the poorest 10 per cent of the British nation earned just 3 per cent of the country's total earnings (see, for example, *Social Trends 28*, 1998: 104; Kellner, 1996: 6–8; Institute of Fiscal Studies, 1997).

One of the most profound contradictions that bedevilled Major's premiership was the irreconcilable tension between the neo-liberal emphasis on the primacy of market forces in the economic sphere, and the Conservative defence of traditional institutions in the social sphere. In the economic sphere, the emphasis remained on modernisation and dynamism, with competition and the profit motive being the *sine qua non* of all economic activity. Yet in the social sphere – to the extent that such a thing as society was acknowledged – the emphasis was on the restoration of the family, and 'back to basics', thus urging respect for established institutions and sources of authority. Economically, Major's premiership purported to look towards the twenty-first century, yet socially, it harked back to the allegedly halycon days of the 1950s (before the wicked 1960s came along and ruined everything).

Major himself famously depicted his image of the England he dreamt of, namely one in which old maids would cycle unhindered to communion along country lanes, while spectators watching cricket on the village green would sup warm ale. Yet the relentless march of market forces and commercialism which Major seemed happy to support was destroying the remnants of this idyll; the country lane was being replaced by a motorway bypass, while attendance at communion was dwindling, not helped by the legalisation of Sunday trading (shopping malls became our new cathedrals). Meanwhile, the village green was being sought by property developers eager for a new plot on which to build yet another private housing estate of 'executive starter homes'. At the same time, the pub serving warm ale was doubtless being transformed into a theme pub, serving designer beers, and replete with deafening 'techno' music, karaoke nights, and huge TV screens showing live sport.

In short, the social vision which Major seemed to subscribe to was being destroyed by the very market forces which he and a great many of his Conservative colleagues worshipped. Once again, the economic triumphed over, and undermined, the social. Roger Scruton was one of the few Conservative commentators to acknowledge the fundamental incompatibility between unbridled economic competition and commerce on the one hand, and social stability and continuity on the other (Scruton, 1980). Similar observations were made throughout the 1990s by John Gray, who insisted that 'Free markets disrupt traditions and nullify the authority of the past', and by 'subjecting people to a containing imperative of job mobility, make settled communities and enduring relationships harder to sustain'. Ultimately, Gray warned, 'free markets work against traditional Tory values', and it is upon this contradiction that contemporary Conservatism has 'foundered' (Gray, 1997: 23–4; Critchley and Halcrow, 1997: 38–40). Yet the Thatcherites who acquired hegemony in the Conservative party during the 1980s and 1990s possessed neither the wisdom nor the willingness to acknowledge such contradictions.

Meanwhile, by the end of Major's premiership, the NHS was widely deemed to be teetering on the brink of collapse, starved as it had been of resources, resulting in regular ward and hospital closures, along with the redundancies of thousands of committed, experienced nursing staff. Yet at the same time, the NHS bureaucracy grew apace, fuelled by the internal markets which – as in other public services – generated new and ever-expanding strata of administrators, accountants and managers whose salaries were partly financed by cutting back on 'front-line' staff. In 1991, the NHS employed 470 000 nursing and midwifery staff, but by 1995, this number had fallen to 421 000. During the same period, the number of clerical and administrative staff increased from 152 000 to 165 000, while the number of managers rose from 16 000 to 26 000 (*Social Trends 27*, 1997: 140).

Here too was a delicious irony, namely that Major and his ministers – like those of the Thatcher governments – regularly railed against bureaucracy, and milked the applause of the Conservative faithful at Party conferences by pledging to slash the red tape which allegedly stifled enterprise and entrepreneurs, yet marketisation of the public sector yielded a relentless increase in paperwork and form-filling. Many public-sector professionals – already suffering plummeting morale and a relentless decline in pay (compared to their private-sector counterparts) – found themselves devoting ever more time and energy behind their desks, writing reports and ticking boxes rather than actually providing the services which they thought they were primarily employed to provide, and which had usually been their primary motivation for entering a public-sector profession. Still, at least patients lying on trolleys in some hospital corridor, waiting for their treatment, could while away the hours playing 'spot the nurse' amid the NHS business managers and grey suits.

Two further contemporary Conservative contradictions were discernible in the increasing hostility towards the European Union which characterised Major's premiership. Firstly, in resisting moves towards closer European integration, Major and his ministerial colleagues repeatedly invoked the principle of subsidiarity, whereby decisions should be taken at the lowest possible level or tier, closest to the people most directly affected by those decisions. Yet without any apparent appreciation of the irony or inconsistency, the Major governments obstinately refused to countenance any devolution of power to Scotland or Wales, or to regional English assemblies. While the British people were to be 'saved' from the centralising and dictatorial tendencies ascribed to the European Commission in Brussels, they were nonetheless to be subject to the very same tendencies as evinced by the Major governments at Westminster and Whitehall.

The second contradiction which became discernible as a consequence of the Major governments' increasing hostility towards the European Union derived from the notions of British sovereignty and national autonomy, which the Conservative right invoked so frequently and passionately. Those on the right of the Conservative party who were most vocal in excoriating the alleged threat posed to Britain's independence by the European Union and Commission were invariably the same Conservatives who lauded globalisation and international free trade, and who insisted that Britain had to compete with – and emulate – the so-called 'tiger economies' of Southeast Asia.

It was most curious that Conservatives who apparently wanted the British people to remain in control of their own historical and economic destiny also wanted to expose the British economy fully to the vagaries of the global economy, whereupon a range of economic factors impacting upon investment, employment, wages and interest rates in Britain would nonetheless be determined, not by the British people or their elected representatives at Westminster, but by the activities and decisions of unelected and unaccountable foreign currency speculators and multi-national corporations, neither of whom respected or acknowledged national boundaries or interests in their relentless search for higher or quicker profits.

No contradiction was acknowledged by Major and his ministers between the avowed goal of valiantly defending Britain's economic interests and independence (*vis-à-vis* the European Union), and insisting that Britain had to rely upon 'inward investment' in order to secure jobs and prosperity. Hence the awful spectacle of 'patriotic' Conservative ministers boasting to other countries about the low wages and minimal employment protection which prevailed in Britain, in the hope that investment would consequently be transferred to the UK. In the same context, an increasing proportion of the industries privatised by the Thatcher and Major governments were subsequently taken over by foreign companies and business tycoons, thereby reducing Britain's economic independence and 'sovereignty' still further.

To put it another way, the political vision implied by Conservative Eurosceptics, whereby Parliament and democratically elected politicians retain control over Britain's economic policies, is incompatible with their economic vision, whereby the performance of the British economy – and thus the economic well-being of the British people – is subject to the interplay of international market forces over which national governments have little, if any, control.

Furthermore, in order to render the British economy more competitive, the Major governments continued with the Thatcherite attacks on the trade unions and the rights of working people. In the name of patriotism and the national interest, British workers were exhorted to work longer hours, sometimes for less pay, and rather than complain at such exploitation, to be grateful that they at least had a job. 'Labour market flexibility' became the mantra of 'employment' policy during John Major's premiership, while the increasingly common phenomenon of 'job insecurity', inducing fear among the white-collar middle classes (many of them hitherto Conservative voters), was insensitively dismissed by ministers as 'a state of mind'.

It thus became increasingly apparent that the Thatcherite right in John Major's Conservative party, however flamboyantly and ostentatiously it donned the Union Jack, viewed the British people with the same contempt and arrogance as it viewed Europe, and foreigners in general. Indeed, it was George Walden – a Conservative MP until he stood down in 1997 – who noted with sadness that 'It is one of the quirks of our national supremacists that they entertain a low opinion of their countrymen . . . a swinish multitude to be fed populist swill, and enjoined to display . . . "plebian patriotism"' (Walden, 1997: 16).

WHY THE CONSERVATIVES LOST IN 1997

In 1997, Major led the Conservatives to a calamitous election defeat, one which left the Party with its lowest share of the vote since 1832, and its lowest number of MPs since 1906. Half of the Conservative party's MPs lost their seats, as did a third of its Cabinet ministers. At the same time, no Conservative MPs were elected in Scotland or Wales.

Loss of Traditional Conservative Support

The 1997 election defeat also reflected an unprecedented loss of support from traditionally Conservative sections of British society. Most notable was the fact that on 1 May 1997, only 25 per cent of the C1s (routine middle class) supported the Conservative party, down from 41 per cent in 1992 (see Table 12.1 opposite). Having apparently personified the stolid, dull, grey conformity of curtain-twitching, car-washing Middle England, John Major found himself abandoned in droves by 'his' people, 47 per cent of whom voted Labour (many of them for the very first time). Meanwhile, although 42 per cent of the ABs (professional and managerial categories)

Table 12.1   Class and voting in the 1997 election, percentages (1992 figures in brackets)

	AB	C1	C2	DE
Conservative	42 (57)	26 (41)	25 (38)	21 (37)
Labour	31 (20)	47 (33)	54 (41)	61 (47)
Lib Dems	21 (21)	19 (24)	14 (18)	13 (15)

Source: NOP/BBC exit poll 1 May 1997 (and 9 April 1992)

remained loyal to the Conservatives on 1 May 1997, this still constituted a 15 per cent decline in support since April 1992.

This loss of middle-class, managerial and professional support was matched by the loss of support among the working classes. For example, whereas in April 1992, 38 per cent of the fabled C2s had supported John Major and the Conservatives, only 25 per cent did so in May 1997. Among the DEs, meanwhile, support for the Conservative party slumped from 37 per cent in 1992 to 21 per cent in 1997.

The Conservatives also suffered a significant loss of support among women voters in 1997, for whereas 44 per cent of women had supported the party in 1992, only 32 per cent did so five years later.

Another measure of the calamity which befell John Major's Conservative party in May 1997 was the extent to which it lost support in those regions where it had previously appeared unassailable. As Table 12.2 reveals, while the Conservatives lost support in all regions of England, the heaviest losses occurred in what were hitherto the heartlands of London, the South-East and East Anglia, along with the East Midlands (although the Conservatives still led Labour by 9.4 per cent in the South-East). Furthermore, the South-East of England was the only one of the nine English regions in which the Conservative party secured more than 40 per cent of the vote, whereas Labour exceeded 40 per cent in no less than six of these regions.

Loss of Economic Competence

John Major's surprise success in the 1992 general election had apparently confirmed Bill Clinton's dictum: 'It's the economy, stupid.' Irrespective of its unpopular social policies or personalities, it

Table 12.2   Vote by region in 1997 (change since 1992 in brackets)

	Conservative	*Labour*	*Liberal Democrats*
North	22.2 (−11.2)	60.9 (+10.3)	13.3 (−2.2)
North-West	26.7 (−10.7)	54.2 (+ 9.3)	14.8 (−1.5)
Yorks/Humberside	27.9 (− 9.9)	51.8 (+ 7.6)	15.9 (−0.8)
East Midlands	35.5 (−11.7)	47.9 (+ 9.0)	12.9 (−1.2)
West Midlands	33.7 (−11.1)	47.8 (+10.4)	13.8 (−1.6)
East Anglia	38.7 (−12.3)	38.3 (+10.3)	17.9 (−1.6)
South-East	41.4 (−13.1)	32.0 (+11.1)	21.4 (−2.0)
London	31.2 (−14.1)	49.4 (+12.5)	14.6 (−0.6)
South-West	36.7 (−10.9)	26.4 (+ 7.2)	31.3 (−0.1)

seemed that provided a government could deliver prosperity – or convincingly promise future prosperity – to a majority of the electorate, then it was likely to be re-elected. Certainly, in 1992, John Major's Conservative party was widely seen by voters as economically more credible and trustworthy than the Labour party, in spite of having presided over a second recession in ten years, and one which particularly affected traditional Conservative supporters in the South-East of England. John Major's government was absolved of much of the blame for this recession, with many voters attributing it either to the policies of Major's predecessor, or to world recession. Even many voters who did consider the government at least partly culpable still thought that the Conservatives would more successfully steer Britain out of recession than a Labour government.

By 1997, however, the Conservatives' reputation for economic competence had been fatally damaged. The bulk of damage had been done on 16 September 1992 (thereafter known by everyone as 'Black Wednesday'), when Britain had ignominiously been forced to withdraw from the European Union's Exchange Rate Mechanism, and the recently re-elected Major government had been effectively required to devalue the pound (devaluation having previously been associated with Labour governments). The Major government never recovered from this humiliation; from this moment onwards, the Conservative party trailed Labour in the opinion polls by double figures.

Major and his ministers clearly anticipated that the damage caused by 'Black Wednesday' would be ameliorated by the next election, when a politically engineered economic recovery would yield a corresponding revival in the electorate's trust in the Conservatives' economic competence. Yet in this – as in so many other areas – Major and his ministers misjudged public opinion.

In the year or so leading up to the 1997 election, a number of economic indicators did suggest that the Major government was presiding over an increasingly healthy economy: inflation was generally below 3 per cent (except for the last quarter of 1996, when it reached 3.2 per cent), GDP increased from 2.0 per cent at the beginning of 1996 to 2.6 per cent by the end of the year, unemployment was falling every month, and average earnings were increasing, leading to a concomitant increase in consumer spending. Major and his ministers thus expected economic recovery to facilitate a corresponding recovery in the Conservative party's political fortunes as the election neared. It was not be.

Whereas in April 1992, many voters had been inclined to absolve Major and his ministers of blame for the recession, by 1997, the electorate seemed reluctant to give them credit for the subsequent economic recovery, perhaps seeing it as being in spite of, rather than because of, the Major governments' policies. After all, in 1992, Major and his ministers had insisted that economic circumstances (at that time, recessionary) were not the responsibility of the government, but a consequence of global forces beyond political control. That being the case, many voters in 1997 may well have assumed that any subsequent economic recovery was also due to economic circumstances and events beyond ministerial control. If the Major government had eschewed responsibility for recession in the 1992 election, why should it garner plaudits from the electorate for an economic upturn five years later?

In private, ministers might well have fulminated against the apparent ingratitude of the 'swinish multitude'. Yet many voters were not even convinced that Britain was 'booming' (as Conservative election posters proclaimed). According to the BBC/NOP exit poll conducted on 1 May 1997, only 25 per cent of voters believed that their (or their family's) standard of living had improved since 1992, while 38 per cent believed that it had deteriorated. The same poll also revealed that 44 per cent of the electorate trusted the Labour Party 'to take the right decisions about the economy' (an 11 per cent increase since 1992) compared to 42 per cent who trusted the Conservatives (down by 11 per cent since 1992).

Nor did its previous reputation as the party of low taxation benefit the Conservatives in 1997. On the contrary, the Labour party appeared to be highly successful in convincing voters that the

Conservatives had imposed no less than 22 tax increases on them since April 1992, either in the form of raising or increasing the scope of existing taxes – most notably VAT – or by introducing new taxes. These increases in indirect taxation outweighed any advantages which the Conservatives expected to accrue as a result of modest reductions in income tax (with further reductions promised if re-elected).

Indeed, when the BBC/NOP exit poll asked voters which party they most trusted 'to take the right decisions about income tax', Labour led the Conservatives by 44 per cent to 36 per cent, this constituting an increase (since 1992) of 13 per cent for Labour, and a reduction of 19 per cent for the Conservative party. At the same time, 59 per cent of voters expected taxes to increase if the Conservatives were returned to office, with 61 per cent anticipating increased taxation under a Labour government. It was no longer the case that voters associated higher taxes exclusively with the Labour party. Furthermore, many voters apparently reckoned that if they were likely to end up paying more taxes irrespective of who won the general election, then they might as well opt for the party which was most likely to spend any tax increases on improving Britain's public services, most notably health and education. Yet while marginally more voters expected taxes to rise under Labour, it was also the case that 9 per cent of voters thought that overall taxation would diminish under a Labour government (doubtless partly reflecting Labour's commitment to reducing VAT and introducing a 10 per cent tax-band to assist the low-paid), compared to 5 per cent who envisaged lower levels of taxation if the Conservatives were re-elected.

At a more general level, as Table 12.3 indicates, voters were more optimistic about the benefits to be accrued from Labour's policies rather than those of the Conservatives, with 24 per cent confident that Labour's policies would make things 'a lot better', while only 8 per cent had similar confidence in Conservative policies. Indeed, whereas 17 per cent of the electorate feared that Labour's policies would make things 'a lot worse', no less than 31 per cent were similarly fearful about the likely impact of Conservative policies.

Issue Saliency

Following on from the Major governments' loss of (perceived) economic competence, a further problem which affected the Conservative

Table 12.3   Voters' expectations in the 1997 election

	Labour policies would make things	Conservative policies would make things
a lot better	24	8
a little better	33	23
no difference	11	19
a little worse	16	18
a lot worse	17	31

Source: BBC/NOP exit poll, 1 May 1997

Table 12.4   Issue saliency in the 1997 election: percentage of voters citing issues as important in helping them to decide who to vote for

1. Health care	70	9. Europe	24
2. Education	62	10. Environment	24
3. Law and order	50	11. Transport	21
4. Unemployment	45	12. Animal welfare	12
5. Pensions	42	13. Northern Ireland	11
6. Taxation	35	14. Trade unions	10
7. Economy	32	15. Devolution	10
8. Housing	28		

Source: *Independent on Sunday*, 6 April 1997

party during the 1997 election campaign was that it was not seen to be sufficiently responsive to, or associated with, the issues which the electorate was most concerned about. As Table 12.4 illustrates, an *Independent on Sunday*/MORI poll conducted shortly after the official launch of the election campaign revealed that the five most important issues to voters were health care, education, law and order, unemployment, and pensions (and on all of these issues, including law and order, the Labour Party was preferred to or trusted more than the Conservatives).

Meanwhile, taxation and the economy were ranked sixth and seventh respectively, and even these issues – as we have just noted – no longer provided the Conservative party with any advantage over Labour. Not only had the Major government lost its former image of competence on these economic issues, they were also of less importance to many voters than in previous elections. In hoping to secure political capital out of economic issues, therefore, the Major government itself experienced a 'double whammy' in 1997.

Furthermore, two of the issues which Major and his ministers did seek to make political capital out of, namely trade unions and devolution, were deemed by voters to be the two least salient issues, while Europe only ranked ninth, a less salient issue than housing. Additionally, the environment was deemed to be as salient as Europe. The Major government's hope that it would benefit on polling day from Euroscepticism among the British electorate was based on an overestimation by 10 Downing Street and Conservative Central Office of the salience or importance of Europe to the voters.

Besides, attempts by the Conservative leadership to make Europe a more central issue in the election campaign merely served to remind voters of disagreements and disunity which permeated the Conservative party over this particular issue. This, in turn, compounded another problem facing the Conservatives during John Major's premiership, namely public perceptions of party unity and 'fitness to govern'.

Perceptions of Party Unity and 'Fitness to Govern'

Whereas throughout the 1980s, the Labour Party had suffered from (entirely justified) public perceptions that it was riven by internal disagreements and in-fighting, which therefore rendered it unfit to govern, by 1997, it was John Major's Conservatives who were now seen as deeply divided, particularly over Europe. While the Conservative party under John Major's leadership moved steadily towards an emphatically Eurosceptic position, as articulated by a number of high-profile ministers and ex-ministers, such as Michael Howard, Peter Lilley, Michael Portillo and John Redwood, there remained a number of senior Conservatives who were equally renowned for their pro-European stance, most notably Kenneth Clarke, Ted Heath, Michael Heseltine and Douglas Hurd.

Thus it was that when the BBC/NOP exit poll asked voters whether they thought the Conservative and Labour parties were united or divided, 84 per cent believed the Conservatives to be divided, compared to 34 per cent who considered Labour to be a divided party. This public recognition of the internal divisions permeating the Conservative party, along with retrospective judgements about the party's performance in office during the previous five years, constituted a fatal weakness in its attempts at securing a fifth consecutive election victory, while reinforcing the image of John Major as a weak leader presiding over a disagreeable and disintegrating Conservative party.

Ideological Disjuncture

As well as having lost the confidence of much of the electorate on economic issues, the Conservative party during John Major's premiership appeared to undergo a process of ideological disjuncture comparable to that experienced by Labour during the 1980s. In fact, even under Thatcher's premiership, opinion polls and attitude surveys indicated that during the course of the 1980s, the British electorate was becoming *less* enamoured with many of the tenets of Thatcherism (Crewe, 1989; Edgell and Duke, 1991; Pattie and Johnston, 1996: 53–6; Studlar and McAllister, 1992), to the extent that the Conservative party's successes at the polls in 1987 and 1992 were, in large part, in spite of public opinion, rather than a reflection of it.

By the 1997 election, however, the gulf between the Conservatism of the Major government and electoral opinion had become too wide. Major's government and the British public had, on most issues, moved further apart. Thus, for example, when the BBC/NOP exit poll asked voters whether the 'new government should or should not carry out any further privatisation', 73 per cent of respondents believed that it 'should not', while in response to the question 'Do you think that the Conservative/Labour Party is good for one class or all classes?', barely 30 per cent thought that the Conservatives were good for all classes, compared to nearly 70 per cent who believed Labour to be so.

Even on the question of whether Britain ought to join a single European currency, only a minority – albeit a sizeable minority – of respondents seemed to share the hostility of much of the Conservative party, with 36 per cent believing that Britain should never join a single currency, while 47 per cent endorsed a 'wait-and-see' stance. In other words, while just over a third of the electorate were totally opposed to British membership of a single European currency, nearly half subscribed to a pragmatic perspective. The same BBC/NOP poll also revealed that 17 per cent of the electorate believed that the new government ought immediately to declare that Britain would join the single European currency.

With regard to the issue of 'tax-and-spend', 72 per cent of voters were of the opinion that the new government should 'increase income tax by 1p-in-the-pound and spend it on Britain's schools', while nearly two-thirds of the electorate believed that the new government 'should redistribute income from the better-off to those who are less well off'.

During the 1990s, this ideological disjuncture become more pronounced, compounded by the consolidation of Thatcherism which Major's premiership wrought. That this ideological disjuncture increased during Major's premiership was partly due to the fact that the negative and corrosive consequences of Thatcherite policies became increasingly apparent as the decade progressed, and impacted upon more and more British people. The Conservative right continued to peddle the myth that 'for the electorate as a whole, Britain is not in disintegration or decay . . . for the most part, it is a society more stable, secure, prosperous (and indeed courteous) than at other periods in its history' (Lawlor, 1997: 28).

Yet most of the British electorate begged to differ, for by the 1997 general election, as we have already intimated, the idiocies of Thatcherite Conservatism stood exposed for all to see: an NHS in which experienced and dedicated nurses were made redundant in order that the Trusts could afford the salaries of another tranche of administrators and 'business managers'; a collapsing education system in which overburdened and totally demoralised teachers were snowed under with paperwork and administration resulting from government reforms, and then harangued – by the ministers responsible – for not spending sufficient time in the classroom actually teaching; a privatised railway system which was, incredibly, even more inefficient and unreliable than the nationalised industry it replaced, and in which, on one infamous occasion, hundred of services were cancelled because the company concerned had made too many of its train-drivers redundant in its desperation to yield immediate profits; the promotion of family life, and the exhortation by the Major government that parents should spend more time with their children (largely in order to prevent delinquency), while the same government was extolling the virtues of 'labour market flexibility' (entailing longer working hours), and vehemently opposing European Union policies on the 48-hour working week and paternity leave, both of which would have enabled parents to have spent more time together with their children.

A number of factors therefore, most notably ideological disjuncture, perceptions of a loss of economic competence, weak leadership, a divided (and unmanageable) parliamentary party, growing socio-economic inequality, allegations of sleaze and corruption, and declining public services, contributed to the Major government's crushing electoral defeat on 1 May. According to one commentator, the decisive termination of the Major premiership was 'an inescapable nemesis ... the fate of a party undone by ideological hubris' (Gray, 1997: 22).

After its surprise election victory in 1992, John Major's Conservative government increasingly turned its back on the British electorate. It was no surprise, therefore, that at the next general election, the British electorate readily reciprocated. John Major's Conservative government had grown tired of governing and had run out of ideas. The electorate had grown tired of John Major's Conservative government and had run out of patience. As John Major himself might have said, for a governing party to render itself so unpopular is a 'not inconsiderable achievement'.

Chronology of John Major's Premiership

1990

13 November   Sir Geoffrey Howe's resignation speech bitterly attacks Margaret Thatcher's leadership, especially her stance towards the European Union.

14 November   Michael Heseltine announces that he will challenge Margaret Thatcher for the leadership of the Conservative party.

20 November   First ballot of Conservative leadership contest: Margaret Thatcher defeats Michael Heseltine by 204 votes to 152, but is four votes short of the necessary 15 per cent majority.

22 November   Margaret Thatcher announces her resignation as Conservative leader.

27 November   John Major wins 185 votes in the second ballot of the Conservative leadership contest, and although this is technically two votes short of an outright majority, the other two contenders, Michael Heseltine and Douglas Hurd, stand down to allow Major to become leader of the Conservative party and Prime Minister.

1991

17 January   Start of the Gulf War against Iraq.

28 February   Ceasefire in Gulf War.

11 March   John Major speaks of his desire to see Britain 'at the very heart of Europe'.

19 March   Norman Lamont's Budget increases VAT from 15 per cent to 17.5 per cent.

1 April   Reforms of the NHS launched: NHS Trusts and GP fundholders established, while hospitals operate internal markets.

23 April   Michael Heseltine announces that the poll tax will be replaced by a council tax from April 1993.

20 May   Publication of White Paper on higher education, presaging the abolition of the 'binary divide' between universities and polytechnics.

22 July   John Major launches the Citizen's Charter.

1 October   Introduction of parliamentary Bill to replace the poll tax with a new council tax.

18 November   Publication of a White Paper, *Competing for Quality*, indicating which government services might become subject to competitive tendering.

9–10 December   Summit of EU leaders at Maastricht, Holland. John Major secures 'opt-out' for Britain from Social Chapter and single European currency.

1992

7 January   Britain signs the Maastricht Treaty.

21 February   Conservative MP Richard Shepherd attempts to introduce

Bill requiring the government to hold a referendum on the Maastricht Treaty.

9 April General election. Conservative party re-elected with a 21-seat majority.

6 May Queen's Speech announces government's intention to privatise British Coal and British Rail.

15 May Margaret Thatcher denounces the Maastricht Treaty in a speech at The Hague (Holland).

21 May 22 Conservative MPs vote against the Second Reading of the Bill to ratify the Maastricht Treaty.

3 June More than 100 Conservative MPs sign an Early Day Motion demanding a 'fresh start' *vis-à-vis* the European Union.

16 September Britain forced to withdraw from the European Exchange Rate Mechanism following a serious run on the pound.

13 October Michael Heseltine announces imminent closure of 31 coal mines, entailing the loss of 30 000 jobs. This proposal is hastily revised following widespread public condemnation and demonstrations.

22 October Opinion poll reveals that 77 per cent of the British public are 'dissatisfied' with John Major's premiership; only 16 per cent are 'satisfied'.

4 November Government wins Commons' debate on Maastricht Treaty by three votes, as 26 Conservative MPs vote against it.

1993

18 February Official statistics reveal that unemployment has risen to 3 062 065.

21 February In the wake of the abduction and murder of two-year old James Bulger by two boys aged 10, John Major suggests that society should 'condemn a little more and understand a little less'.

9 March Two teaching unions vote to boycott 'key stage' tests in June.

17 March Norman Lamont's Budget imposes VAT on domestic fuel.

1 April Launch of 'Care in the Community' programme.

6 May Liberal Democrats win the Newbury by-election with swing (from the Conservatives) of 28.4 per cent.

27 May Norman Lamont replaced as Chancellor of the Exchequer by Kenneth Clarke.

9 June In a speech from the backbenches, Norman Lamont criticises John Major's leadership, alleging that Major conveys the impression of 'being in office but not in power'.

22 July Major's Government is defeated by 324 votes to 316 in House of Commons vote over the Social Chapter. John Major immediately announces that the issue will be presented the following evening as a 'vote of confidence'.

23 July Major wins 'vote of confidence' by 339 votes to 299.

25 July John Major alleged to have called, in an off-the-record conversation with a television presenter, three of his Cabinet colleagues 'bastards'.

29 July Liberal Democrats win Christchurch by-election with a swing (from the Conservatives) of 35 per cent.

2 August Britain ratifies the Maastricht Treaty.

8 October   John Major's speech at Conservative party's annual conference launches 'back to basics' initiative.

15 December   John Major and the Irish Prime Minister, Albert Reynolds, sign the 'Downing Street Declaration'.

1994

29 January   Norman Lamont describes John Major as 'weak and hopeless', in an interview in *The Times*.

12 May   John Smith, leader of the Labour party, dies from a heart attack.

27 May   John Major speaks of the 'offensive problem' of begging on Britain's city streets, claiming that there was 'no justification' for it.

31 May   John Major suggests that the move towards European integration should proceed on a 'multi-track, multi-speed, multi-layered' basis.

9 June   Elections to the European Parliament, in which the Labour party wins 62 seats compared to the Conservatives' 18.
Liberal Democrats win by-election in Eastleigh, Hampshire, with a swing (from the Conservatives) of 16.3 per cent.

24 June   John Major effectively vetos the appointment of Belgian Prime Minister, Jean-Luc Dehaene, as successor to Jacques Delors as President of the European Commission.

21 July   Tony Blair elected leader of the Labour party.

4 August   A Gallup poll indicates that the Labour party has a 33 per cent lead over the Conservatives.

16 September   John Major announces the end of the six-year broadcasting ban on members of Sinn Fein.

3 November   Cabinet shelves plans to privatise the Post Office, following strong opposition to the proposal from Conservative MPs representing rural constituencies.

28 November   Eight Conservative MPs have the party whip withdrawn after abstaining from the vote on the Second Reading of the European Communities (Finance) Bill, even though John Major had effectively made support for the Bill a vote of confidence. A ninth Conservative MP voluntarily resigns the party whip.

7 December   Government defeated in Commons vote on Budget measure to increase VAT on gas and electricity to 17.5 per cent.

15 December   Labour party wins by-election in Dudley, West Midlands, with a swing (from the Conservatives) of 29 per cent.

1995

6 April   Labour party wins 20 of the 29 new Scottish local authorities, while the Conservatives win none, winning only 81 of the 1159 seats being contested.

24 April   Conservative whip restored to the eight MPs who had abstained from a crucial vote in November.

22 June   John Major resigns as Conservative leader in order to force a leadership contest, telling his critics in the party to 'put up or shut up'.

26 June   John Redwood resigns as Secretary of State for Wales in order to challenge John Major for the leadership of the Conservative party.

4 July   John Major is re-elected as Conservative leader, having polled 218 votes to John Redwood's 89. However, with 20 abstentions, critics claimed that over 100 Conservative MPs – one-third of the parliamentary party – had declined to support Major.

7 October   Alan Howarth, Conservative MP for Stratford-on-Avon, announces that he is joining the Labour party, due to the Conservatives' continued drift to the right.

29 December   Emma Nicholson, Conservative MP for Devon West and Torridge, announces that she is joining the Liberal Democrats, due to the Conservative's abandonment of 'one-nation' Toryism.

1996

19 February   Education Secretary, Gillian Shephard, announces that Sir Ron Dearing is to chair a committee of inquiry into the future of Higher Education.

20 March   Health Secretary, Stephen Dorrell, says in Parliament that there is a link between Creutzfeld-Jakob Disease and BSE (mad cow disease).

27 March   The European Commission announces a ban on the export of British beef (and related products).

11 April   Labour wins by-election in Staffordshire South-East with a swing (from the Conservatives) of 22 per cent. John Major's government now has a parliamentary majority of one.

21 May   John Major announces that, in retaliation for the EU's ban on exports of British beef, his government will veto all EU decisions requiring unanimous support.

13 June   Two Conservative MPs, Sir John Gorst and Hugh Dykes, threaten to withdraw their support from the government in protest against the possible closure of the casualty ward at a hospital in Edgware, North London.

22 July   David Heathcoat-Amory resigns as Paymaster-General due to the government's refusal to rule out completely Britain's future membership of the single European currency.

6 October   Lord McAlpine, a former Conservative party treasurer, announces his defection to the Referendum party.

12 October   Peter Thurnham, Conservative MP for Bolton North-East, joins the Liberal Democrats (having resigned the Conservative whip in February).

14 October   The House of Commons' select committee on standards and privileges launches an inquiry into allegations that a former junior minister, Neil Hamilton, accepted 'cash for questions'.

13 November   In the vote following a Commons' debate critical of its management of the BSE/beef crisis, the Major government has a majority of one.

6 December   Conservative MP Sir John Gorst announces that he is withdrawing his support for the government in protest over its policy towards a hospital in his constituency (although he does not actually resign the Conservative whip).

1997

16 January   Conservative MP Iain Mills dies; John Major's government technically in a minority (of −1).

21 January   Two Conservative MPs have to be brought to Westminster in an ambulance in order to vote on a debate on the NHS.

22 January   Government shocked by public hostility to Defence Secretary Michael Portillo's announcement that the Royal Yacht *Britannia* was to be replaced by a new yacht, costing taxpayers £60 million.

29 January   Chancellor Kenneth Clarke's sanguine views about a single European currency (expressed in a *Financial Times* interview) further infuriate Conservative Eurosceptics.

26 February   Armed Forces Minister Nicholas Soames admits that he misled Parliament over Gulf War syndrome/sickness, but claims that he was not briefed properly by his officials and military leaders.

17 March   John Major announces that the general election will be held on 1 May.

22 March   Tim Smith, a former Northern Ireland Minister, announces that he will not be standing for re-election as an MP, having admitted that he received between £18 000 and £25 000 from Mohammed Al-Fayed in 1987.

29 March   Chairman of the Scottish Conservative party, Michael Hirst, resigns following revelations that he had had a gay relationship.

17 April   John Major tries to placate Conservative Eurosceptics by promising a free vote on whether Britain should join the single European currency.

1 May   Labour win a 179-seat majority in the general election, with a swing of 10.6 per cent. A number of senior cabinet ministers lose their seats, as does the chairman of the Conservative 1922 Committee.

2 May   John Major announces his imminent resignation as leader of the Conservative party.

19 June   John Major replaced as Conservative party leader by William Hague.

Bibliography

Adam Smith Institute (1989) *Wiser Councils* (London: Adam Smith Institute).

Adam Smith Institute (1989) *Shedding a Tier* (London: Adam Smith Institute).

Adams, Gerry (1986) *The Politics of Irish Freedom* (Dingle: Brandon).

Alderman, K. (1996a) 'The passage of the European Communities (Finance) Act (1995) and its aftermath', *Contemporary British History* 10(3).

Alderman, K. (1996b) 'The Conservative Party leadership election of 1995', *Parliamentary Affairs* 49(2).

Andrews, G. (ed.) (1990) *Citizenship* (London: Lawrence & Wishart).

Arthur, Paul & Jeffrey, Keith (1996) *Northern Ireland since 1968* (Oxford: Blackwell).

Audit Commission (1993a) *Passing the Buck: the Impact of Spending Assessments on Economy, Efficiency and Effectiveness* (London: HMSO).

Audit Commission (1993b) *Realising the Benefits of Competition: the Client Role for Contracted Services.*

Baggott, Rob (1992) 'The measurement of change in pressure group activity', *Talking Politics* 5(1).

Baggot, Rob (1995) 'From confrontation to consultation? Pressure group relations from Thatcher to Major', *Parliamentary Affairs* 48(3).

Baker, David, Fountain, Imogen, Gamble, Andrew & Ludlam, Steve (1995a) 'Sovereignty – the San Andreas Fault of Conservative ideology', unpublished paper presented to the Political Studies Association (PSA) Conference, York.

Baker, David, Fountain, Imogen, Gamble, Andrew & Ludlam, Steve (1995b) 'Backbench Conservative attitudes to European integration', *Political Quarterly* 66(2).

Baker, David, Fountain, Imogen, Gamble, Andrew & Ludlam, Steve (1996) 'The blue map of Europe: Conservative parliamentarians and European integration', in Colin Rallings, David Farrell, David Denver & David Broughton (eds) *British Elections and Parties Yearbook 1995* (London: Frank Cass).

Baker, David, Gamble, Andrew & Ludlam, Steve (1993) 'Whips or scorpions?: the Maastricht vote and Conservative MPs', *Parliamentary Affairs* 46(2).

Baker, David, Gamble, Andrew & Ludlam, Steve (1994) 'The parliamentary siege of Maastricht 1993: Conservative divisions and British ratification', *Parliamentary Affairs* 47(1).

Baker, Kenneth (1993) *The Turbulent Years* (London: Faber).

Banham, John (1995) 'An opportunity to be seized', *Public Finance*, 30 June.

Barber, S. & Millns, T. (1993) *Building the New Europe* (London: Association of County Councils).

Barnett, N. & Harrison, S. (1996) 'The Citizen's Charter in local government' in J. A. Chandler (ed.) *The Citizen's Charter* (Dartmouth: Aldershot).

Baston, Lewis (1996) 'The Party coming apart at the seams', *Parliamentary Brief*, March.

BBC (1993) *File on 4*, 14 December.

Beer, Samuel (1969) *Modern British Politics* (London: Faber).

Bennett, R. (1997) 'The relation between government and business associations in Britain: an evaluation of recent developments', *Policy Studies* 18(1).

Bew, Paul & Gillespie, Gordon (1993) *Northern Ireland: a Chronology of the Troubles 1968–1993* (Dublin: Gill & Macmillan).

Bew, Paul & Gillespie, Gordon (1996) *The Northern Ireland Peace Process 1993–1996: a Chronology* (Dublin: Gill & Macmillan).

Bew, Paul, Gibbon, Peter & Patterson, Henry (1995) *Northern Ireland 1921–1995: Political Forces and Social Classes* (London: Serif).

Bew, Paul, Patterson, Henry & Teague, Paul (1997) *Between War and Peace: the Political Future of Northern Ireland* (London: Lawrence & Wishart).

Blake, Robert (1972) *The Conservative Party from Peel to Churchill* (London: Eyre & Spottiswoode).

Bogdanor, Vernon (1979) *Devolution* (Oxford: Oxford University Press).

Bolton, Eric (1993) 'Imaginary gardens with real toads' in Clyde Chitty & Brian Simon (eds) *Education Answers Back* (London: Lawrence & Wishart).

Bradbury, Jonathan (1997) 'Conservative governments, Scotland and Wales', in Bradbury, J. and Mawson, J. (eds) British Regionalism and Devolution (London: Jessica Kingsley).

Bradbury, J. & Mawson, J. (eds) (1997) *British Regionalism and Devolution* (London: Jessica Kingsley).

Bradshaw, Jonathan *et al.* (eds) (1993) *Support for Children: a Comparative Approach*, Department of Social Security Research Report 21 (London: HMSO).

Brittan, Samuel (1975) 'The economic contradictions of democracy', in *British Journal of Political Science*, vol. 5 (2).

Brittan, Samuel (1988) *A Restatement of Economic Liberalism* (London: Macmillan).

Broughton, David (1995) *Public Opinion Polling and Politics in Britain* (Hemel Hempstead: Harvester Wheatsheaf).

Broughton, David, Farrell, David, Denver, David, & Rallings, Colin (eds) (1995) *British Elections and Parties Yearbook 1994* (London: Frank Cass).

Brown, J. Andrew (1992) 'The Major effect: Changes in party leadership and party popularity', *Parliamentary Affairs* 45(4).

Butler, David & Kavanagh, Dennis (1992) *The British General Election 1992* (London: Macmillan).

Butler, D., Adonis, A., & Travers, D. (1994) *Failure in British Government: the Politics of the Poll Tax* (Oxford: Oxford University Press).

Cabinet Office (1991) *The Citizen's Charter: Raising the Standard*, Cmnd 1599. (London: HMSO).

Cabinet Office/OPSS (1994) *Next Steps: Moving On* (London: HMSO).

Chandler, J. (1996a) (ed.) *The Citizen's Charter* (Aldershot: Dartmouth).

Chandler, John (1996b) *Local Government Today* (Manchester: Manchester University Press).

Chitty, Clyde & Simon, Brian (1993) *Education Answers Back* (London: Lawrence & Wishart).

Clark, Alan (1993) *Diaries* (London: Weidenfeld & Nicolson).

Clarke, Harold, Stewart, Marianne & Whiteley, Paul (1997) 'Error-correction models of party support: the case of New Labour' in Charles Pattie, David Denver, Justin Fisher & Steve Ludlam (eds) (1997) *British Elections and Parties Review; Volume 7* (London: Frank Cass).

Cockett, Richard (1997) 'Major: the verdict of history', *Independent on Sunday*, 11 May.

Commission for Local Democracy (1995) *Taking Charge: the Rebirth of Local Democracy: Final Report* (Municipal Journal Books).

Conservative Research Department (1996) *A New Wales*, Politics Today Series, No. 10 (London: Conservative Research Department).

Cooke, Alistair (1997) *The Campaign Guide: 1997* (London: Conservative Research Department).

Cowley, Philip (1995) 'Marginality, mortality and majority: the effect of by-elections on government majorities', *Politics* 15(2).

Cowley, Philip (1996a) 'The mystery of the third hurdle: re-electing the Conservative leader', *Politics* 16(2).

Cowley, Philip (1996b) 'How did he do that?: the second round of the 1990 Conservative leadership election' in David Farrell, David Broughton, David Denver & Justin Fisher (eds) (1996) *British Elections and Parties Yearbook 1996* (London: Frank Cass).

Cowley, Philip (1996c) '111 not out: the press and the 1995 Conservative leadership contest', *Talking Politics* 8(3).

Cowley, Philip (1997) 'The Conservative Party: decline and fall', in A. Geddes & J. Tonge (eds) *Labour's Landslide* (Manchester: Manchester University Press).

Cowley, Philip & Garry, J. (1998) 'The British Conservative Party and Europe: the choosing of John Major', *British Journal of Political Science* 28(2).

Cowley, Philip & Norton, Philip (1996) *Are Conservative MPs Revolting?* Hull: University of Hull, Centre for Legislative Studies.

Coxall, Bill & Robins, Lynton (1998) *British Politics since the War* (London: Macmillan).

Crewe, Ivor (1998) 'Has the electorate become Thatcherite?' in Robert Skidelsky (ed.) *Thatcherism* (London: Chatto & Windus).

Crewe, Ivor (1989) 'Values, the crusade that failed' in Dennis Kavanagh & Anthony Seldon (eds) *The Thatcher Effect: a Decade of Change* (Oxford: Oxford University Press).

Crewe, Ivor, Norris, Pippa, Denver, David & Broughton, David (eds) (1992) *British Elections and Parties Yearbook 1991* (Hemel Hempstead: Harvester Wheatsheaf).

Crewe, Ivor (1996) '1979–1996' in Anthony Seldon (ed.) *How Tory Governments Fall* (London: Fontana).

Crewe, Ivor (1992) 'A nation of liars? Opinion polls and the 1992 election', *Parliamentary Affairs* 45(4).

Crewe, Ivor (1997) 'The opinion polls: Confidence restored?', *Parliamentary Affairs* 50(4).

Crick, Michael (1997) *Michael Heseltine* (London: Hamish Hamilton).

Criddle, Brian (1992) 'MPs and candidates', in David Butler & Dennis Kavanagh, *The British General Election of 1992* (London: Macmillan).

Critchley, Julian (1992) *Some of Us* (London: John Murray).

Critchley, Julian (1994) *A Bag of Boiled Sweets* (London: Faber).

Critchley, Julian & Halcrow, Morrison (1997) *Collapse of the Stout Party* (London: Victor Gollancz).

Curtice, John & Steed, M. (1992) 'Appendix 2: the results analysed' in David Butler & Dennis Kavanagh, *The British General Election of 1992* (London: Macmillan).

Curtice, John (1996) 'What future for the opinion polls? The lessons of the MRS Inquiry' in Colin Rallings, David Farrell, David Denver & David Broughton (eds) *British Elections and Parties Yearbook 1995* (London: Frank Cass).

Curtice, John, Sparrow, Nick, & Turner, John (1997) 'The missing Tories in opinion polls: Silent, forgetful or lost?' in Charles Pattie, David Denver, Justin Fisher & Steve Ludlam (eds) *British Elections and Parties Review, Volume 7* (London: Frank Cass).

Davies, N. (1997) *Europe: a History* (London: Pimlico).

Denver, David, Norris, Pippa, Broughton, David & Rallings, Colin (eds) (1993) *British Elections and Parties Yearbook 1993* (Hemel Hempstead: Harvester Wheatsheaf).

Department of Education & Science (1991) *Higher Education: a New Framework* Cmnd 1541 (London: HMSO).

Department of Employment (1988) *Employment for the 1990s* (London: HMSO).

Department of Employment (1991) *Industrial Relations in the Nineteen Nineties* (London: HMSO).

Department of Employment (1992) *People, Jobs and Opportunity* (London: HMSO).

Department of Health, Department of Social Security, Scottish Office, & Welsh Office (1989) *Working for Patients*, Cmnd 555 (London: HMSO).

Devine, F., White, C. & Ritchie, J. (1997) 'Voter volatility and decision-making in the 1997 general election', paper presented at the Elections, Public Opinion and Parties (EPOP) Annual Conference, University of Essex, 26–8 September.

Dicey, A. V. (1885) *Law of the Constitution* (Oxford: Oxford University Press).

Doern, B. (1993) 'The UK Citizen's Charter: Origins and implementation in three Agencies', *Policy and Politics* 21(1).

Doig, A. (1995) 'Continuing cause for concern? Probity in local government', *Local Government Studies* 21(1).

Dorey, Peter (1991) 'Corporatism in the United Kingdom', *Politics Review* 3(2).

Dorey, Peter (1993) 'One step at a time: the Conservative reform of industrial relations since 1979', *Political Quarterly* 64(1).

Dorey, Peter (1995a) *British Politics since 1945* (Oxford: Blackwell).

Dorey, Peter (1995b) *The Conservative Party and the Trade Unions* (London: Routledge).

Dorey, Peter (1996) 'Exhaustion of a tradition: the death of "one nation" Toryism', *Contemporary Politics* 2(4).

Dorey, Peter (1998) 'The new "enemies within": the Conservative attack on single parents' in *Revue Française de la Civilisation Britannique* 9(4), April.

Dorey, Peter (forthcoming) *The Politics of Pay: Governments and Wage Determination in Post-War Britain*.

Duigan, Sean (1996) *One Spin on the Merry-Go-Round* (Dublin: Blackwater Press).

Dutton, David (1997) *British Politics since 1945*, Second edition (Oxford: Blackwell).

Eckstein, H. (1960) *Pressure Group Politics: the Case of the British Medical Association* (Stanford: Stanford University Press).

Edgell, S. & Duke, V. (1991) *A Measure of Thatcherism: a Sociology of Britain* (London: HarperCollins).

Efficiency Unit (1991) *Making the Most of Next Steps* (London: HMSO).

Efficiency Unit (1993) *Career Management and Succession Planning Study*.

Efficiency Unit (1996) *Competing for Quality: Policy Review* (London: HMSO).

Evans, Brendan & Taylor, Andrew (1996) *From Salisbury to Major* (Manchester: Manchester University Press).

Farrell, David, Broughton, David, Denver, David & Fisher, Justin (eds) (1996) *British Elections and Parties Yearbook 1996* (London: Frank Cass).

Field, Frank (1997) *Reforming Welfare* (London: Social Market Foundation).

Forsyth, Michael (1996) *Fighting for Scotland* (London: Conservative Political Centre).

Fry, M. (1989) 'Claim of Wrong' in O. D. Edwards (ed.) *A Claim of Right for Scotland* (Edinburgh: Polygon).

Gamble, Andrew (1996) 'An ideological Party' in Steve Ludlam & Martin J. Smith (eds) *Contemporary British Conservatism* (London: Macmillan).

Game, C. (1997) 'How many, where and how? Taking stock of local government', *Local Government Policy Making* 23(4).

Garry, J. (1995) 'The British Conservative Party: Divisions over European policy', *West European Politics* 18(4).

Giddens, Anthony (1984) *The Constitution of Society* (Cambridge: Polity).

Gilmour, Ian & Garnett, Mark (1997) *Whatever Happened to the Tories: the Conservatives since 1945* (London: Fourth Estate).

Gipps, Caroline (1993) 'Policy-making and the use and misuse of evidence' in Clyde Chitty & Brian Simon (eds) *Education Answers Back* (London: Lawrence & Wishart).

Goode Committee (1993) *Report of the Pension Law Review Committee*, Cmnd 2342-1/2 (London: HMSO).

Gorman, Teresa, with Kirby, Heather (1993) *The Bastards* (London: Pan).

Graham, D. & Tytler, D. (1993) *A Lesson for Us All* (London: Routledge & Kegan Paul).

Gray, A. & Jenkins, B. (1996) 'Public administration and Government 1994–95', *Parliamentary Affairs* 49(2).

Gray, John (1997) 'Conservatism R.I.P.', *New Statesman*, 12 September.

Greenwood, John & Wilson, David (1994) 'Toward the contract state: CCT in local government', *Parliamentary Affairs* 47(3).

Greer, P. (1994) *Transforming Central Government: the Next Steps Initiative* (Buckingham: Open University Press).

Hague, M. (1996) 'Labour's dangerous plans for Wales' in Conservative Political Centre, *The Battle for the Constitution* (London: Conservative Political Centre).

Hague, Rod & Berrington, Hugh (1995) 'A Treaty too far? Opinion, rebellion and the Maastricht Treaty in the backbench Conservative Party 1992–94', unpublished paper presented to the PSA conference, York.

Hall, W. and Weir, S. (1996) *The Untouchables: Power and Accountability in the Quango State* (London: Scarman Trust).

Hambleton, R. (1996) 'Reinventing local government – lessons from the USA', *Local Government Studies* 22(1).

Hansard Society (1993) *Making the Law: the Report of the Hansard Society Commission on the Legislative Process* (London: Hansard Society).

Harvie, C. (1989) 'Thoughts on the union between law and opinion in Dicey's last stand' in Colin Crouch & David Marquand (eds) *The New Centralism* (Oxford: Blackwell).

Haughton, G. & Strange, I. (1997) 'Turf wars: the battle for control over English local economic development', *Local Government Studies* 23(1).

Hay, Colin (1995) 'Structure and agency' in David Marsh & Gerry Stoker (eds) *Theory and Method in Political Science* (London: Macmillan).

Heator, Derek (1990) *Citizenship* (Harlow: Longman).

Hebbert, M. (1993) '1992: Myth and aftermath', *Regional Studies* 27(8).

Hennessy, Peter (1986) *The Great and the Good: an Inquiry into Britain's Establishment* (London: Policy Studies Institute).

Hennessy, Peter, Hughes, R. & Seaton, J. (1997) *Ready, Steady, Go! New Labour and Whitehall* (London: Fabian Society).

Hills, John & Mullings, Beverley (1990) 'Housing', in John Hills (ed.) *The State of Welfare* (Oxford: Clarendon Press).

Hogg, Sarah & Hill, Jonathan (1995) *Too Close to Call* (London: Little, Brown, & Co.).

Hogwood, Brian (1997) 'The machinery of government 1979–97', *Political Studies* XLV(4).

Holliday, Ian (1993) 'Organised interests after Thatcher', in Patrick Dunleavy, Andrew Gamble, Ian Holliday & Gillian Peele (eds) *Development in British Politics 4* (London: Macmillan).

Howarth, – (1996) 'Will you join the dance?' *The Guardian*, 4 January.

Howe, Geoffrey (1995) *Conflict of Loyalty* (London: Pan).

Independent, The (1993) 'Monks ready to test Tory open door' 9 September.

Institute for Management Development (1996) *World Competitiveness Yearbook* (Lausanne: IMD).

Institute of Fiscal Studies (1997) *Inequality in the UK* (London: Institute of Fiscal Studies).

Isaac-Henry, K. (1984) 'Taking stock of the local authority associations', *Public Administration* 62(2).

Jenkins, S. (1996) *Accountable to None* (Harmondsworth: Penguin).

John, Peter (1994a) 'Central–local government relations in the 1980s and 1990s: Towards a policy learning approach', *Local Government Studies* 20(3).

John, Peter (1994b) *The Europeanisation of British Local Government: New Management Strategies* (York: Joseph Rowntree Foundation).

Johnson, Nevil (1980) 'Constitutional reform: Some dilemmas for a Conservative philosophy' in Zig Layton-Henry (ed.) *Conservative Party Politics* (London: Macmillan).

Johnston, Ron, Pattie, Charles & Rossiter, David (1997a) 'Sleaze, constituency and dissent: Voting on Nolan in the House of Commons' *Area* 29.

Johnston, Ron & Pattie, Charles (1997b) 'Anchors aweigh: Variations in strength of party identification and in socio-political attitudes among the British electorate, 1991–94' in Charles Pattie, David Denver, Justin Fisher & Steve Ludlam (eds) *British Elections and Parties Review, Volume 7* (London: Frank Cass).

Jones, P. & Hudson, J. (1996) 'The quality of political leadership: a case study of John Major', *British Journal of Political Science* 26(2).

Jordan, G. (1994) 'From Next Steps to Market Testing: Administrative reform as improvisation', *Public Policy and Administration* 9(2).

Junor, Penny (1993) *The Major Enigma* (London: Michael Joseph).

Junor, Penny (1996) *John Major: from Brixton to Downing Street* (London: Penguin).

Kavanagh, Dennis (1994) 'A Major Agenda?' in Dennis Kavanagh & Anthony Seldon (eds) *The Major Effect* (London: Macmillan).

Kavanagh, Dennis (1997) *The Reordering of British Politics* (Oxford: Oxford University Press).

Kavanagh, Dennis & Seldon, Anthony (eds) (1994) *The Major Effect* (London: Macmillan).

Kellner, Peter (1996) 'The Tory report', *Independent on Sunday* (Supplement), 6 October 1996.

Kemp, Sir Peter (1993) *Beyond Next Steps: a Civil Service for the 21st Century* (London: Social Market Foundation).

Kemp, Sir Peter (1994) 'The Civil Service White Paper: a job half finished', *Public Administration* 72(4).

King, Desmond (1993) 'Government beyond Whitehall' in Patrick Dunleavy, Andrew Gamble, Ian Holliday & Gillian Peele (eds) *Developments in British Politics* 4 (London: Macmillan).

Klug, F., Starmer, K. & Weir, S. (1996) 'Civil liberties and the parliamentary watchdog: the passage of the Criminal Justice and Public Order Act 1994', *Parliamentary Affairs* 49(4).

Kohli, M. *et al.* (1991) *Time for Retirement: Comparative Studies in Early Exit from the Labour Force* (Cambridge: Cambridge University Press).

LAMSAC (1982) *Performance Review and the Elected Member* (London: LAMSAC).

Lang, Ian (1994) *The Swinton Lecture*, Delivered at the University College of Ripon and York St. John, 3 July (London: Conservative Political Centre).

Lanoue, D. & Headrick, B. (1994) 'Prime Ministers, parties and the public: the dynamics of government popularity in Great Britain', *Public Opinion Quarterly* 58.

Lansley, S., Goss, S. & Wolmar, C. (1989) *Councils in Conflict: the Rise and Fall of the Municipal Left* (London: Macmillan).

Lawler, Sheila (1997) 'Big government has had its day', *The Observer*, 23 March.

Lawson, Nigel (1992) *The View From No. 11* (London: Bantam Press).

Leach, S. (1993) 'Local government reorganisation in England', *Local Government Policy Making* 19(4).

Leach, S. (1994) 'The Local Government Review: a critical appraisal', *Public Money and Management* 41(1).

Leach, S. & Barnet, N. (1997) 'The new public management and the local government review', *Local Government Studies* 23(3).

Leigh, Edward (1993) 'The judgement of others', *The Spectator* 5 June.

Lewis, Derek (1997) *Hidden Agendas* (London: Hamish Hamilton).

Lilley, Peter (1993) *Benefits and Costs: Securing the Future of Social Security* (London: Mais Lecture).

Lister, Ruth (1994) 'The family and women' in Dennis Kavanagh & Anthony Seldon (eds) *The Major Effect* (London: Macmillan).

Local Government Management Board (1993) *Challenge and Change* (Luton: LGMB).

Local Government Management Board (1995) *Tomorrow's Town Hall* (Luton: LGMB).

Local Government Training Board (1985) *Good Management in Local Government: Successful Practice and Action* (Luton: LGTB).

Local Government Training Board (1988) *Learning from the Public* (Luton: LGTB).

Loveday, B. (1994) 'Ducking and diving: Formulating a policy for police and criminal justice in the 1990s', *Public Money and Management* 41(4).

Loveday, B. (1996) 'Business as usual? The new police authorities and the "Police and Magistrates' Courts Act"', *Local Government Studies* 22(2).

Lowndes, V. (1997) 'Change in public service management: New institutions and new managerial regimes' *Local Government Studies* 23(2).

Ludlam, Steve (1996) 'The spectre haunting Conservatism: Europe and backbench rebellion', in Steve Ludlam & Martin J. Smith (eds) *Contemporary British Conservatism* (London: Macmillan).

Ludlam, Steve & Smith, Martin J. (1996) 'The character of contemporary Conservatism' in Steve Ludlam & Martin J. Smith (eds) *Contemporary British Conservatism* (London: Macmillan).

Major, John (1992) *The Next Phase of Conservatism: the Privatisation of Choice* (London: Conservative Political Centre).

Major, John (1993) *Conservatism in the 1990s: Our Common Purpose* (London: Carlton Club/Conservative Political Centre).

Major, John (1995) *Speech to Grant-Maintained Schools Foundation* Birmingham, 12 September 1995 (mimeo).

Major, John (1997) *Our Nation's Future* (London: Conservative Political Centre).

Maloney, W., Jordan, W. & McLaughlin, A. M. (1994) 'Interest groups and public policy: the insider/outsider model revisited', *Journal of Public Policy* 14(1).

Marr, Andrew (1995) *The Independent*, 17 November.

Marsh, David & Rhodes, Rod (1992) 'The implementation gap: Explaining policy change and continuity' in David Marsh & Rod Rhodes, *Implementing Thatcherite Policies: Audit of an Era* (Buckingham: Open University Press).

Marshall, T. H. & Bottomore, Tom (1992) *Citizenship and Social Class* (London: Pluto).

Martin, S. & Pearce, G. (1994) 'The demise of the lone ranger: prospects for unitary authorities in the "New Europe"', *Local Government Policy Making* 20(5).

McGarry, John & O'Leary, Brendan (1995) *Explaining Northern Ireland* (Oxford: Blackwell).

McGregor-Riley, Victoria (1997) *The Politics of Medical Representation: the Case of the British Medical Association 1979 to 1995*, unpublished PhD thesis (Leicester: De Montfort University).

McIlroy, John (1995) *Trade Unions Today*, 2nd edition (Manchester: Manchester University Press).

McSmith, Andy (1996) 'Tory Right "repeating Labour's mistakes"', *The Observer*, 23 March.

Meikle, J. (1997a) 'Local government: All in the balance', *The Guardian*, 26 March.

Meikle, J. (1997b) 'Local government: Work in progress', *The Guardian*, 16 April.

Melding, D. (1996) 'Towards a federal Britain', *Agenda*, Winter.

Melhuish, D. & Cowley, Philip (1995) 'Whither the "new role" in policy-making?: Conservative MPs in Standing Committees, 1979 to 1992', *Journal of Legislative Studies* 1.

Millward, Neil *et al.* (1992) *Workplace Industrial Relations in Transition* (Aldershot: Dartmouth).

Mitchell, James (1995) 'Unionism, assimilation and the Conservatives' in Jill Lovenduski & Jeffrey Stanyer (eds) *Contemporary Political Studies* (Belfast: PSA).

Mitchell, N. (1987) 'Changing pressure group politics: the case of the TUC 1976–1984', *British Journal of Political Science* 17(4).

Mitchell, P. (1992) 'The lottery of competition', *Public Finance and Accountancy*, 24 January.

Montgomery-Massingberd, H. (1986) 'Top and bottom of the Tory class', *The Spectator*, 3 May.

Morris, T. (1994) 'Crime and penal policy' in Dennis Kavanagh & Anthony Seldon (eds) *The Major Effect* (London: Macmillan).

Mount, Ferdinand (1992) *The British Constitution Now* (London: Mandarin).

Mountfield, R. (1997) 'The new senior civil service: Managing the paradox', *Public Administration* 75(2).

Murray, Charles (1984) *Losing Ground* (New York: Basic Books).

Nadeau, R., Niemi, R. & Amato, T. (1996) 'Prospective and comparative or retrospective and individual? Party leaders and party support in Great Britain', *British Journal of Political Science* 26(2).

National Consumer Council (1986) *Measuring up Consumer Assessment of Local Authority Services: a Guideline Study*, NCC.

Negrine, Ralph (1995) 'The "gravest political crisis since Suez": the press, the Government and the pit closures announcement of 1992', *Parliamentary Affairs* 48(1).

Neville, L. (1997) 'Rebellions', in Martin Linton (ed.) *The Election* (London: Fourth Estate).

Nicholson, Emma (1996) *The Secret Society* (London: Indigo).

Norris, Pippa, Crewe, Ivor, Denver, David & Broughton, David (eds) (1992)

British Elections and Parties Yearbook 1992 (Hemel Hempstead: Harvester Wheatsheaf).

Norris, Pippa (1997) 'Anatomy of a Labour landslide', *Parliamentary Affairs* 50(4).

Norton, Philip (1975) *Dissension in the House of Commons 1945–74* (London: Macmillan).

Norton, Philip (1978) *Conservative Dissidents* (London: Temple Smith).

Norton, Philip (1980) *Dissension in the House of Commons 1974–79* (Oxford: Oxford University Press).

Norton, Philip (1990) '"The lady's not for turning": But what about the rest? Margaret Thatcher and the Conservative Party 1978–89', *Parliamentary Affairs* 43(1).

Norton, Philip (1992) 'The Conservative Party from Thatcher to Major' in Anthony King, David Denver, Kenneth Newson, Philip Norton, David Sanders & Patrick Seyd, *Britain at the Polls 1992* (London: Chatham House).

Norton, Philip (1995) 'Working without the whip', *The House Magazine*, 9 January.

Norton, Philip (1996) 'History of the Party III: Heath, Thatcher, Major' in Philip Norton (ed.) *The Conservative Party* (Hemel Hempstead: Prentice Hall/Harvester Wheatsheaf).

Norton, Philip (1997) 'The Conservative Party: "In Office, but not in power"', in Anthony King (ed.) *New Labour Triumphs: Britain at the Polls* (Chatham, New Jersey: Chatham House).

O'Leary, Brendan (1997) 'The Conservative stewardship of Northern Ireland, 1979–97', *Political Studies* 45(4).

O'Leary, Brendan, & McGarry, John (1993) *The Politics of Antagonism: Understanding Northern Ireland* (London: Athlone)

Olson, Mancur (1982) *The Rise and Decline of Nations* (New York: Yale University Press).

Organization for Economic Co-operation & Development (OECD) (1992) *Education at a Glance: OECD Indicators* (Paris: OECD).

Ozbudun, E. (1970) *Party Cohesion in Western Democracies: a Causal Analysis* (New York: Sage).

Parry, R., Hood, C. & James, O. (1997) 'Reinventing the Treasury', *Public Administration* 75(3).

Patten, John (1993) 'Must think harder', *The Spectator*, 2 October.

Patten, John (1995) *Things to Come* (London: Sinclair-Stevenson).

Patterson, Henry (1997) *The Politics of Illusion: a Political History of the IRA* (London: Serif).

Pattie, Charles & Johnston, Ron (1996) 'The Conservative Party and the electorate' in Steve Ludlam & Martin J. Smith (eds) *Contemporary British Conservatism* (London: Macmillan).

Pattie, Charles, Denver, David, Fisher, Justin, & Ludlam, Steve (eds) (1997) *British Elections and Parties Review, Volume 7* (London: Frank Cass).

Pearce, Edward (1991) *The Quiet Rise of John Major* (London: Weidenfeld & Nicolson).

Pearce, Edward (1992) *Election Rides* (London: Faber & Faber).

Pirie, Madsen (1988) *Micropolitics: the Creation of Successful Policy* (Aldershot: Wildwood House).

Plowden, William (1994) *Ministers and Mandarins* (London: Institute for Public Policy Research).

Prior, James (1986) *A Balance of Power* (London: Hamish Hamilton).

Public Accounts Committee (1994) *The Proper Conduct of Business* (London: House of Commons *154*, 1993–94).

Public Service Committee (1996) *Ministerial Accountability and Responsibility* (London: House of Commons *313*, 1995–96).

Public Services Committee (1997) *The Citizen's Charter* (London: House of Commons *78*, 1996–97).

Radcliffe, J. (1996) 'Community care and new public management: the local government response', *Local Government Studies* 22(4).

Rallings, Colin, Farrell, David, Denver, David & Broughton, David (eds) (1996) *British Elections and Parties Yearbook 1995* (London: Frank Cass).

Rallings, Colin & Thrasher, Michael (1997a) 'Strong case for second place', *Local Government Chronicle*, 9 May.

Rallings, Colin & Thrasher, Michael (1997b) 'The local elections', *Parliamentary Affairs* 50(4).

Ranson, S. & Thomas, H. (1989) 'Education reform: consumer democracy or social democracy?' in J. Stewart & G. Stoker (eds) *The Future of Local Government* (London: Macmillan).

Rawlings, Richard (1994a) 'Legal politics: the United Kingdom and ratification of the Treaty on the European Union (part one)', *Public Law* 1994.

Rawlings, Richard (1994b) 'Legal politics: the United Kingdom and ratification of the Treaty on the European Union (part two)', *Public Law* 1994.

Read, Melvyn & Marsh, David (1997) 'The Family Law Bill: Conservative splits and Labour Party cohesion', *Parliamentary Affairs* 50(2).

Rhodes, Rod (1986) 'Corporate bias in central–local relations: a case study of the Consultative Council on Local Government Finance', *Policy and Politics* 14(2).

Rhodes, Rod (1994) 'The hollowing out of the state: the changing nature of public service in Britain', *Political Quarterly* 65(2).

Rhodes, Rod (1997) *Understanding Governance: Policy Networks, Governance, Reflexivity and Accountability* (Buckingham: Open University Press).

Richards, S., Smith, P. & Newman, J. (1996) 'Shaping and reshaping market testing policy', *Public Policy and Administration* 11(2).

Richardson, J. J. & Jordan, G. (1979) *Governing under Pressure* (Oxford: Martin Robertson).

Richardson, J. J. (1990) *Government and Groups in Britain: Changing Styles*, Strathclyde Papers on Government and Politics 69 (Glasgow: Strathclyde University).

Richardson, J. J. (1993) 'Interest group behaviour in Britain: continuity and change' in J. J. Richardson (ed.) *Pressure Groups* (Oxford: Oxford University Press).

Riddell, Peter (1992) 'The Conservatives after 1992', *Political Quarterly* 63(4).

Riddell, Peter (1994) 'Major and Parliament', in Dennis Kavanagh & Anthony Seldon (eds) *The Major Effect* (London: Macmillan).

Riddell, Peter (1997) 'Tories have yet to face up to their new status', *The Times*, 9 October.

Ridley, Nicholas (1988) *The Local Right* (London: Centre for Policy Studies).

Ridley, Nicholas (1991) *My Style of Government* (London: Hutchinson).

Robbie, K. & Wright, M. (1996) 'Local authorities, compulsory competitive tendering and buy-outs', *Local Government Studies* 22(1).

Roberts, P. (1997) 'Whitehall et le désert Anglais' in J. Bradbury & J. Mawson (eds) *British Regionalism and Devolution* (London: Jessica Kingsley).

Rogaly, Joe (1994) Game beyond patience', *The Financial Times*, 7 December.

Rose, Richard (1985) 'From government at the centre to nation-wide government' in Yves Meny & Vincent Wright (eds) *Centre–Periphery Relations in Western Europe* (London: Allen & Unwin).

Rouse, J. (1997) 'Performance inside the quangos: Tension and contradictions', *Local Government Studies* 23(1).

Routledge, Paul (1995) *Madam Speaker* (London: HarperCollins).

Routledge, Paul (1997) *John Hume: a Biography* (London: HarperCollins).

Rowan, Brian (1995) *Behind the Lines: the Story of the IRA and Loyalist Ceasefires* (Belfast: Blackstaff).

Russel, Trevor (1978) *The Tory Party: Its Policies, Divisions and Future* (Harmondsworth: Penguin).

Sanders, David (1996) 'Economic performance, management competence and the outcome of the next general election', *Political Studies* 44(2).

Scruton, Roger (1980) *The Meaning of Conservatism* (London: Macmillan)

Seldon, Anthony (1997) *John Major: a Political Life* (London: Weidenfeld & Nicolson).

Settle, M. (1995) 'Major will have to face Welsh MPs says Hague', *Western Mail* 1 December.

Seymour-Ure, Colin (1997) 'Leaders and leading articles: the characterisation of John Major and Tony Blair in the editorials of the national daily press, 17 March–2 May 1997', paper presented at the Elections, Public Opinion and Parties (EPOP) Annual Conference, University of Essex, 26–8 September.

Sharrock, David & Devonport, Mark (1997) *Man of War, Man of Peace? The Unauthorised Biography of Gerry Adams* (London: Macmillan).

Shepherd, Robert (1991) *The Power Brokers* (London: Hutchinson).

Skelcher, C. & Davies, H. (1996) 'Understanding the new magistracy: a study of characteristics and attitudes', *Local Government Studies* 22(2).

Sowemimo, Matthew (1996) 'The Conservative Party and European integration', *Party Politics* 2(1).

Stephens, Philip (1996) *Politics and the Pound: the Conservatives' Struggle with Sterling* (London: Macmillan).

Stephens, P. (1997) *Politics and the Pound* (London: Macmillan).

Stoker, Gerry (1993) 'Introduction: Local government reorganisation as a garbage can process', *Local Government Policy Making* 19(4).

Stewart, J. (1992) *The Rebuilding of Public Accountability* (London: European Policy Forum).

Stewart, J. (1995) Appointed boards and local government', *Parliamentary Affairs* 48(2).

Stewart, J. D. (1958) *British Pressure Groups: Their Role in Relation to the House of Commons* (Oxford: Clarendon Press).

Stewart, M. & Clarke, Harold (1992) 'The (un) importance of party leaders: Leader images and party choice in the 1987 British election', *Journal of Politics* 54(2).

Studlar, T. & McAllister, Ian (1992) 'A changing political agenda? The structure of political attitudes in Britain, 1974–87', *International Journal of Public Opinion Research*, vol. 4.

Talbot, C. (1995) 'Central Government reforms' in P. Jackson & M. Lavender (eds) *Public Services Yearbook 1995–96* (London: Chapman & Hall).

Talbot, Colin (1997) 'Central Government', in Peter Jackson and Michael Lavender (eds) *Public Services Yearbook 1997–98* (London: Pitman).

Taylor, Peter (1997) *The Provos: the IRA and Sinn Fein* (London: Bloomsbury)

Taylor, Robert (1994) 'Employment and industrial relations policy' in Dennis Kavanagh & Anthony Seldon (eds) *The Major Effect* (London: Macmillan).

Tebbit, Norman (1991) *Unfinished Business* (London: Weidenfeld & Nicolson).

Thatcher, Margaret (1993) *The Downing Street Years* (London: Harper-Collins).

Thatcher, Margaret (1995) *The Path to Power* (London: HarperCollins).

Thatcher, Margaret (1996) 'How to woo the middle classes', *The Daily Telegraph*, 12 January.

Theakston, Kevin (1995) *The Civil Service since 1945* (Oxford: Blackwell).

Theakston, Kevin (1998) 'New Labour, New Whitehall?', *Public Policy and Administration*, 13(1).

Thompson, Helen (1995) 'Joining the ERM: analysing a Core Executive policy disaster', in R. A. W. Rhodes & Patrick Dunleavy (eds) *Prime Minister, Cabinet and Core Executive* (London: Macmillan).

Thornton, Sir Malcolm (1993) 'The role of government in education' in Clyde Chitty & Brian Simon (eds) *Education Answers Back* (London: Lawrence & Wishart).

Tilson, B., Beazley, M., Burfitt, M., Collinge, C., Hall, S., Loftmann, P., Mawson, J., Nevin, B. & Srbljanin, A. (1997) 'Partnerships for regeneration: the Single Regeneration Budget Challenge Fund, round one', *Local Government Studies* 23(1).

Travers, Tony (1996) 'Town hall turns red', *The Guardian*, 11 December.

Travers, Tony (1997) 'The new agenda: local government; capping doesn't fit', *The Guardian* 7 May.

Treasury & Civil Service Committee (1993) *The Role of the Civil Service: Interim Report* (London: House of Commons *390*, 1992–93).

Treasury & Civil Service Committee (1994) *The Role of the Civil Service* (London: House of Commons *27*, 1993–94).

van Kersbergen, Kees (1995) *Social Capitalism* (London: Routledge).

Walden, George (1997) 'Backing Britain unto oblivion', *New Statesman*, 9 May.

Waldegrave, William (1994) 'Transforming the public sector', speech to Oxford Deregulation Seminar, 7 January.

Walkland, Stuart (1975) 'Government legislation in the House of Commons', in Stuart Walkland (ed.) *The House of Commons in the Twentieth Century* (Oxford: Clarendon Press).

Walters, Alan (1990) *Sterling in Danger* (London: Fontana).

Ware, R. (1996a) 'The road to Maastricht: Parliament and the Intergovernmental Conferences of 1991', in Philip Giddings & Gavin Drewry (eds) *Westminster and Europe* (London: Macmillan).

Ware, R. (1996b) 'Legislation and ratification: the passage of the European Communities (Amendment) Act 1993', in Philip Giddings & Gavin Drewry (eds) *Westminster and Europe* (London: Macmillan).

Watkins, Alan (1991) *A Conservative Coup* (London: Duckworth).

Watson, George (1987) 'The Conservative contradiction', *Encounter* November.

Welfare, D. (1992) 'An anchronism with relevance: the revival of the House of Lords in the 1980s and the defence of local government', *Parliamentary Affairs* 54(2).

Whiteley, Paul (1997) 'The Conservative campaign', *Parliamentary Affairs* 50(4).

Widdicombe, D. (1986) *The Conduct of Local Authority Business* Cmnd 9797, HMSO.

Wilson, David (1996a) 'The Local Government Commission: examining the consultative process', *Public Administration* 74(2).

Wilson, David (1996b) '"Structural" solutions for local government: an exercise in chasing shadows', *Parliamentary Affairs* 49(3).

Wilson, David & Game, Chris *et al.* (1994) *Local Government in the United Kingdom* (London: Macmillan).

Wilson, J. (1996) 'Citizen Major? The rationale and impact of the Citizen's Charter', *Public Policy and Administration* 11(1).

Wincott, Daniel (1991) *After Maastricht: British Party Politics and European Union*, Leicester Papers in Politics No. P91/2.

Wincott, Daniel (1994) 'Is the Treaty of Maastricht an adequate "constitution" for the European Union?', *Public Administration* 72(4).

Wincott, Daniel (1996) 'Federalism and European Union: the scope and limits of the Treaty of Maastricht', *International Political Science Review*.

Wyatt, Petronella (1997) 'I've been vindicated: John Major gives his first interview since the general election', *The Spectator*, 20/27 December.

Index

Action Centre for Europe 106
Adam Smith Institute 50
Adams, Gerry 110, 111, 113–14, 121, 122, 123
advisory committees 75
agencies *see* Next Steps agencies
Amalgamated Engineering Union 180
Ancram, Michael 122, 123
Anglo-Irish Agreement (AIA) (1985) 109–11, 112–13, 117

'back to basics' 84, 153, 154, 228, 236
Baker, Kenneth 60, 151–2
Banham, Sir John 50, 51, 82
Barnes, John 225
Baston, Lewis 16
benefits 166; and fraud 177; increase in people on sickness 168; streamlining of administration of 177–8; *see also* individual types
Benefits Agency 29, 32
Bichard, Michael 36
'Black Wednesday' (1992) 99–103, 103–4, 138, 199, 242–3
Blair, Tony 43, 61, 125, 142, 200, 208, 213
Blatch, Baroness 152
BMA (British Medical Association) 71–2, 79–80
Body, Sir Richard 13
Bolton, Eric 157
Bourn, Sir John 35
Brooke, Peter 111, 112, 115
Brunson, Michael 7
BSE crisis 105, 217
Budgets: (1991) 48; (1993) 79; (1994) 38; (1995) 38
Bundesbank 88, 101, 102, 103
bureaucracy 238

business lobby 84–5
Butler, Sir Robin 29, 35, 37, 40, 41
by-elections 200–1

Callaghan, James 19, 41
Campbell, John 216, 224–5
'care in the community' 58
CBI 72, 85
CCT (compulsory competitive tendering) 52–4, 57, 66, 82, 228
Chamberlain, Joseph 128
Chandler, John 65–6
Chilcot, Sir John 40
Child Benefit 169
Child Support Act (1991) 169, 172–3
Child Support Agency (CSA) 28–9, 30, 172–3, 230–1, 234
Choice and Diversity (White Paper) (1992) 148
Churchill, Winston 132
Citizen's Charter 30–2, 34, 39, 43, 67, 207, 215
citizenship 31
civil service 26–44, 227; compromising of political impartiality 41; *Continuity and Change* White Paper (1994) 35–6, 37, 42; creation and reorganisation of Senior Civil Service 36, 39; in crisis 42–3; cuts in running costs 38; introduction of new code of conduct 42; and market testing 32–5, 36, 43, 53; Next Steps agencies *see* Next Steps agencies; reduction in size 38–9; relationship between ministers and officials 40–1; relationship with organised interests 73; steps towards a more open

Civil Service – *continued*
  government 39–40; Thatcher's
  legacy 26–7
Clarke, Kenneth   33, 35, 42, 72–3,
  79, 156, 217
coal-mines   12
collective bargaining   181, 182,
  185, 186–8, 229
Combined Loyalist Military
  Command (CLMC)   120
Committee of the Regions   137
committees of inquiry   69, 75
Common Fisheries Policy   14
Competing for Quality (White
  Paper)   32–3
compulsory competitive tendering
  see CCT
'Conservative Mainstream'   222
Conservative Party: consequences
  of election (1992) 6–7; divisions
  within 1–2, 223, 233; ejections
  and defections 14–16, 85, 220,
  221–2; rebellions within *see*
  rebellions; responses to policy
  failure 234–5; weakening of 85
Constitution   144
consultation   68–86, 230; and
  Major government   74–85;
  Thatcher's legacy 69–73
consultative documents   70, 76–7
Continuity and Change (White
  Paper)   35–6, 37, 42
Cooksey, Sir David   51
council houses   57
Council of Ministers   104
council tax   48–9, 63, 228
crime   60–1; creation of victims'
  helpline   83
Criminal Justice Act (1991)   83
Criminal Justice and Public Order
  Act (1994)   83–4
Critchley, Julian   221
Currie, Edwina   222

Dangerous Dogs Bill (1991)   5
Dearing Report   159
Dearing, Sir Ron   81, 164
Dehaene, Jean-Luc   105
Delors, Jacques   97

Democratic Audit   61
Denmark: referendum on
  Maastricht Treaty   8, 96–7, 104
Devine, F. *et al.*   216
devolution   126–45, 231–2, 238;
  Conservative ideology 127–30;
  and Forsyth in Scotland 139–42;
  and Heath 129–30; and
  Maastricht Treaty 137; Major's
  commitment to Union of
  England and Scotland 133,
  134–5, 140, 144, 145, 232; and
  Major's first government 132–5;
  and Major's second government
  135–7; Thatcher's legacy 130–2;
  Welsh and Scottish Committee
  reforms 136–7, 144
Dicey, A. V.   127, 128, 129, 144
Dorrell, Stephen   32, 80
Downing Street Declaration
  (1993)   116–19, 120, 123, 144,
  231
Dudley by-election   201
Duncan Smith, Iain   7, 14
Dykes, Hugh   222, 223

economy   239–40; competence in
  managing 209–12, 234, 242–4;
  improvement 201, 215, 243
education   146–64, 212, 228–9,
  248; attack on bad schools 150;
  attack on 'progressive' teaching
  151–2, 153, 154; and Dearing
  Report 159; emphasis on 'moral'
  150, 153–5; expenditure on
  163–4; increase in class sizes
  163; introduction of market
  criteria 147; Major's concern
  over 162; more emphasis on
  '3 Rs' 153, 228; and 'opting-out'
  process 147–8, 149, 150, 228;
  and parental choice 147, 148,
  164; reform and expansion of
  higher 159–62; reform of
  National Curriculum 157–9;
  relations between government
  and teaching profession 80–1,
  154, 155–6, 156–7, 162–3, 229;
  on sex education 154–5;

teacher-training and teaching methods 150–2
Education Act (1988) 70, 72, 80, 146–8, 149, 155, 156, 157
Education Act (1993) 148–50
Education Associations 149
Efficiency Unit 33, 34
elderly 166, 167; care for 176
elections
  (**1992**) 201; consequences of for Party 6–7; devolution issue 134–5; economy issue 242; polls 202; small majority 7, 68, 74, 233
  (**1997**) 64, 201, 240–9; class and voting 240–41t; consequences of ERM débâcle 199–200; and Constitution 144; economic competence issue 210, 211, 242–4, 246; and Europe 107, 246; ideological disjuncture 247–9; issue saliency 245–6; and non-economic issues 212–13; and pensions 167; perceptions of party unity and fitness to govern 246–7; and press 216; reasons for defeat 249; result statistics 199; Scottish and Welsh votes 126; trade union issue 197; vote by region 241, 242t; voters' expectations 245t
employment 183, 195, 240, 249; job insecurity 195–6, 240; working hours 194–5; *see also* unemployment
Employment Act (1990) 184
ERM (Exchange Rate Mechanism) 8, 87, 88, 89; sterling's suspension from ('Black Wednesday') 99–104, 199, 206, 208, 209, 215–16, 232, 233, 234, 242
EU (European Union) 62–3, 90, 92, 105
Europe 87–100, 143, 232–3, 238–9; backbench attitudes towards integration 12, 13t;

backbench rebellions over 5, 8–9, 12, 207; divisions over 1–2, 4, 106–7, 126, 214, 232; elitist strategy towards 97–9, 106; and Eurosceptics *see* Eurosceptics; Major's strategy 90–2, 96–9, 105, 107; and (1997) election 107, 246; and pro-Europeans 105–6, *see also* ERM; Maastricht Treaty
European Communities Bill (1972) 8, 9, 16
European Communities (Finance) Bill 13, 22
European Court of Justice 14, 92, 193
European elections (1994) 105, 201
European Regional Development Fund 63
Eurosceptics 7, 17, 87, 88, 90, 98–9, 106–7, 232–3

Family Homes and Domestic Violence Bill 14, 22
federalism 128–9, 130
firearms control: rebellions over 14, 19
First Division Association (FDA) 41, 42
Fitzgerald, Garret 109
Fogden, Mike 28
Forsyth, Michael 28, 131, 139–42
  48-hour week 193–4, 197, 229, 249
Fraser Report (1991) 28
'Fresh Start' group 17
Funding Agency for Schools 149
Further and Higher Education Act (1992) 160

GCHQ 26
Germany 94, 101, 103
Gilmour, Ian 219–20, 226
GLC: abolition of 50
Goode Committee 176
grant-maintained schools 146, 149, 150

Gray, John 237
Green Papers 70, 76, 77
Gummer, John 51, 56

Hague, William 136, 142–3, 201
Hansard Society Commission 70, 86
health 58, 188; consultation with doctors 79–80; and pay determination 188
Heath, Edward 19, 20, 23, 129–30, 145
Hepplewhite, Ros 29
Heseltine, Michael 18, 27, 48; and business sector 85; characteristics 214; and civil service 30, 35, 37, 41, 42, 43; elevated to President of Board of Trade 55; on Europe 214; and leadership contest (1990) xv, 2, 4, 48; and local government 48, 50, 55, 67; and privatisation of agencies 27–8; view of by Thatcherites 219
higher education 159–62, 164
Hogg, Baroness Sarah 67
Holland, Sir Geoffrey 41
Holliday, Ian 182–3
housing 57, 167, 169–70
Housing Act (1980) 57
Housing Act (1989) 57
Housing Action Trusts (HATs) 66
housing benefit 169, 170, 173–4
Housing, Land and Urban Development Act (1992) 57
Howard, Michael 95; as Employment Secretary 94, 184; and local government 55–6; and prisons 29, 60; relationship with civil servants 40, 41
Howarth, Alan 220, 221
Hume, John 110, 111, 114, 116, 123
Hurd, Douglas xv, 2, 35, 42, 219

incapacity benefit 171
Income Support scheme 170, 172

'independent reviews' 75
industrial relations *see* trade unions
inflation 207, 211
Inner London Education Authority (ILEA) 147
Institute for Management Development 164
invalidity benefit 168, 171
IRA 110, 111, 231; and decommissioning of arms 120, 123–4, 125; and Downing Street Declaration 119; involvement in talks 113–16
Irish Home Rule 127, 128

job-seekers' allowance 168, 170–1
Jones, P. and Hudson, J. 204–5
judiciary 60

Kavanagh, Dennis xvii
Kemp, Sir Peter 33, 35
Kinnock, Neil 208, 213

Labour Party: and Citizen's Charter 31; and election (1997) 199, 244; modernisation of under Blair 208, 213; public opinion on handling of economic problems 209, 211; public opinion on handling of non-economic problems 212, 213; rebellions 23; and trade unions 213; upward trend in support 200
Laird, Gavin 190
Lamont, Norman 48, 90, 207, 224; and ERM 102, 103, 104; resignation 138
Lang, Ian 133–4, 135, 136, 139, 186, 220
law and order 59–61, 213; relationship between police associations and government 82–4
Lawson, Nigel 189–90
leadership contests: (1990) xiv, xv, 2–4, 45, 48; (1995) 2, 17–18, 106, 142

'league tables' 148
legal profession 82–3
Leigh, Edward 224
Lestor, Jim 223
Levene, Peter 33
Lewis, Derek 29
Liberal Democrats 9, 201
Lilley, Peter 29, 38, 165–6, 167, 168, 171, 177, 178
local authorities: relations and consultation with Major government 72, 81–2
local elections 63–5, 201
local government 45–67, 227–8; and CCT 52–4, 57, 66, 82, 228; early portents 47–8; and education 147–8; and elected mayors 56; emergence of 'new magistracy' 56–61; and EU 62–3; low number of Conservative councillors 201; management and leadership 55–6; post-war erosion of autonomy 65; replacement of poll tax by council tax 48–9, 228; restructuring of 50–2; and Thatcher 46, 47, 50, 65–6
Local Government Act (1988) 53
Local Government Act (1992) 53, 57
Local Government Association (LGA) 67, 82
Local Government Commission (1992) 75, 81–2
Local Government Finance and Valuation Act (1991) 49
Local Government, Planning and Land Act (1980) 53, 59

Maastricht Treaty 8–12, 92–6; achievement by Major 94, 95, 232; and Danish referendum 8, 96–7, 104; and establishment of Committee of the Regions 137; negotiations over 90–1, 92–5; ratification of 6, 8–9, 12, 104, 207; rebellions over 1–2, 5, 8–9, 10t–11t, 12, 22, 23; Social Agreement 94–5; Social Chapter

9, 79, 93, 94–5, 191–4, 229; and subsidiarity principle 63, 93–4, 232, 238; and Thatcher 96–7, 98
MacGregor, John 73
Macleod Group 222
Macleod, Iain xiii, 218, 220
Magistrates' Association 83
Major, John 45, 67, 107; background xiv; belief and support of Union of England and Scotland 133, 134–5, 140, 144, 145, 232; characteristics and personality xiv; Conservative disillusion with 218–26; consolidation of Thatcherism 226–35, 248; contradictions of consolidation of Thatcherism 236–40; as a conviction politician 145; criticism of by 'one-nation' Conservatives 220–3, 225–6; decline in public satisfaction with performance 206–7, 233; defence of premiership 225; disadvantages suffered during premiership 216; disillusionment of right in 218–19, 223–4; education experience 162; honeymoon period 4–6; initial public approval of 205–6, 233; interview with *The Independent* 144; personal commitment to the way officialdom deals with the public 30; personal qualities 202, 204, 215; political style xvii, 40, 73–4, 215; press hostility towards 216; public image 204–5, 213, 217, 233, 247; reasons why considered 'one-nation' Conservative xiii–xv; resignation and re-election 17–18, 106, 206–7; *Spectator* interview 107; and Thatcher 47, 138, 205, 215, 218, 223, 226
mayors, elected 56
manufacturing industry: decline of 180, 181, 182
market testing 32–5, 36, 43, 53
Maxwell, Robert 176

Mayhew, Sir Patrick　112, 115,
　121, 123
Meacher, Michael　37
Millward, Neil *et al.*　181
minimum wage　197
ministerial responsibility　43, 227
Mitchell Commission Report
　(1996)　124
Mitchell, James　131
Molineux, James　118, 119
monetary union　12, 91, 94, 102,
　106
Morris, T.　84
Murray, Charles　172

National Curriculum　80, 81, 146,
　148, 228; reform of　157–9
National Curriculum Council　70
National Economic Development
　Council (NEDC)　69–70, 75,
　79, 183, 189–90, 197, 229
National Lottery　215
New Urban Left　46
Next Steps agencies　26–8, 31–2,
　33, 36, 75, 227; privatisation
　37–8, 43; relationship with
　departments　28, 29–30
NHS (National Health
　Service)　58, 212, 237–8, 248
NHS trusts　58, 188
Nichol, Sir Duncan　41
Nicholson, Emma　220, 221
Nolan Committee　62, 75
Northern Ireland　29, 108–25,
　231; and Anglo-Irish Agreement
　109–11, 112–13, 117; Brooke/
　Mayhew talks process 111–13;
　ceasefires (1994) 108, 119–21,
　123, 125; collapse of ceasefire
　122–4, 125; decommissioning of
　arms issue 120, 123–4, 125; and
　Downing Street Declaration
　116–19, 120, 123, 144, 231;
　Framework Document 119,
　121–2; involvement of IRA in
　talks 113–16; Major's
　commitment to peace process
　108–9; and Mitchell Report 124;
　Thatcher's legacy 109–10, 111;

violence and bombing campaign
　113
nursery vouchers　81

Oliver, F. S.　128
Open Government (White Paper)
　(1993)　39–40
organised interests　68–86,
　229–30; relations with Thatcher
　government　69–73; relations
　with Major government　73–85
owner-occupation　170, 174, 231

part-time employment　169,
　192–3, 197
party leaders: impact of　203–4
Passport Agency　30
Patten, Chris　73
Patten, John　148, 152, 153–4,
　156–7, 158
pay determination　186–9
Pension Act (1995)　176
pensions　166, 167, 175–6, 211,
　231
People, Jobs and Opportunity
　(White Paper) (1992)　187–8
Pimlott, Ben　216
Plaid Cymru　136, 137, 143
Plowden, William　40, 43
police　60; and Sheehy Report
　(1993) 60–1, 83
Police and Magistrates' Court Bill
　(1993)　61, 83–4
poll tax　27, 45, 48, 72, 92, 132,
　228
polytechnics　160
poor: gap between rich and　236
Portillo, Michael　178, 192, 193
Positive European group　106
post office: privatisation　13, 22
prisons　29, 60, 234
Private Members' Bills　14
private sector: earnings gap
　between public and　189
Public Accounts Committee report
　(1994)　35
Pym, Francis　128

quangos　190, 228

railway industry 188, 222, 248
Ramsden, John 225
rebellions 12–14, 18, 22–4, 233;
  honeymoon period 4–6; levels of
  in post-war parliaments 18–19t;
  number of dissenting votes cast
  20–21t; over Europe 1–2, 5,
  8–12, 22, 23, 207; size of
  (1992–97) 19–20t
Recruitment and Assessment
  Service (RAS) 38
Redwood, John: and leadership
  contest (1995) 17, 18, 106,
  142; in Wales 138–9, 142, 143,
  144
Research Assessment Exercise
  (RAE) 162
Reynolds, Albert 116, 118, 120,
  122, 144
Rhodes, Rod 65
Richardson, J. J. 73
Ridley, Nicholas 224
Rifkind, Malcolm 131, 133–4
Rogaly, Joe 23
Royal Commissions 69, 75
Ryder, Richard 5

Santer, Jacques 105
SATs (standard assessment
  tasks) 80–1, 157, 158–9
Scotland 52, 81, 231–2;
  devolution issue 126, 129–30,
  133–5, 136–7, 139–42, 231–2;
  and Forsyth 139–42; Thatcher's
  legacy 131–2
Scottish Grand Committee 136,
  141, 144
Scruton, Roger 237
SDLP 110–11, 112
Seldon, Anthony 225
SERPS (state earnings-related
  pension scheme) 166, 167,
  175
service sector: expansion 181,
  182
sex education 154–5
Sheehy Report (1993) 60–1, 83
Shephard, Gillian 95–6, 150, 185
Shepherd, Richard 5, 96

Single European Act (1986) 191
single European currency 222,
  247–8
single parents 138–9, 169, 172–3,
  230–1
Sinn Fein 109, 110, 114, 119,
  120, 121, 123, 231
sleaze allegations 207–8, 215
Smith, John 41, 208, 213
SNP (Scottish National
  Party) 129, 130, 135, 137, 140,
  143, 145, 201
Social Agreement 94–5
Social Chapter 9; rejection
  of 79, 93, 94, 191–4, 229
Social Fund 74
social security 165–78, 230–1;
  growth in expenditure 165,
  166–7; restraining of
  expenditure 32, 38, 167–70, 177,
  178
Social Security Act (1986) 167,
  175
Social Security (Incapacity for
  Work) Act (1994) 171
*Social Services – Achievement and
  Challenge* (White Paper)
  (1997) 58
Staffordshire South-East
  by-election (1996) 201
Standard Spending Assessments
  (SSAs) 49
Stewart, John 57
strikes 186, 196
student loans 160–1
subsidiarity, principle of 63,
  93–4, 232, 238

taxation 211, 244, 248
Taylor, Robert 79
Taylor, Sir Teddy 20
teacher-training 150–2
Teaching Quality Assessments
  (TQAs) 161
Tebbit, Norman 151, 224
Thatcher, Margaret 7, 18; and
  civil service 26–7; and
  devolution 130–2; and education
  150–1; and Europe 92, 96, 98;

Thatcher, Margaret – *continued*
  isolation of 91–2; and leadership
  election (1990) 2; and local
  government 46, 47, 50, 65–6;
  and Major 47, 138, 205, 215, 218,
  223, 226; and Northern Ireland
  109–10, 111; public image 205,
  206t; reasons for downfall xvi, 4;
  and social security 166; view of
  Scotland 133
Thatcherism 247; contradictions
  of Major's consolidation of
  236–40; Major's consolidation
  of 226–35
think tanks 84, 230
Thomas, Lord Elis 136
Thurnham, Peter 221–2
Trade Union Act (1984) 179
Trade Union Reform and
  Employment Rights Act
  (1993) 184–5, 190
trade unions 179–90, 197;
  abolition of National Economic
  Development Council 75, 183,
  189–90, 197, 229; decline in
  membership 180–1; employees'
  views on objectives of 196t;
  exclusion from consultative
  process 71; and Labour Party
  213; public's views on
  government restrictions on
  196–7; reduction in density
  181; reform under Major
  184–6; relationship with
  Major government 77–8, 183,
  185, 198, 229, 240; and
  Thatcher 69, 179–80; and
  undermining of collective
  bargaining 187–8
Trades Union Congress
  (TUC) 71
Training and Enterprise Councils
  (TECs) 59, 66, 79, 190
Transport & General Workers'
  Union 180
Travers, Tony 49
Treasury 39

Trosa Report (1994) 28
True, Nick 134

Ulster Unionist Party (UUP) 112
unemployment 180, 194, 211;
  benefits 168, 170–1
'unit fine' scheme 83
universities 160–1, 164
urban development 58–9
Urban Development Corporations
  (UDCs) 59, 66
Urban Regeneration Agency
  (URA) 59

victims' helpline 83

Wages Act (1986) 190–1
Wages Councils: abolishment 79,
  185, 190–1, 198, 229
Waldegrave, William 27, 39–40,
  73
Walden, George 240
Wales 52, 81, 132–3, 135; and
  devolution 126, 131, 139, 143,
  231–2; 'Grand Committee'
  strategy 136–7; and Hague
  142–3; and Redwood 138–9,142,
  143, 144
Walker, Peter 132, 133
Walters, Alan 100–1
Watson, George 235
Welsh Grand Committee 136–7,
  142, 144
Welsh Language Act (1993)
  135–6, 144
Whiteley, Paul 200
Whitmore, Sir Clive 41
Widdicombe Report (1986) 46
Williams, Sir David 67
Wilson, David and Game,
  Chris 50
Wilson, Harold 19
Wilson, Richard 40
working class 241
working hours 194–5
Working for Patients (White Paper)
  (1989) 58